Where the Whales Are

*Your Guide to Whale-Watching Trips
in North America*

by Patricia Corrigan

With a Foreword by Roger Payne

Illustrations by David Peters

A Voyager Book

The
Globe
Pequot
Press

Chester, Connecticut

To the world's whales,
and to those who dare to watch them

———————

Text copyright © 1991 by Patricia Corrigan
Illustrations copyright © 1991 by David Peters

Library of Congress Cataloging-in-Publication Data

Corrigan, Patricia.
    Where the whales are : your guide to whale-watching trips in North America /
by Patricia Corrigan : with a foreword by Roger Payne; illustrations by David
Peters. — 1st ed.
            p.   cm.
    Includes bibliographical references and index.
    ISBN 0-87106-318-2
    1. Whale watching—North America—Guide-books. 2. Whales—North America.
I. Peters, David, 1954-   . II. Title.
QL737.C4C67 1991
599.5'097—dc20   90-49961
                                                                        CIP

Front cover photograph of humpback whale breaching courtesy of The Pacific Whale
Foundation

Back cover photograph of humpback whale feeding courtesy of the New England
Aquarium

Manufactured in the United States of America
First Edition/Second Printing

Contents

List of Illustrations

Note: On any given page, the whales are not necessarily drawn to scale.

Foreword

If after reading this book you cannot meet the whale of your dreams when and where you wish, it may be time to reprioritize your life.

Every time I approach the guide books in a bookstore and scan the new offerings, I wonder the same thing: Did the person who undertook this daunting task do a thorough job, or did he or she get partway into it and run out of gas?

Pat Corrigan has done her job. She did not run out of anything. The clarity with which she writes and the fresh, concise way she sets forth her information means that you and I can find what we're looking for at once. But better: Not only does she think out what you and I want to know more clearly than we do, she presents it straight, succinctly, and without ever saying too much, or being patronizing. What a treat for us, when a fine writer and journalist decides to do a book like this.

She tells us the basics about whales and the areas they frequent and then offers good advice on everything surrounding whale watching: how to choose among the competing tours, what to wear, what to bring with you, what to eat, how to avoid seasickness, and so on. She garnishes it with remarks such as "Inhale deeply of the fresh air and taste the salt on your lips. Memorize the moment with your every pore, and it won't matter whether or not the photographs turn out."

Good advice, that.

That it is possible to get so much solid information about a subject as specialized as whale watching is one of life's little delights. It says that in spite of all the disappointments that sprout like weeds in our society, we still grow some straight-grained hardwood. Pass over the weeds and buy this guide and then follow its advice. You won't be disappointed, and you will see whales.

Roger Payne
President, Whale and Dolphin Conservation Society

Acknowledgments

Heartfelt gratitude and deep affection are due to the following parties for the reasons noted here.

My son, Joel Krauska, named this book and loves learning about and watching whales as much as I do. The wonderful tour operators listed in this book—my new extended family—sent me not only tidily filled-out questionnaires but warm words of encouragement, updates on whale conservation issues, invitations to visit, snapshots of whales, T-shirts, and audio and video tapes of assorted whale songs and behaviors. And some of them called, just to chat, or to tell me that they remember meeting me or that they grew up in St. Louis, too.

Linda Piel Gwyn somehow knew I should write books and pestered me until I did. My agent, Jeanne Hanson, found me and then found me a publisher. My editor, Betsy Amster, began her first letter to me, "Hallelujah! I'm very glad that we'll be publishing *Where the Whales Are.*" Laura Strom, also at Globe Pequot, and copy editor Jay Howland graciously guided me through the sometimes murky waters of manuscript preparation.

My only aunt, Betty Ann Dameris, prayed this book into being and on its way. Joan Bray rescued me from an untimely technical difficulty. Many of my special friends provided emotional support, cheerfully attended all my whale parties, and bought me great whale presents. And some of them even went whale watching!

David Peters, who illustrated this book so well, also painted a glorious 8-foot-long humpback whale on my bedroom wall for $10 and a Pepsi. Sue Kelley at the Pacific Whale Foundation on Maui, Corinne Wadsworth at Seven Seas Whale Watch in Gloucester, Massachusetts, and Ken Wright, whale-watch captain at the New England Aquarium, all sent me gorgeous color slides for the book's cover before I had a chance to ask.

Roger Payne and Stephen Leatherwood spared time for me and

my questions, both on and off whale-watch boats. Dr. Peter C. Beamish at Ocean Contact Ltd., Dr. Scott Krause at the New England Aquarium, and Dr. Richard Sears at the Mingan Island Cetacean Study Inc. all reviewed the chapter on whale biology. Carol Perkins lugged home pounds of material on beluga whales from a conference in Canada and presented it all to me.

Bob Wilds and the crew of the *Mystery* escorted me on my first whale-watch trip on September 25, 1982. Erich Hoyt directed me to several later whale-watching adventures. Robert Packard wrote the article on whale watching that first captured my imagination. My editors at the St. Louis Post-Dispatch, Jim Creighton and Bob Duffy, allowed me to spout periodically about whales in a Midwestern newspaper.

And I would be remiss if I failed to mention the whales, who chose me to write this book so you could go find them.

Welcome to Whale Watching

Whales! The greatest show on earth is in the water, and anyone willing to go where whales are will see it. Whales—swimming, all sea-shiny and slick; diving, flashing enormous fan-shaped tails; spouting, baptizing one and all with a hearty expulsion of air and water as the mighty mammals breathe; whales with vast open mouths feeding on microscopic shrimp; whales hurtling their fifty-ton bodies up, up, and completely out of the water, then falling back with a thunderous crash.

Blue whales, fin whales, rare right whales, humpbacks, gray whales, killer whales, minkes, and beluga whales—I've seen them all, in the Atlantic Ocean off Cape Cod, in Hawaiian waters, in Alaska's Prince William Sound, off the coast of British Columbia, in Canada's St. Lawrence Seaway, near Peninsula Valdes in Argentine waters, in the Southern Pacific Ocean off Baja California, off the coast of San Diego, and just yards from the Oregon shore.

I am not a marine biologist, research scientist, conservation specialist, wildlife photographer, or anyone at all with a specialized entree to the world of whales. I do watch whales, as often as I can manage, and so can you. Extraordinary experiences are available to anyone willing to go where the whales are.

The first whale I ever met was a finback, a creature just slightly smaller than the 80-foot, seventy-six-ton boat on which I was a passenger. The whale came toward us, dived, swam under the boat, and was gone before we could comprehend what we had seen. Finback whales are the second largest creatures ever to live on earth, surpassed in size only by the mighty blue whales, and they are among the fastest swimmers in the sea, reaching speeds of twenty knots (thirty miles per hour).

That trip was in 1982, out of Barnstable Harbor, off Cape Cod. We spent much of the day watching humpback whales feeding, their huge open mouths rising up through the columns of bubbles they blow under water to trap krill and tiny fish. The humpbacks also waved their tails ("threw their flukes") over and over, and two swam and dived together in unison, as though their dance had been choreographed. It was a magic day.

Once I had seen whales, I wanted to see more, to experience again the awe and exhilaration, the sense of deep privilege I felt when I was among them. Seeing whales became a priority, and I began to seek out opportunities to go where whales were whenever possible.

In 1984, during a three-day business trip to Maui, I boldly abandoned my traveling companions and headed for Lahaina, where I signed on for back-to-back whale-watch trips, a day's worth of expeditions. The morning trip reaped only a few far-distant flukes, and the afternoon threatened to be even less satisfying. But just as the captain started the boat's engine to leave, a humpback whale in the distance breached—hurled itself completely out of the water—seven times.

One look at that was simply not enough. Two years later, in May of 1986, I was on a ferryboat trip across Prince William Sound in Alaska when a humpback whale approached the boat and stayed nearby for forty-five minutes. Right in front of us, only yards from the boat, the whale breached over and over, slapped its 15-foot flippers on the water, waved its tail each time it dived, and smacked its tail repeatedly at the water's surface. Just before the graceful behemoth swam away, it appeared to wave "goodbye" with one long flipper.

The captain said that in his seventeen years of crossing the sound, he hadn't ever seen such a breathtaking spectacle. The thirty passengers, most of us strangers when we had boarded, were all hugging one another and laughing and crying. The cap-

When a humpback whale breaches—heaves its entire body out of the water—it falls back with a thunderous crash.

tain joined in the celebration by declaring a round of drinks on the house, and we all offered up toasts to "our" whale.

In 1987, I returned to Cape Cod with my then-twelve-year-old son in tow. We took whale-watch trips on four consecutive days, and we saw whales every day. One afternoon, a humpback that had been lolling around several hundred yards away suddenly surfaced alongside the boat, so we had an unusual up-close look at the whale's impressive 40-foot length. We also saw five fin whales and at least thirty Atlantic white-sided dolphins.

From the back decks of cruise ships, I've seen orcas (killer whales), gray whales, common dolphins, and blue whales. Surely, sighting blue whales is one of the rare privileges in life. In June of 1987, I was on the St. Lawrence River, aboard the S.S.

Bermuda Star. The ship's pilot from Quebec had warned me that it was too early in the season to see any whales, yet four blue whales showed up on my thirty-ninth birthday, and I also saw a dozen or so belugas arching their backs out of the sun-sparkled water at the mouth of the Saguenay River.

How did a nice Midwestern woman living on the banks of the Mississippi River become entranced with these magnificent marine mammals?

In July of 1982, I read an article in the *New York Times* travel section about a whale-watch trip off Cape Cod. A photograph of a whale leaping out of the water accompanied the article. After reading just a few paragraphs, I became obsessed with the idea of meeting a whale. The first opportunity was a week-long business trip to Washington, D.C., that autumn. I made arrangements to add a two-day visit to Cape Cod to the end of the trip. Then I headed for the library for books on whales, so that I would know what I was looking at in case I saw one.

I did see a whale, and it changed my life. Now I want to change yours.

Humpbacks sometimes smack their fifteen-foot flippers on the water's surface.

How to
Use This Book

This is a book for people who watch whales, people who have been inexplicably moved, often deeply touched, by the sight of these glorious animals in their natural habitat. This is also a book for people who want to watch whales and for people who are about to discover that they too are fascinated with the mighty beasts. What you hold in your hands is a nature guide, a travel planner, an adventure book, and an inspirational text in the broadest sense.

Listed here are more than two hundred commercial whale-watch tour operators who are ready and waiting to escort you on more than two hundred fifty trips to see whales off the coasts of the United States (including Alaska and Hawaii), Canada, and Mexico. (Note: If we missed you, or if you know of a tour operator who is not included in this book, please see the note at the end of the book so we can include you in revised editions.)

You may use this book to plan a single whale-watching expedition, to devise an entire itinerary devoted to watching whales, or to find information on package tours and research expeditions. You pick a trip, pick a place or time, or pick a certain whale species that you want to see, and the book will point the way.

Guidelines for picking and choosing are in this chapter, and what to expect when you go whale watching (including what to wear) is covered in the next. The following chapter, "Whale Tales," includes information on sixteen species of whales and dolphins. The book's final chapter is a calendar of sorts, indicat-

Where the Whales Are

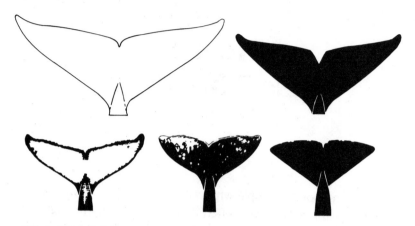

Whale tails, or flukes, come in different sizes and shapes. **Top row:** *Blue whale, right whale.* **Bottom row:** *Humpback whale, gray whale, sperm whale.*

ing what whales are where, when. This book also includes information on thirty museums and aquariums that have special whale exhibits or programs about marine life, names and addresses to write for tourism information, names and addresses of more than seventy whale conservation and research organizations, information on nine adopt-a-whale programs, a bibliography, and list of fifteen tour operators who sponsor package whale-watch trips in areas not covered here.

The Directory

The chapters cover the following geographic areas: Northeast U.S. Coast, Pacific Northwest, California, Hawaii, Alaska, Canada, and Mexico. Most of the listings are arranged north to south, and maps are included in each chapter.

Each listing includes the tour operator's name, address, and telephone number; what sort of whales you can expect to see; what time of year the trips are available; the type of boat (or boats) on which they take place; a daily schedule, if available; the cost; whether or not reservations are recommended or advised; the point of departure (with simple directions to that point); and a note about whether or not a naturalist or narrator is on board. Symbols indicate what you may expect in the way of a sheltered area on board, food, drink, binoculars, and hydrophones to let you hear the whales while you watch them, and whether or not a brochure is available from the tour operator.

Physically disabled whale watchers are welcome and are made comfortable on many boats, including kayaks. On some boats that do not have ramps accessible to wheelchairs, tour operators are willing to carry the passenger aboard if possible. If you will need help boarding or if you are concerned about finding a safe place for a wheelchair, please call the tour operator in advance.

All prices and departure times are subject to change. Since this book went to press, some tour operators may have added boats to their fleet or replaced less-comfortable vessels with sleek new boats designed for whale watching. Still others may have merged or gone into another line of work. The moral of this paragraph is this: Call or write to tour operators before you arrive at the pier. If you call or write off-season, you may not get an immediate response. Keep at it—whale watching is worth it.

Pick a Trip

Whale-watch trips may last one hour, two hours, half a day, a full day, two or three days, or on up to ten or fourteen days. You may spend as little as $7 per person for an hour-long trip or as much as $3,000 for a two-week expedition with several stops. Vessels listed in this book include large excursion boats, small excursion boats, fishing boats, small motor craft, sailboats, motorized rafts, and sea kayaks.

Some trips are strictly for pleasure, some are research oriented, and some successfully combine both elements. Most whale-watch tours listed here are family-run businesses; some are sponsored by scientific institutions and research organizations. Most of the trips are suitable for almost everyone, from the exceptionally sea hardy to those who rely on pills or patches to stave off the possibility of motion sickness. Trips to the Farallon

Sometimes humpbacks (and other whales) stick their heads out of the water, a behavior called "spyhopping."

Islands off San Francisco are particularly rigorous; the outings within the confines of Depoe Bay off the coast of Oregon can be remarkably calm. Otherwise, you pay your money and you take your chances—and chances are you'll be just fine.

Pick a Place or Time

Most of the trips are listed according to the point of departure. The exceptions are trips in Mexico, all of which are sponsored by tour operators in the United States and Canada. These trips are organized by destination. Otherwise, if you already know where you are going, you can look up that city (or one close by) and see what's available in the way of whale watching. If you don't have a destination in mind, you can check the calendar to see where whales are when and make your plans accordingly.

In some communities where whale watching is big business, local hotels and motels offer package deals, usually in the form of discount coupons for some tours. Where available, these packages are noted in the listings. Usually guests are given a choice of departure times but not of tour operators. Call or write to the tour operators, rather than the hotels, for details.

Pick a Whale
If you've met humpback whales and you want to watch gray whales next time out, you can turn immediately to the listings for tours off the west coast of the United States and in the lagoons of Baja California, Mexico. If you want a peek at the rarest whale in the world, the northern right whale, look for trips

Dolphins in all the world's oceans enjoy bow riding, frolicking in the wake made by boats and ships.

in the North Atlantic. Blue whales can be found with some certainty in Canada and occasionally off the coast of California, and orcas patrol the waters off the San Juan Islands. Humpbacks and minkes? Head for Alaska, Hawaii, or the northeast coast of the United States. These are just general guidelines, as the migration paths of the world's whales meander through all the oceans.

About Picking and Choosing

A word is in order about the nature of "naturalists." The term generally refers to the person or persons on board who narrate the whale-watch trips, providing educational information about the whales, their behaviors and habitat, and the other creatures that share the marine environment. Some naturalists are marine biologists or oceanographers. Some are affiliated with, and trained by, research organizations and scientific institutions. On some trips, narration is provided by knowledgeable captains, people who have been going to sea with whales for years and have made a point of educating themselves so they can answer passengers' questions correctly. On some trips where no narration is provided, tour operators show an educational video on whales and hand out written materials provided by whale conservation organizations.

Probably it is unwise to judge a trip's worth based solely on whether or not a naturalist is on board. Once, when I was on a commercial trip off Cape Cod with a "certified" naturalist, said naturalist identified a passing whale as a humpback. My son, then with only one previous whale-watch trip under his belt, took a good look at the animal and insisted it was a finback, based on its color and the shape of its dorsal fin. Off he went to talk to the "expert." Moments later she was back on the public address system, admitting her mistake.

Some tour operators work with scientific research organizations and advertise that affiliation. The tie-in may be full-time and permanent, in that each whale-watch trip is a fact-finding research mission; or it may be that the boat has been chartered from time to time by organizations for its members. Boarding a boat that actively shares in a research effort or donates part of each day's profits to that research doesn't necessarily mean that you'll have a more rewarding trip, unless participating in research is exactly what you have in mind.

Also, booking passage on a whale-watch trip that boasts the presence of a naturalist is no reason not to educate yourself before you get on the boat. Many wonderful books about whales and whale biology are in print, available at libraries and bookstores all over the country. (For sixty-five such titles, see the Bibliography.) Learning about the animals ahead of time makes the experience that much richer and will allow you to ask more specific questions if there is a naturalist on the trip you take.

Other Considerations

In any given area, all the tour boats go to the same places, sometimes staying in radio contact with one another in case someone sights whales that others have overlooked. For the most part, all whale-watch tour operators are infused with enthusiasm for the sport and are proud to be sharing the experience with their passengers. Cooperation among tour operators, rather than cutthroat competition, is most often the case. Therefore, if you're not particularly concerned about the size of the boat or the credentials of the naturalist, you might choose a trip that simply departs at a time convenient for you or that charges a fare that suits your budget. If you're a skeptic, seek out those tour operators who "guarantee" that you'll see a whale or they'll give you a free trip—not an uncommon offer in those areas where whales are practically willing to keep appointments with tour operators, year after year. And if you can afford it and you're so inclined, sign up for more than one trip. Because of the nature of the beast, every trip is unique.

What to Expect on a Whale Watch

Before you can do any whale watching, you will likely have to do some whale waiting. While you're waiting, watch the water's surface for flying fish, other marine mammals, or even shark fins. Confronted with a vast expanse of ocean, many people initially think that "there's nothing out there." But that's just not true. Everything is out there. A whole world is just beneath the water's surface, and if you watch carefully, you will see evidence of that world. Also, look up and meet assorted seabirds that you're not likely to see flying over landlocked cities.

En route to where whales are supposed to be, you can always scan the horizon, just in case a whale might have meandered into new territory. Whales are blissfully ignorant of our schedules and calendars and maps, and they often pop up when and where we least expect them. An experienced captain once assured me we were well past the area off British Columbia where orcas are sighted, and thirty minutes later, four tall dorsal fins came into view along the shore.

Another orca spent a recent summer off Provincetown, Massachusetts, playing in the surf and delighting tourists and townspeople alike. Government officials actually met several times to determine what to do about the whale, which wasn't where it "should" have been at that time of year. Some gray whales appear to take a liking to the coast of Oregon and Washington and spend twelve months in residence, rather than joining their species' annual trek between Alaska and Mexico.

Keep your eyes open and watch for that first thrilling sight of a whale spout against the horizon. One naturalist once described it as similar to a car radiator "blowing off steam"; after the steam subsides, look for a glimpse of what appears to be a shiny black stretch limo.

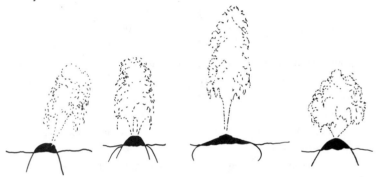

The blows, or spouts, of the great whales are distinctive. **From left:** *Sperm whale, bowhead whale, blue whale, and gray whale.*

What Not to Expect

What you can't expect is to see whales where you want them to be exactly when you want them to be there. This is nature, real life; not a multimillion-dollar theme park where every surprise is scheduled. Patience must rule the day. When you do see whales, you will realize they were worth the wait. Also, you will return to shore exhilarated, better educated about a fascinating animal, and more aware of what's at stake if we lose even one species to extinction.

What You Need to Know Ahead of Time

Sometimes people are disappointed when they first see a whale spout. "That's it?" they say. "That little puff of steam that the wind blew away?" But when you've had a chance to do some whale watching, you will find out that each of the great whales has a distinctive spout. Literally a large roomful of air and mist is exhaled each time a whale breathes. If you're familiar with the

13

height and shape of the different blows, and if the wind isn't too strong, and if you're facing the whale head on, sometimes you can tell exactly what sort of whale you're seeing even if you don't get a glimpse of the body or the dorsal fin or some other telltale sign. And sometimes, of course, you can't.

If you know what to expect, if you know that the great whales range in size from 45 to 90 or 100 feet and weigh as much as 1.5 tons per foot, you're less likely to be disappointed at the sight of a spout. If you know that a blue whale can weigh as much as thirty-two elephants or that a toddler could crawl through the arteries of any full-grown great whale or that a humpback's flipper is more than twice the height of the tallest person you know, then your sense of excitement about even a distant sighting will increase.

Chances are good—guaranteed at some spots during certain times of year—that you will see much more than a spout. Take binoculars, if you have them, to get a closer look at whales in the distance. If you don't have binoculars, don't despair. Most likely you won't need them.

Human beings are only as large as some of the smallest cetaceans. Shown here, from top to bottom, are the blue whale, sperm whale, bottlenose dolphin, humpback whale, and orca.

There are laws that restrict how close whale-watch boats may approach the animals. For the most part, the laws are designed to protect the whales from harassment by overeager whale-watch vessels and small pleasure craft. Whales, unaware of our laws and good intentions, often approach idling boats for what appears to be a closer look at whale watchers. In the words of Dr. Peter Beamish, who operates Ocean Contact Ltd. out of Trinity Bay in Newfoundland, "Whale watching is free in Newfoundland. you can sit on a cliff near Trinity all day and watch whales. We guide people into our spectacular marine environment so that the whales can watch them."

What to Wear

Of course, no matter how close whales come to the boat, you can't watch them comfortably if you're not dressed appropriately. No matter how sunny and warm it is in town or even at the dock, once you're out on the water the temperature may be cooler by ten to twenty degrees. If the wind is blowing, it may be even chillier. Also, there is always the possibility that you will get wet, either from occasional spray or from the unanticipated rain cloud.

When you pack a backpack or tote for whale watching, put in the obligatory sunscreen, a hat or visor, a sweatshirt or sweater, and a waterproof windbreaker, poncho, or jacket. Ear-muffs, mittens, and scarves may come in handy too. And if you forgo the gloves, remember to smear some sunscreen on your hands, even if they are the only part of you that is exposed. Wear sunglasses, long pants or jeans, a comfortable shirt, socks, and rubber-soled shoes. Female whale watchers clad in dresses, pantyhose, and tasteful grown-up-lady shoes—and whale watchers of both sexes in cutoffs and tank tops—have a hard time staying on a spray-splashed deck long enough to enjoy the trip.

As you sail over the bounding main, you may be aware of how wild the ocean seems, how uncontrollable a force it is to reckon with. For most people, that's part of the thrill. If you're not accustomed to being at sea, or if you've never managed it comfortably, plant your feet firmly on the deck and keep your knees loose and slightly bent. That way, you're not fighting the motion—and it's fun!

What to Bring

A camera is the obvious answer, and this from a person who has an album fully of fuzzy, out-of-focus pictures of whales and pictures of where whales just were. Unless you are a professional nature photographer accustomed to shooting from boats rocking gently (and not so) on the sea, you probably won't get professional-quality nature photos. However, you probably will get perfectly acceptable snapshots of tail flukes, dorsal fins, a flipper or two, and maybe even a whole whale at midbreach. And so you should bring your camera.

That said, it is also true that documenting whale behavior through a camera lens is not nearly as exciting as taking in the experience with all your senses turned up high. At some point, put down the camera and bring your mind's eye into sharp focus. Stare hard at the creature, noting the texture and color of its skin, any scars or scratches, the flash of baleen when it opens its mouth, the way the water streams down the ventral pleats under the whale's chin, or the places where barnacles are gathered. Listen to that most amazing sound when the whale breathes, the explosion of air and water that may well rain down upon you. Inhale deeply of the fresh air and taste the salt on your lips. Memorize the moment with your every pore, and it won't matter whether or not the photographs turn out.

What Not to Bring

In order for motion sickness pills to be effective, you must take them at least thirty minutes before you board the boat. After you've put out to sea (or worse, started feeling bad), it's too late to take a pill, so be sure to swallow yours in time. Dramamine makes most people sleepy; Bonine makes only some people sleepy. Both are available over the counter. Medicated patches, worn behind the ear, are generally effective if they don't cause a reaction and make the wearer sick. Ginger has a reputation for

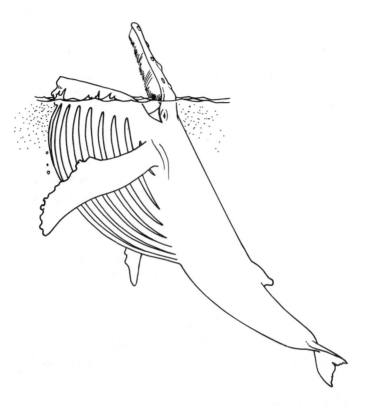

The humpback whale has a pleated throat that expands when the animal feeds. The whale then filters out the water through its baleen plates.

preventing motion sickness, and is available in capsule form at most health food stores. On a positive note, even the queasiest passengers feel better when the whales show up.

Of course, many people who take no precautions at all never become seasick. Please don't stay home because you are worried that you might get sick—after all, you might not. If you do start to feel uncomfortable, stay outside in the open air, keep your eyes on the horizon, and breathe deeply. Nibble on plain soda crackers. Stave off panic by thinking about anything except being sick. If none of that works, comfort yourself with the thought that everyone, even experienced sailors, gets seasick at least once.

Few children under age five enjoy being confined on a boat for an extended period of time. As for older children, please take into consideration the individual child's behavior in public, level of intellectual curiosity, and need for unrestricted space. If you do decide to bring along a young child, tell him or her what to expect on the expedition and what behavior will be expected.

Most whale-watch boat operators allow passengers to smoke cigarettes in a restricted area out on deck, but they discourage pipe or cigar smoking.

What You Will See from Shore

Sometimes people who have seen whales from shore, either from an official lookout or just meandering along the beach one day, feel that they've had the whole experience and think that they don't need to book passage on a whale-watch boat. Certainly, seeing a whale from shore is a thrill. I actually spotted a gray whale once through a living room window. But it's not the same. Watching whales from shore instead of going out to sea is something like watching a play on television instead of going to the theater and seeing the live performance. Watching from shore is fun, but it's a passive experience, not nearly as exciting as being smack in the middle of the action.

After the chapter about the kinds of whales you are likely to see, the rest of this book is set up to help you get to where the whales are. Make plans to go soon—and let me know what happens.

Whale Tales

Say "whale" and what comes to most people's minds is an image of a sperm whale. Moby Dick was a sperm whale, and the distinctive shape of Herman Melville's Great White Whale is so familiar that illustrations of that one species are often used to represent all whales. In fact, the mighty sperm whale, with its rectangle-shaped head and its long, narrow lower jaw, is unique among whales.

What the sperm whale has in common with all other whales is that it is a mammal. Aristotle was the first to record the observation that whales were not giant fish; that they did not breathe through gills. Whales are warm-blooded, air-breathing creatures that spend most of their time under water, rising to the surface to exhale and then take in great gasps of fresh air before submerging again.

More than 345 million years ago, an amphibian relative of the land vertebrates climbed out of the water and began to adapt to life on land. One group of mammals eventually returned to the water, and those were the early ancestors of today's whales. Over time, the noses of these air-breathing mammals moved from the front to the top of the head. A special valve evolved, so the whales can seal off their air passages when they are under water, and their external ears disappeared completely. Some whales hear with dense bones located on each side of their heads, where their external ears once were, picking up the smallest of vibrations.

All whales are cetaceans, a word derived from their biological order, Cetacea, from the Greek ketos or the Latin cetus, which both mean "whale." The order includes at least seventy-three species of whales, porpoises, and dolphins. One ancient suborder of whales disappeared more than twenty million years ago, but two suborders survive today. The existing suborders are Odontoceti ("toothed whales") and Mysticeti ("mustached whales").

The "mustache" is actually baleen—hard, keratinous fibers that overlap in the whales' mouths and serve as a sieve. When the whales eat, the hundreds of strips of baleen filter water out and leave behind the krill and small fish. Baleen was once known as "whalebone," and whales were butchered so the baleen could be used in corsets, shirt collar stays, brushes, and buggy whips and as ribs for umbrellas and lamp shades.

Baleen varies widely in size among whales. Shown here, to scale, are baleen strips from the bowhead whale (top), the blue whale (left), and the gray whale (right).

Except for sperm whales, all larger whales are baleen whales. All baleen whales—except for gray whales, right whales, bowhead whales, and pygmy right whales—are rorquals, whales with ventral (underside) pleats that allow their throats to expand while feeding. Baleen whales have two external blowholes. Toothed whales—sperm whales, orcas, narwhals, beluga whales, dolphins, and porpoises—have just one.

Whales are generally believed to be intelligent, curious, and nonaggressive toward humans. Most whales travel in "pods," social or family groups. Among behaviors common to some species of the larger whales are spyhopping, where a whale lifts its

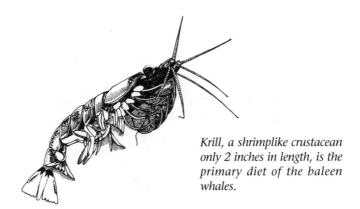

Krill, a shrimplike crustacean only 2 inches in length, is the primary diet of the baleen whales.

massive head out of the water and appears to look around, and breaching, where the whale leaps completely out of the water and then falls back with a thunderous crash. Several species raise their broad tails completely out of the water when they "sound," or begin a deep dive. Some whales stick their flippers or tails out of the water or slap them against the water's surface.

Scientists can't explain any particular behavior of whales, though they have formulated theories based on years of research. Because whales are difficult to study in their natural habitat, we actually know very little about the live animals.

We know a great deal about dead whales. The United States was once the world's greatest whaling power. By the nineteenth century, Yankee whalers no longer killed whales for meat, to survive, but for oil for lamps and machines and for by-products used in candles, crayons, dog food, fertilizer, cosmetics, and perfume. With hand-held harpoons thrown from wooden whaleboats, Yankee whalers had almost depleted the right and bowhead populations; then the modern age of whaling ushered in the exploding harpoon and the fleets of mechanized factory ships that have contributed to the slaughter of millions of whales in the twentieth century.

Today there is a relatively inexpensive substitute for every product once sought from whales. Yet eight of the twenty species

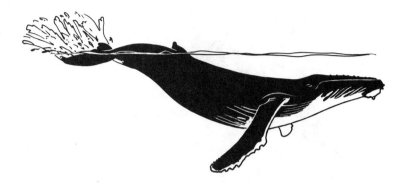

"Tail lobbing" is what scientists call the humpback's penchant for smacking its tail on the water's surface.

of "great whales"—the larger whales—are endangered, close to extinction. And in spite of a moratorium on commercial whaling declared in 1986, Japan, Norway, and Iceland continue to kill whales, claiming "scientific research" is their purpose.

But whales and dolphins also face other threats. Oil spills, such as the one in 1989 from the *Exxon Valdez* in Prince William Sound, kill whales, as do nylon fishing nets (also known as ghost nets) that drift through the open seas, entangling marine mammals and seabirds. Even more insidious are the tens of thousands of human-produced toxic substances that we dump into the sea—chemicals that, if we continue dumping, will practically guarantee the eventual extinction of marine mammals and all other life in the ocean. As we sit poised at the top of the food chain, we must ask ourselves, "Will we be next?"

The organizations listed in Appendix 2 believe that it's not too late to save whales and, by extension, to save ourselves. Write to those that interest you to learn how you can help.

Some of what scientists do know about sixteen species of whales and dolphins follows here. This general information relates to the species you are most likely to see on the whale-watch trips in this guidebook, listed according to size: blues, fin-backs, rights, bowheads, sperm whales, humpbacks, gray whales, minkes, orcas, pilot whales, narwhals, belugas, bottlenose dolphins, common dolphins, white-sided dolphins (Atlantic and Pacific), and harbor porpoises. By no means is this information complete. Several fine books on whale biology are listed in the Bibliography.

Population estimates, where available, are based on statistics from the International Whaling Commission. Still, many of the figures are speculative, as estimates change frequently. The range in length and weight of the different species is based, unfortunately, primarily on measurements taken from dead whales.

Blue whale *(Balaenoptera musculus).* The blue, or sulphur-bottom, whale is the largest creature ever to live on earth. Blue whales are blue-gray, often with gray mottling. Though they can attain a length of more than 100 feet and weigh between 130 and 150 tons, most of the largest blue whales were killed before the species was granted protected status. Today, most blue whales sighted are between 70 and 90 feet long.

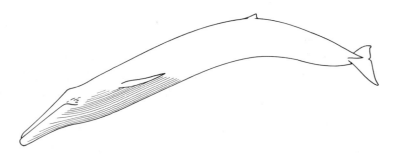

The blue whale is the largest creature ever to live on earth and eats as much as two tons of food a day.

The heart of a blue whale is about the size of a Volkswagen Beetle, and there is room on its tongue for a full-grown elephant to stand. A newborn blue whale measures 20 to 25 feet and weighs about three tons. The calf gains as much as 200 pounds a day while nursing, and an adult blue whale can eat as much as two tons of krill a day.

Blue whales are an endangered species. Only between 4,000 and 6,000 are left.

Fin whale *(Balaenoptera physalus).* Though the fin, or finback, whale has to settle for being the second largest animal on earth, it is the fastest of the large whales. The sleek finback can attain a speed of 30 miles an hour, a record only occasionally threatened by the sei whale. Fin whales grow to 80 feet in length and weigh sixty to seventy tons.

The fin whale is the second largest animal ever to live on earth and is known as "the greyhound of the sea" because it swims so swiftly.

Fin whales are dark gray to brownish black, with a characteristic white lower right jaw. A narrow ridge on the animal's back extends from the dorsal fin to the tail and gives the whale its nickname of "razorback."

The United States considers fin whales endangered, though they have not been granted that status internationally. An estimated 120,000 live in the seas of the world, down from a preexploitation population of 548,000.

Right whale *(Eubalaena glacialis/australis)*. Unfortunately, the right whale got its name from nineteenth-century whalers who considered it the "right" whale to kill because it swims slowly, it has abundant oil, and its carcass floats. The arched upper jaw holds baleen that grows to 7 feet long.

Northern and southern right whales, black in color, attain a length of 50 to 60 feet and weigh as much as forty-five tons. They have callosities, patches of thickened skin, that grow in the same places that human males have facial hair—mustaches, eyebrows, beard, and sideburns. The callosities are often covered with cyamid crustaceans, or whale lice. The distinctive number, size, shape, and placement of callosities on each right whale make it possible to recognize individual whales.

The North Atlantic right whale is the rarest of all whales because the whaling industry slaughtered so many of the animals.

The right whale is the most rare of all the whales. Both southern and northern right whales are endangered. When the Pilgrims landed in what is now Massachusetts, the North Atlantic Ocean was home to an estimated 20,000 right whales. A journal entry noted that one could almost walk across Cape Cod Bay on the backs of the animals, so plentiful were they. Today, only about 300 right whales live in the North Atlantic, and fewer than 2,000 live in the Southern Hemisphere. Some scientists fear that it is too late to save the species from extinction.

Bowhead whale *(Balaena mysticetus)*. Bowheads take their name from the exaggerated arch of the jaw, which houses baleen that grows up to 14 feet long. These whales are primarily black, with a white band underneath the chin. They grow as large as 65 feet long and weigh as much as sixty-five tons.

The bowhead whale boasts the longest baleen of all whales, with each individual strip growing 12 feet or even longer.

These mighty giants aren't easy to find, but you may be lucky enough to see one if you travel in the arctic regions. Bowhead whales are endangered, but they are still hunted by Alaskan Eskimos, who are allotted a certain number of "subsistence" kills each year. The Eskimos particularly enjoy muktuk, a delicacy consisting of the outer skin layers of bowhead whales: a tough outer layer, the true skin, and oily blubber. Muktuk may be eaten fresh, frozen, cooked, or pickled. The baleen is used to make intricately woven baskets. As someone once noted, "Nothing is wasted except the whale."

Fewer than 7,000 bowhead whales are believed to exist today, compared with a preexploitation population of 30,000.

Sperm whale *(Physeter macrocephalus)*. The rectangle-shaped head of the 50- to 60-foot sperm whale accounts for about one-

26

third of the animal's length and contains a "case" full of rich oil. Some scientists think that during dives below the surface of the ocean, the waxlike oil solidifies, which reduces buoyancy and helps the whale extend the distance of its dives.

One-third of the sperm whale's body is the head, which holds a huge "case" of waxy oil.

Male sperm whales weigh as much as fifty-nine tons and have the largest brain of any creature on earth. They are dark grayish-brown to brown and have a wrinkled skin behind the head. The animal's lower jaw is long and narrow and contains up to sixty conical teeth, which fit into corresponding sockets in the upper jaw. Sperm whales feed on giant squid; the squid can grow to 55 feet and weigh some 4,500 pounds.

Those teeth were once prized by whalers, who carved miniature scenes on them, an art known as scrimshaw. Another once-valued product from sperm whales is ambergris, a product from the intestinal bile used by the perfume industry to make permanent blends of various fragrances. The United States considers sperm whales an endangered species; fewer than one million live in the world's oceans. The peak of exploitation was reached in the 1960s, when 29,000 sperm whales were killed each year.

Humpback whale *(Megaptera novaeangliae)*. The "big-winged New Englander" is perhaps the most gregarious of all the large whales. If you've seen a whale breach, slap the water with its flipper or tail, poke its head up to watch you watching it, and raise its beautiful scalloped tail high out of the water before a long dive, chances are you've seen a humpback whale. The males also sing long, haunting songs.

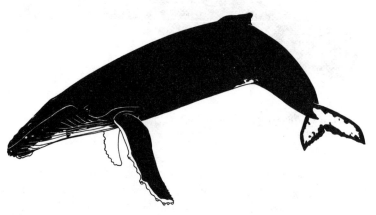

The humpback whale has distinctively long flippers and a reputation for curiosity about whale-watch boats.

Humpback whales, basically black or gray with some white on the throat or belly, flippers, and tail, grow to about 50 feet and can weigh as much as forty-five tons. The animal boasts the longest flippers of any whale, sporting 15-foot "wings" that have scalloped edges and are often white underneath. The "stovebolt" knobs on the humpback's head usually hold hair follicles, and some scientists think the single hair that protrudes from each may be a sensor. The pattern on the underside of each humpback's tail is unique, and individual whales are easily recognizable.

Humpback whales are endangered, down to about 10,000 compared to 65,000 estimated to have lived prior to the rise of the whaling industry.

Gray whale *(Esrichtius robustus)*. The gray whales are the conservationists' success story. Though the North Atlantic population was brought to extinction in the 1600s, the North Pacific populations have recovered twice from near extinction. In the mid-nineteenth century, so many gray whales were killed that they became classified as "economically extinct," which meant that there were so few left, it wasn't worth the time or trouble to hunt them. The species began to recover, only to be nearly wiped out again in modern times with the advent of mechanized

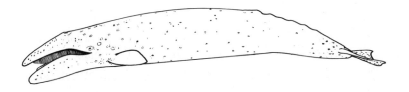

Some scientists believe the gray whale is the most closely related to the archaic whales.

whaling techniques. The government stepped in, and today between 17,000 and 24,000 gray whales migrate each year from the Bering, Chukchi, and western Beaufort seas to breeding grounds off Baja California.

Some scientists believe the gray whales are primitive in many ways and may be direct descendants of the ancient ancestral baleen whales. The body, flippers, and flukes (tail) of the stocky animals are mottled, with gray and white splotches. The whale's head is bumpy and warty, with bristly facial hairs, and patches of barnacles, algae, and whale lice cover much of the rest of the body. Gray whales grow to lengths of 45 to 50 feet and weigh about a ton per foot.

Beauty is only skin deep, of course, and gray whales delight more than two million whale watchers off the U.S. west coast each year. In the quiet lagoons off Baja California, some gray whales known as "the friendlies" have been known to approach Zodiac rafts full of whale watchers and come in close enough to be petted. And you may recall that the international effort expended off Point Barrow, Alaska, in the fall of 1988 was on behalf of three gray whales trapped in the ice.

In the United States, gray whales are still considered an endangered species, but the International Whaling Commission has reclassified them from "protected stock" to the status of "sustained management" stock.

Minke whale *(Balaenoptera acutorostrata)*. Legend has it that a Norwegian whaler named Minke mistook this smallest of the baleen whales for a mighty blue, and his amused peers promptly named the whale after him to commemorate forever his error.

Minkes are black to dark gray on the back, white on the belly and across an "armband" on the flipper (in the Northern Hemisphere). There may be as many as three subspecies of minkes, but generally these streamlined animals grow to about 30 feet and

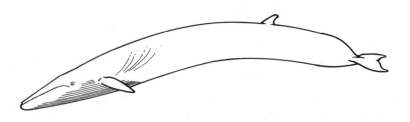

Minke whales are often mistaken for other, larger, baleen whales.

weigh up to seven tons. Some minkes have a reputation for being feisty, swimming close to shore in inlets and bays and popping up right in front of moving boats.

These whales are not considered endangered, and many are killed each year by those nations still active in commercial whaling. Also, several minke whales have been held in captivity in Japan, as they are the only member of the genus small enough to be displayed and researched.

Orca whale *(Orcinus orca).* Some orcas, or killer whales, spend their lives in show business at theme parks and oceanariums, and many people have seen the shiny black and white whales up close. Orcas are members of the dolphin family, and like dolphins they are acrobatically inclined. Still, orcas in captivity rarely achieve their full growth potential.

Orcas, commonly called "killer whales," often swim in family groups within the pod.

In the wild, male orcas grow to about 30 feet, weigh up to eight tons, and sport striking 6-foot dorsal fins. Females are slightly smaller. The animals have ten to thirteen conical teeth on each side of each jaw, and they prey on fish, squid, birds, seals, turtles, porpoises, and, occasionally, whales.

Research has shown that orcas kill for food, not for sport, and they do not go after human beings without extreme provocation. Legend has it that these whales were originally known as "whale killers" and that over time the name was reversed to the more ominous version. No population estimates are available, and orcas are not considered an endangered species.

Pilot whale *(Globicephala melaena and G. macrorhynchus).* At aquariums and theme parks, you can distinguish between long-finned and short-finned pilot whales because there will be large signs identifying them, but at sea even experts find it nearly impossible to tell the two species apart. A good guess is possible, however, because the long-finned pilot whale is generally found in nontropical waters and the short-finned pilot whale is seen in tropical waters.

The long-finned pilot whale is one of the largest animals ever kept in captivity. You may have met one in a marine life park.

Both species have large bulbous foreheads, stocky elongated bodies, and prominent dorsal fins and are slate gray to black in color. The short-finned pilot whales, not surprisingly, have shorter flippers than long-finned pilot whales. Males of both species reach a length of 19 or 20 feet, with females slightly smaller. Both species feed on squid and schooling fish and travel in herds of up to several hundred individuals, often in the company of bottlenose dolphins.

Narwhal *(Monodon monocerus)*. Male narwhals go through life armed to the teeth, so to speak. The adult male of this unusual species boasts a tooth that grows through the upper lip into an 8-foot-long tusk. No one is sure of the tooth's function, though males have been seen battling with their built-in swords. Eskimo and Alaskan Indian tribes prized the narwhal's tusk most highly, and such a gift to the chief or the tribal elder was considered a great tribute.

The male narwhal has an 8-foot-long tusk, unique among whales, that may have inspired the legend of the unicorn.

Narwhals are stocky animals, slow swimmers, that range in color from dark blue-gray in juveniles to mottled dark brown in adults. Males grow to about 15 feet, excluding the tusk, and weigh about 3,500 pounds. Females are slightly smaller. The whales live in arctic waters, where they feed on squid, fish, shrimp, and crab.

Beluga whale *(Delphinapterus leucas)*. The only true "white" whales are the belugas. The whales are born gray or brown and turn white as they mature.

Belugas, which are not the source of the famous caviar that comes from sturgeons, are also known as "sea canaries" because of their impressive range of vocalizations. They squeal and chirp and are considered among the most vocal of all whales.

The animals are stocky, with a disproportionately small head. Generally they grow to about 16 feet and weigh as much

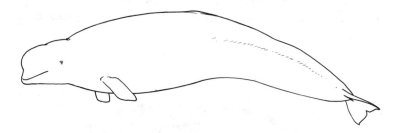

The beluga whale, also known as the sea canary, is famous for its raucous songs.

as 2,400 pounds, though there are size differences among different geographical populations. Scientists estimate there are about 50,000 belugas, all living in arctic or subarctic water: The 500 left in the St. Lawrence River are believed to be at the greatest risk because of the toxic pollutants in the river.

Bottlenose dolphin *(Tursiops truncatus)*. Remember Flipper? That particular bottlenose dolphin may have been the first, last, and only bottlenose dolphin to star in its own television series, but it was largely responsible for the fond associations many people have with the species.

Again, the animals vary slightly in different geographical regions of the world, and at least two distinct subspecies may

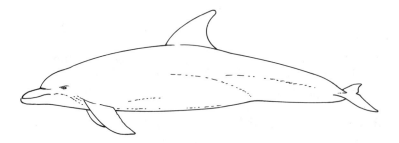

Flipper, star of his own television show, was a bottlenose dolphin.

exist. In general, bottlenose dolphins range from dark to lighter gray in color. They grow to about 13 feet and weigh as much as 1,400 pounds. They live in shallow water and are often seen riding the surf.

Common dolphin *(Delphinus delphis).* These are the aerial acrobats that Herman Melville probably had in mind when he wrote, "They always swim in hilarious shoals which upon the sea keep tossing themselves to heaven like caps in a Fourth of July crowd." The pods, or herds, may number as many as two thousand individuals. In addition to the acrobatics, common dolphins are said to change course for the opportunity to ride the bow wave of a passing ship, or even of a passing larger whale, for that matter.

The common dolphin is found in many areas.

Common dolphins are often tricolored: black, gray, and cream. They reach a length of 7 to 8 feet and weigh 200 to 300 pounds. Unlike the bottlenose dolphin, common dolphins do not thrive in captivity. They live in temperate and tropical waters of all oceans.

White-sided dolphin *(Lagen-orhynchus acutus and L. obliquidens).* Atlantic and Pacific white-sided dolphins are not classified as the same species, but they share more than a name.

Both are primarily black on top and white on the underbelly, with a gray stripe running from behind the eye to the beginning of the tail. The Atlantic white-sided dolphin has a characteristic yellow patch that begins just under the dorsal fin and extends back. Both species have dorsal fins that are tall and quite pointed, and both travel in herds of up to one thousand animals.

Atlantic white-sided dolphins are the larger of the two, growing to 10 feet and weighing 400 to 550 pounds. Pacific white-sided dolphins are 7 to 8 feet in length and weigh at least 330 pounds. Both species feed on hake, squid, and sardines.

Top: The Atlantic white-sided dolphin is often sighted in the North Atlantic Ocean. Bottom: The Pacific white-sided dolphin is a frequent bow-wave rider on whale-watch trips off the California coast.

Harbor porpoise *(Phocena phocena).* The harbor porpoise is the most commonly seen of all porpoises, and though it does not ride the bow waves of ships, it has been known occasionally to approach small boats. The stocky little animal is usually brown or dark gray, with lighter gray coloring at the flanks.

Harbor porpoises grow to about 6 feet in length and weigh up to 200 pounds. They surface to breathe about every fifteen seconds and do not stay submerged longer than three or four minutes. The animals have been described as generally undemonstrative, with a "businesslike" approach to life.

The harbor porpoise is one of the smallest species of whale.

Directory
of
Tours

KEY

 Sheltered area

 Food

 Beverages

 Coffee only

 Binoculars

 Hydrophone

 Brochure

Northeast U.S. Coast

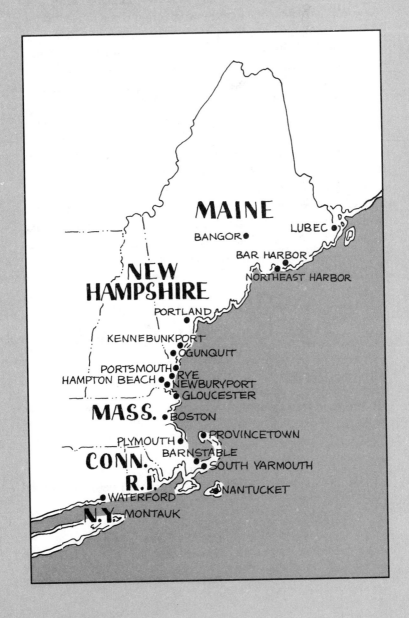

Northeast U.S. Coast

Commercial whale-watch tours are said to have originated on the Northeast Coast, and today four New England states plus New York take advantage of the whales that come to feed in the Gulf of Maine from April through October. Whale-watch trips depart from numerous cities and towns in Connecticut, Maine, Massachusetts, New Hampshire, and New York, setting out to see humpbacks, finbacks, minkes, the occasional rare right whale, and assorted dolphins.

Massachusetts leads the way, with more than twenty whale-watch tours. Provincetown, on Cape Cod, boasts five! Maine is active in the industry, with trips originating from seven cities along the coast. Four tours operate out of New Hampshire and one each from Connecticut and New York.

The whale-watch tours on the Northeast Coast range from trips sponsored by small charter companies to research-oriented trips run by institutions and organizations. Here, too, are excursion boats built specifically for whale watching.

TOURISM INFORMATION

Connecticut

Connecticut Department of Economic Development
865 Brook Street, Rocky Hill, CT 06067
(800) CT–BOUND

Southeastern Connecticut Tourism District
27 Masonic Street, P.O. Box 89, New London, CT 06320
(800) 222–6783
(203) 444–2206

Maine

Maine Office of Tourism
189 State Street, Augusta, ME 04333
(207) 289–5710

Maine Publicity Bureau
97 Winthrop Street, Hallowell, ME 04347
(207) 289–2423

Massachusetts

Massachusetts Office of Travel & Tourism
100 Cambridge Street, 13th Floor, Boston, MA 02202
(800) 447–MASS
(800) 632–8038 in Massachusetts

Cape Cod Chamber of Commerce
Hyannis, MA 02601
(508) 362–3225

New Hampshire

New Hampshire Office of Vacation Travel
P.O. Box 856, Concord, NH 03301
(603) 271–2666

New York

Department of Economic Development
One Commerce Plaza, Albany, NY 12245
(518) 474–5676

Long Island Tourism & Convention Commission
213 Carleton Avenue, Central Islip, Long Island, NY 11722
(516) 234–4959

Lubec, Maine

Lubec Marine Services

9 High Street, Lubec, ME 04652; (207) 733–5584

Whales:	Humpback, finback, right, minke, Atlantic white-sided dolphin
Season:	June 1 through September 30
Boats:	One boat; 20–25 passengers
Trips:	One 3- to 4-hour trip daily at 1 P.M. A second 8- to 9-hour trip to the Bay of Fundy is available on Saturday only from August 1 through September 30, leaving at 8 A.M. On Saturdays the shorter trip is the busier.
Fare:	Shorter trip: adults, $15; children: 5 to 12, $5; under 5, free. Longer trip: adults, $40; children 5 to 12, $20 (the trip is not recommended for children under 5). Reservations advised.
Departure:	Trips leave from the Lubec Public Landing. Take Route 1 to Route 189.
Naturalist:	Yes

Edwin "Butch" Huntley, in business for more than fifteen years, says Lubec Marine Services is the only business of its kind in the area.

Bar Harbor, Maine

Acadian Whale Watcher

Golden Anchor Pier, 56 West Street, Bar Harbor, ME 04644; (207) 288–9794 or 9776

Whales:	Humpback, fin, minke, right, Atlantic white-sided dolphin

Season:	Mid-May through late October
Boats:	One boat, the *Acadian Whale Watcher;* 150 passengers
Trips:	Two 4-hour trips daily in summer at 8 A.M. and 1:30 P.M. and a shorter sunset cruise that leaves about 5 P.M. In May and October, only the sunset cruise may be available. Midweek is busiest.
Fare:	Adults, $25; senior citizens, $20; children: ages 9 to 14, $18; ages 6 to 8, $15; 5 and under, free. Group rates and private charter rates. Reservations advised.
Departure:	Trips leave from the Golden Anchor Pier on West Street in Bar Harbor, at the foot of Rodick Street about half a mile from Route 3.
Naturalist:	Yes

"The *Acadian* is a new vessel that is perfect for the sightseer," says naturalist Robert Wilds, "as we sail around Acadia National Park on our way to the whales' feeding grounds. Also, we whale watch in an area where there are very few vessels." Tapes of the *Acadian* trips are for sale, available free to groups who charter the boat.

Note: This same Robert Wilds served as the naturalist on my first whale watch, out of Barnstable Harbor in 1982. The experience can be habit forming!

Frenchman Bay Company
1 West Street, P.O. Box 153, Bar Harbor, ME 04609;
(207) 288–3322

Whales:	Fin, humpback, right, minke, Atlantic white-sided dolphin
Season:	Mid-May through mid-October
Boats:	Six boats; 49–210 passengers each
Trips:	One 4- to 5-hour trip daily at 12:15 P.M. during off season (late May to late June and early September to

mid-October). Two 4-hour trips daily at 8:15 A.M. and
2:15 P.M. from late June to early September. Midweek
is busiest in the summer.

Fare: Adults, $25; children: under 12, $18; under 5, free.
Private charter rates available. Reservations advised.

Departure: Trips leave from the Frenchman Bay Company pier at
the corner of Main and West streets on the waterfront
in Bar Harbor.

Naturalist: Yes

"You'll leave the port of Bar Harbor, past magnificent summer homes
and the rocky shores of Acadia National Park. Keep an eye peeled for
eagles, ospreys, and seals on the way out," advises Captain Marc
Brent. "Once at sea, we'll look for shearwaters, petrels, and puffins.
About forty-five minutes after we leave Frenchman Bay, we'll arrive
in the area where whales abound."

Northeast Harbor, Maine

Maine Whalewatch
P.O. Box 78, Northeast Harbor, ME 04662; (207) 228–5803

Whales: Finback, humpback, right, minke, harbor porpoise

Season: June 1 through September 30

Boats: Two boats; 38 passengers each

Trips: One 9-hour trip daily at 8:30 A.M. The busiest day is
Friday.

Fare: $30 per person: Children under 5, free. Reservations
advised.

Departure: Trips leave from the Sea Street Pier (the Municipal
Wharf) in Northeast Harbor. When entering town,
take the only road to the left and head for the water.

Naturalist: Naturalists from Allied Whale, the cetacean research group at the College of the Atlantic

"Maine Whalewatch was founded by researchers from Allied Whale. The main motivation behind the trips was, and continues to be, to supply researchers a platform to study whales and to educate students and the general public about marine endangered species," says Captain Bob Bowman.

"We can't guarantee whales, but our sighting average is very high, and passengers feel that even on the possible few days without whales, their time was enjoyably spent." Harbor porpoise and harbor and gray seals are seen on virtually every trip, as are myriad seabirds.

Richard M. Savage & Sons

P.O. Box 321, Northeast Harbor, ME 04662; (207) 276–3785

Whales:	Fin, humpback, minke
Season:	June through September
Boats:	One boat, the *Poor Richard*; 20 passengers
Trips:	One full-day trip daily, by charter only. Sunday is the busiest day.
Fare:	$450 per day. Reservations required.
Departure:	Trips leave from the town landing at Northeast Harbor. Take Sea Street due east to the water.
Naturalist:	Captain narrates trips.

"We're the only vessel that offers private daily charters with a licensed vessel and captain and optional lobster picnics," notes Richard Savage II. Captain Savage, an island native, has been in business since 1970 and has extensive cruising experience on Maine waters.

Bangor, Maine

Seafarers Expeditions
P.O. Box 691, Bangor, ME 04401; (207) 942–7942

Whales:	Finback in July; right and humpback in August
Season:	July and August
Boats:	The 42-foot *Sea Princess*, a commercial fishing boat set up for whale watching
Trips:	Two 5-day trips to Grand Manan Island. Participants stay in motels at night. Trips conclude in Bangor, Maine.
Fare:	$655 per person. Price includes meals, lodging, ground transportation, boat trips, and professional guides; does not include airfare.
Departure:	Trips leave from Bangor, Maine.
Naturalist:	Experienced naturalists accompany both trips.

"This trip continues to be one of our most popular, as it offers you the chance to observe a multitude of whale, dolphin, and seabird species in a beautiful setting," notes Seafarers Expeditions founder Scott Marion.

Founded in 1981, Seafarers Expeditions is headed by Marion, a naturalist who has led whale and bird tours throughout the North Atlantic for many years. Scott Mercer, owner and head naturalist of New England Whale Watch, works with Scott Marion, as does Scott Krause at the New England Aquarium. Half a dozen other consulting whale biologists, none named Scott, are also involved.

Portland, Maine

Odyssey Whale Watch
Commercial Street, P.O. Box 1084, Portland, ME 04104;
(207) 775–0727

Whales:	Finback, humpback, minke, right, Atlantic white-sided dolphin
Season:	Mid-May through mid-October
Boats:	One, the *Odyssey*; 95 passengers
Trips:	One 7¹/₂-hour trip daily at 8 A.M., and a 4¹/₂-hour sunset trip at 4:30 P.M. Wednesday through Sunday. Weekend day trips are the busiest.
Fare:	Adults, $30; senior citizens, $25; children: 13 to 17, $25; 12 and under, $20 on the day trips. Sunset cruises cost $25 for adults; $20 for senior citizens; children: 13 to 17, $20; 12 and under, $18. Reservations advised.
Departure:	Trips leave from Long Wharf on Commercial Street in Portland. From the Maine Turnpike, take Exit 7, then take the exit ramp for Route 295. Take Exit 4 off 295 and follow signs for Route 1A, Commercial Street, or the waterfront. Ticket booth is next to Key Bank, by DeMillo's Restaurant.
Naturalist:	Yes

"We are the only whale watch in Portland, and we are a small family-run business," notes Daniel Libby. "Our sightings regularly feature seals, dolphins, sharks, and numerous seabirds as well as whales."

The owner and skipper is a marine biology teacher at the local high school.

Kennebunkport, Maine

Indian Whale Watch
P.O. Box 2672, Kennebunkport, ME 04046; (207) 967–5912

Whales:	Humpback, fin, minke, right, Atlantic white-sided dolphin
Season:	June through October
Boats:	One boat, the *Indian;* 72 passengers
Trips:	One 5- to 6-hour trip daily at 10 A.M. The busiest day is Saturday.
Fare:	Adults, $25; senior citizens (60 and older), $20; children: 13 to 18, $20; 6 to 12, $15; under 6, free. Group rates and private charters available. Reservations advised.
Departure:	Trips leave from Arundel Wharf Restaurant on Ocean Avenue in Kennebunkport.
Naturalist:	Yes

"We try to make every trip a good time as well as an educational experience," says owner Karla Kay Brindle. "Each member of my crew is an enthusiastic whale lover and they have been with us for years. Our naturalist is a marine mammal biologist with a strong ecology background. He gives a commentary as well as answers questions, and every day we offer a free ticket to anyone who can stump the crew."

Brindle adds, "Our feeling is that everyone should experience whales—these wondrous creatures—and if we didn't have to make a living, I would take everyone out for free." Whale sightings are guaranteed.

Nautilus Whale Watch
P.O. Box 2777, Route 9, Kennebunkport, ME 04046;
(207) 967–0707

Whales:	Humpback, fin, minke, Atlantic white-sided dolphin
Season:	Mid-May through late September
Boats:	One boat; 100 passengers
Trips:	One 5- to 6- hour trip daily at 10 A.M.
Fare:	Adults, $25; senior citizens, $22.50; children under 12, $15. Reservations advised.
Departure:	Trips leave from Arundel boatyard, off Route 9.
Naturalist:	Captain serves as naturalist.

"All personnel are trained to answer questions about the whales and provide information, but generally, our captain is the official naturalist and handles the microphone," notes Nautilus staffer Diane Emery. Whale sightings are guaranteed.

Ogunquit, Maine

Ugly Anne
P.O. Box 863, 9 King's Lane, Ogunquit, ME 03907;
(207) 646–7202

Whales:	Humpback, fin, minke
Season:	May 1 through November 1
Boats:	One, the *Ugly Anne*; 35 passengers
Trips:	Two 4-hour trips daily at 8 A.M. and 1 P.M.
Fare:	$25 per person. Reservations required.

Departure:	Trips leave from Perkins Cove in Ogunquit. Take Shore Road to Oarweed to the dock.
Naturalist:	No

Owners Jeanne and Ken Young, Sr., note, "The *Ugly Anne* is primarily a charter fishing boat, but we do see a lot of whales in August and September." Charters are available. And you can buy *Ugly Anne* T-shirts and sweatshirts.

Portsmouth, New Hampshire

Oceanic Whale Watch Expeditions
Isles of Shoals Steamship Company, 315 Market Street, P.O. Box 311, Portsmouth, NH 03801; (800) 441–4620, (603) 431–5505

Whales:	Humpback, fin, minke, right, Atlantic white-sided dolphin
Season:	Late April through October 31
Boats:	Two boats; 149 and 349 passengers
Trips:	One 6-hour trip daily at 9:30 A.M. (Departure time may vary according to the season.) Saturday is the busiest day.
Fare:	Adults, $21.50; senior citizens, $20; children, $14.50. Reservations required on weekends; advised at all times. Guests at the Sheraton Hotel receive a discount on whale watch.
Departure:	Trips leave from Barker Wharf, 315 Market Street in Portsmouth. Off Interstate 95 (going north or south)

take Exit 7 and turn toward downtown Portsmouth.
Go about 1 mile. Office is across from the Sheraton
Hotel.

Naturalist: Yes

"Though we cannot guarantee sightings, as the oldest whale watchers in New England, we do have a 99 percent success rate, and with our naturalist, we can always guarantee an educational day at sea," notes sales director Maureen McGinty.

The naturalist, with field experience dating back to 1965, is also knowledgeable about bird identification and local history.

Rye, New Hampshire

Atlantic Fleet
P.O. Box 678, Rye, NH 03870; (603) 964–5220

Whales:	Humpback, fin, minke, right
Season:	May 1 through early October
Boats:	Two boats; 30 and 149 passengers
Trips:	One 4-hour trip at 5:30 P.M. Monday through Friday. The most popular day is Wednesday.
Fare:	Adults, $18; senior citizens, $16; children, $13. Reservations are advised.
Departure:	Trips leave from Rye Harbor State Marina on Route 1A, the coastal highway.
Naturalist:	Yes

Owner Brad Cook notes, "Our naturalist provides a precruise discussion and orientation, narration during the trip, and answers questions one-on-one on the return trip. Also, we have fast aluminum vessels, which provide more time on the whale grounds."

New Hampshire Seacoast Cruises
Rye Harbor State Marina, Box 232, Rye, NH 03870;
(603) 964–5545

Whales:	Finback, humpback, minke, Atlantic white-sided dolphin, harbor porpoise
Season:	May 1 through mid-October
Boats:	One boat, the *Granite State*; 150 passengers
Trips:	One 6-hour trip daily from 8 A.M. to 2 P.M. A second trip is offered on Thursdays and Saturdays during July and August from 5 to 9 P.M.
Fare:	Adults, $20; children, $14; under 4, free. Ten percent discount for senior citizens. Reservations advised.
Departure:	Trips leave from Rye Harbor State Marina on Route 1A between Hampton Beach and Portsmouth, next to Saunders' Restaurant. Look for the giant American flag.
Naturalist:	Yes

"Every whale watch is led by an experienced professional research/ naturalist, and the cruise is preceded by a lecture with graphics," says owner Leo Axtin. "Also, we are the nearest mainland port to the Isles of Shoals, the southernmost harbor seal nesting area in the North Atlantic. Almost every whale trip takes us past these islands."

Hampton Beach, New Hampshire

Al Gauron Deep Sea Fishing
State Pier, Hampton Beach, NH 03842; (603) 926–2469

Whales:	Humpback, finback, right, minke, Atlantic white-sided dolphin
Season:	March through November
Boats:	Four boats; three carry 77 passengers; one, 120
Trips:	Three 4- to 5-hour sunset whale-watch cruises each week as weather permits. Boats are otherwise available for private charter.
Fare:	Adults, $17; senior citizens, $16; children, $12. Reservations advised.
Departure:	Trips leave from Hampton Harbor, by the Hampton River bridge in Hampton Beach.
Naturalist:	Captain narrates trips.

"We have four boats in our fleet and have one of the best reputations on the East Coast," says Captain Rocky Gauron. "We are family owned and operated, and all our captains have piloted their boats on at least one hundred whale watches. They are able to handle narrations very capably."

Newburyport, Massachusetts

New England Whale Watch
P.O. Box 825, Hampton, NH 03842; (508) 465–7165

Whales:	Humpback, finback, minke, right, harbor porpoise, Atlantic white-sided dolphin

Where the Whales Are

Season:	April through October
Boats:	One boat, the 100-foot *Capt. Red;* could carry 300, but passengers restricted to 145.
Trips:	Two daily, 9 A.M. to 3 P.M. and 3:30 to 8:30 P.M. The Saturday morning trips are busiest.
Fare:	Adults, $23; senior citizens, $20; children 16 and under, $18; $15 per person for school groups. Reservations advised.
Departure:	Trips leave from the dock at Hilton's Fishing Parties, 54 Merrimac Street in Newburyport, along the Merrimac River half a mile east of U.S. Route 1, next to Captain's Quarters Restaurant.
Naturalist:	Professional biologists actively involved in marine research serve as naturalists.

New England Whale Watch, formerly New Hampshire Whale Watch, was founded in 1978 and was one of the very first whale-watch businesses in New England. The cruises are research and education oriented, and the researchers on board photographically track and identify individual humpback and right whales, both endangered species.

"We have highly experienced guides with broad experience in the field," says Scott Mercer, founder and owner of New England Whale Watch. Mercer, who is a researcher, author, lecturer, and university professor, is one of those knowledgeable guides.

Gloucester, Massachusetts

American Cetacean Society Expeditions
P.O. Box 2639, San Pedro, CA 90731; (213) 548–6279

Whales:	Right, humpback, fin
Season:	Late August

Boats: The *Yankee Freedom*, which sleeps 40 passengers

Trips: One annual 4-day trip to Browns Bank (off Nova Scotia), the Bay of Fundy, and Stellwagen Bank. Trip concludes in Gloucester, Massachusetts.

Fare: $750 for members of the American Cetacean Society. (A family membership is $25 a year.) Nonmembers pay 10 percent more.

Departure: Trips leave from Cape Ann Marina Complex in Gloucester, Mass. From Boston, take I–95 north to Route 128; go north to Exit 14 and head toward Gloucester, about $2^1/2$ miles. Look for the Yankee Fleet office on the left.

Naturalist: Naturalists from the American Cetacean Society accompany the trip.

Founded in 1967, the American Cetacean Society is based in San Pedro, California, and has regional chapters across the country. The group has conducted trips for groups to see whales since 1973. "Our trips are designed for people who are interested in the world about them and want an adventure with whales and nature!" a spokeswoman notes.

Cape Ann Whale Watch

P.O. Box 345, Rose's Wharf, Gloucester, MA 01930
(508) 283–5110

Whales: Humpback, finback, minke, right, Atlantic white-sided dolphin

Season: Early May through mid-October

Boats: Two boats; 130 passengers each

Trips: Two 4-hour trips daily in the summer at 8:30 A.M. and 1:30 P.M. Usually one midmorning trip in early spring and late fall. Weekend afternoon trips are the busiest.

Where the Whales Are

Fare:	Adults, $18; senior citizens over 60, $13; children under 16, $10. Reservations required. Guests at the Twin Light Manor/Best Western Motel receive a discount.
Departure:	Trips leave from Rose's Wharf, 415 Main Street in historic downtown Gloucester. From Boston, follow Route 128 north to Gloucester. At Exit 10, bear right onto Eastern Avenue, then bear right onto Main Street. Rose's Wharf is about .2 mile on the left, opposite the Old Colony gas station.
Naturalist:	Naturalists from the Cetacean Research Unit

Captain Jim Douglass notes, "All trips are research oriented and are led by members of the Cetacean Research Unit, the most experienced naturalists in the area. Also, we were the first whale-watching company in the Gloucester area and the second on the East Coast. We've been in this business since 1978."

A percentage of each fare is donated to the Cetacean Research Unit.

Captain Bill & Sons Whale Watch Cruises
9 Travers Street, Gloucester, MA 01930; (508) 283–6995

Whales:	Humpback, finback, right, minke
Season:	May 1 through mid-October
Boats:	Four boats; 120, 110, 105, and 70 passengers
Trips:	Two 4-hour trips daily at 9 A.M. and 2 P.M. in summer; additional trip on Saturdays according to demand. One trip daily in spring and fall, at varied times. Saturday afternoon trips are the most popular.
Fare:	Adults, $18; senior citizens, $10; children under 16, $10. Reservations advised.

Departure: Two of the boats leave from Rose's Wharf and two from the Cape Ann Marina. To reach Rose's Wharf from Boston, take Route 128 north past two rotaries to the stoplights. Turn right and go 1/4 mile to sign for Rose's Wharf. To reach the Cape Ann Marina, from Boston take Route 128 north to Exit 14. Turn right and head toward Gloucester; go about 2½ miles to marina.

Naturalist: Naturalist on board from Cetacean Research Unit

Captain Bill Cunningham noted in 1989, "Captain Bill's boasts a superb sighting record: 100 percent from 1979 to 1985; 99.5 percent in 1986; 99.4 percent in 1987 and 100 percent in 1988. Our deep-sea fishing boats that leave the dock at 5 A.M. radio back the location of the whales, so we know where to go before we leave the dock."

Videotapes of whale behavior are shown throughout the trip on a color television in the spacious main cabin.

Seafarers Expeditions

P. O. Box 691, Bangor, ME 04401; (207) 942–7942

Whales: Sperm, finback, minke, humpback, pilot, orca, right, dolphin

Season: Early July and late August

Boats: The *Yankee Freedom*; sleeps 40 passengers

Trips: One 3-day trip to Georges Bank in July and one 4-day trip to Browns Bank in Nova Scotia in late August. Trips start and conclude in Gloucester, Massachusetts.

Fare: $595 per person for Georges Bank trip; $725 for Browns Bank trip. Price includes meals, ground transportation, boat trips, and professional guides; does not include airfare.

Where the Whales Are

Departure:	Trips leave from Cape Ann Marina complex, Gloucester, Mass. From Boston, take I–95 north to Route 128; go north to Exit 14 and head toward Gloucester, about 2¹/₂ miles. Look for the Yankee Fleet office on the left.
Naturalist:	Experienced naturalist accompanies all trips.

Founded in 1981, Seafarers Expeditions is headed by Scott Marion, a naturalist who has led whale and bird tours for many years throughout the North Atlantic. Scott Mercer, owner and head naturalist of New England Whale Watch, works with Scott Marion, as does Scott Krause at the New England Aquarium.

"Our 1988 expedition to Georges Bank broke our long-standing record by sighting twelve different whale species, and our Browns Bank trip that same year observed the largest courtship group of right whales ever recorded, involving more than thirty-five fifty-ton right whales," Marion says.

Seven Seas Whale Watch
Seven Seas Wharf, Gloucester, MA 01930; (508) 283–1776

Whales:	Humpback, finback, minke, right, pilot
Season:	May through mid-October
Boats:	Two boats; 100 and 149 passengers
Trips:	Three 4-hour trips daily at 8 A.M., 1 P.M., and 2 P.M. Sunset cruises at 6 P.M. on weekends. The 1 P.M. trip on weekends is the busiest.
Fare:	Adults, $18; senior citizens, $12; children under 16, $10. Group rates and school rates available. Reservations advised.
Departure:	Trips leave from the historic Seven Seas Wharf downtown on Route 127. Take Exit 11 off Route 12 and proceed downtown.

Naturalist: Naturalist on board

"We offer the only steel-hulled vessel on Cape Ann, and we were the first to originate the 'guaranteed sightings' policy," notes Corinne Wadsworth, office manager. "You are guaranteed to see whales on every expedition or you receive a rain check for another trip."

Yankee Whalewatch

The Yankee Fleet, 75 Essex Avenue, Gloucester, MA 01930; (800) 942–5464 (in the northeast) or (508) 283–0313

Whales:	Humpback, finback, minke, right, Atlantic white-sided dolphin
Season:	May 1 through October 31
Boats:	Seven boats; 70, 125, 144, or 150 passengers
Trips:	Two or three 4 1/2-hour trips daily on weekdays, three to five trips on Saturdays, two to four on Sundays—as demand warrants throughout the season. Generally, departure times are 8:30 A.M., 1:30 P.M., 2:30 P.M., and 5:30 P.M. The Saturday 1:30 P.M. trip is the busiest.
Fare:	Adults, $18; senior citizens over 65, $13; children under 16, $10. Reservations advised. Package deal available for guests at the Cape Ann Marina Resort. $45 fare includes rental of a camcorder, which crew members will help you operate.
Departure:	Trips leave from Cape Ann Marina complex. From Boston, take I–95 north to Route 128; go north to Exit 14 and head toward Gloucester, about 2 1/2 miles. Look for the Yankee Fleet office on the left.
Naturalist:	Naturalists from the Atlantic Cetacean Research Center are aboard to narrate and answer questions.

"The Yankee Fleet has been family-owned and operated since 1944, and we use our newest, fastest vessels for whale watching," says Candace Garrett, programs director. "In 1990, we instituted a general environment awareness program to educate passengers about things everyone can do to make a difference in protecting and cleaning up our environment."

From time to time, the Yankee Fleet offers extended whale-watch trips in conjunction with Seafarers Expeditions. See Seafarers listing for details.

Boston, Massachusetts

A. C. Cruise Line
28 Northern Avenue, Boston, MA 02210;
(800) 422–8419, (617) 426–8419

Whales:	Humpback, finback, Atlantic white-sided dolphin
Season:	Mid-April through mid-October
Boats:	Two boats; 146 and 400 passengers
Trips:	One 8-hour trip at 10 A.M. Wednesdays through Sundays. Weekends are busiest.
Fare:	Adults, $20; children, $12. Reservations advised.
Departure:	Trips leave from Pier 1, 28 Northern Avenue at the bridge in the South Station area of Boston. Take the John F. Fitzgerald Expressway to either Northern Avenue or Congress Street.
Naturalist:	Captain serves as naturalist.

Captain Alan Circeo cruises among the harbor islands and out to Stellwagen Bank to view the humpbacks and fin whales feeding.

"It's possible to see dolphins, various seabirds, ships, yachts—there's always a surprise every trip," he says. Whale sightings are guaranteed, and the *Cape Ann* and *Virginia C II* are both available for private charters.

Co-Sponsors: Dirigo Cruises
39 Waterside Lane, Clinton, CT 06413; (203) 669–7068

Oceanic Society Expeditions
Fort Mason Center, Building E, San Francisco, CA 94123; (415) 441–1106

Whales:	Humpback, fin
Season:	August
Boats:	The 95-foot schooner *Harvey Gamage*; 30 passengers, housed primarily in double cabins
Trips:	Two 1-week educational whale-watch voyages with stops at Salem, Marblehead, Gloucester, and Nantucket. Participants live aboard.
Fare:	$695 per person per week. Senior citizens and young adults under 18, $595; children under 12 sharing a cabin, $250. Price does not include airfare to Boston.
Departure:	Trips leave from Pier 7 at 290 Northern Avenue in Boston. Take the John F. Fitzgerald Expressway to either Northern Avenue or Congress Street. Pier 7 is about 1/2 mile from the South Station.
Naturalist:	Naturalists from the Oceanic Society accompany trips.

Marge O'Connor at Dirigo Cruises notes, "The marine biologist on board will be familiar with all the marine mammals and birds, and you can expect daily lectures on various aspects of the world of whales and seabirds. We will also have sailing instruction and some great guest lectures. There is also a library of related materials for your use, as well as charts of the area."

New England Aquarium
Central Wharf, Boston, MA 02110; (617) 973–5277

Whales:	Humpback, finback, minke, right, Atlantic white-sided dolphin
Season:	Mid-April through late October
Boats:	One boat, the *Voyager;* 150 passengers
Trips:	One 5½-hour trip at 9 A.M. each weekday; one trip at 8 A.M. on Saturdays, Sundays, and holidays. In summer there may be a second trip at 2 P.M. on weekends and holidays. During April and most of October, trips start at 11 A.M. Weekends, especially holidays, are busiest.
Fare:	Adults, $22; senior citizens, military service personnel, and college students, $18; children, $16.50. Group rates available. Reservations advised.
Departure:	Trips leave from the New England Aquarium's dock, just to the left of the Aquarium building, which is on Central Wharf on Boston's waterfront, off Atlantic Avenue.
Naturalist:	Naturalist from the Aquarium staff on board

"During the trip, our experienced staff will teach you how to identify the different species of whales and the other marine life that inhabit the area," notes Captain Ken Wright. "On the rare occasion that whales are not seen during your voyage, we will be happy to reschedule you for another trip."

The New England Aquarium is a private, nonprofit organization dedicated to education, conservation, and research; it has sponsored whale-watch trips since 1978.

Plymouth, Massachusetts

Captain John Boats
117 Standish Avenue, Plymouth, MA 02360;
(800) 242–2469, (508) 746–2643

Whales:	Humpback, fin, minke, right, Atlantic white-sided dolphin
Season:	April 1 through October 31
Boats:	Eight boats, 65 to 250 passengers
Trips:	Two to five 4-hour trips daily, usually at 8:30 A.M., 9:30 A.M., 11:30 A.M., 1:30 P.M., and 4:30 P.M. Departures vary according to demand. The 1:30 P.M. trip on weekends is the most popular.
Fare:	Adults, $18; senior citizens, $15; children under 12, $13. Group rates available. Reservations advised.
Departure:	Trips leave from Plymouth Town Wharf, at the end of Route 44 or via Route 3. (Captain John Boats also has a berth at Provincetown's MacMillan Wharf where they take interested ferryboat passengers on a whale watch.)
Naturalist:	Naturalist on board

Doug Hall, director of sales, notes that Captain John Boats is the largest fleet of whale-watching and fishing vessels in Massachusetts. "Since 1977, Captain John Boats has logged sightings of whales and dolphins on more than 98 percent of the excursions."

Captain Tim Brady & Sons, Inc.

254 Sandwich Street, Plymouth, MA 02360; (508) 746–4809

Whales:	Humpback, fin, right, minke, orca, Atlantic white-sided dolphin
Season:	April through November
Boats:	One boat, the *Mary Elizabeth*; 49 passengers
Trips:	One 4¹/₂-hour trip daily at 2 P.M.; with one additional trip each Saturday and Sunday according to demand. Saturday is busiest.
Fare:	Adults, $17; senior citizens 62 and older, $15; children under 12, $12. Ten percent discounts for families.
Departure:	Trips leave from Plymouth's historic Town Wharf, at the end of Route 44 or via Route 3.
Naturalist:	Marine biologist serves as naturalist.

Captain Timothy C. Brady says, "We are the only 45-foot-long whale watcher in the area—new, modern, and fast. We usually take only about thirty-five passengers per trip so no one is crowded. And we can videotape your whale watch."

Massachusetts Whale Watching Center

Box 1328, Plymouth, MA 02360; (508) 224–8477

Whales:	Humpback, right, fin, minke, Atlantic white-sided dolphin
Season:	Late April through October 31
Boats:	Three boats; 140 or 250 passengers
Trips:	Three 4¹/₂-hour trips daily on weekdays; five on Saturdays and Sundays at 8:30 A.M., 11 A.M., 1:30 P.M., 2 P.M., and 4 P.M. Sunday is busiest.
Fare:	Adults, $18; senior citizens 62 and older, $15; children under 12, $13. Special rates for school groups. Reservations required.

Departure:	Trips leave from Plymouth's historic Town Wharf, at the end of Route 44 or via Route 3, just 100 yards north of the Mayflower.
Naturalist:	Naturalist on board from the Plymouth Marine Mammal Research Center

"The Massachusetts Whale Watching Center is the only whale-watching operation which is owned by biologists involved with direct research on local populations of marine mammals," notes director David N. Wiley. "We consider research to be an important component of each whale-watching trip. Our naturalists are specialists in coastal geology, seabird biology, and ecological relationships as well as marine mammals."

Barnstable, Massachusetts

Cape Cod Whale Watcher Cruises
P.O. Box 254, Barnstable, MA 02630; (508) 362–6088

Whales:	Humpback, finback, minke, right
Season:	April through early November
Boats:	One boat; 300 passengers
Trips:	Two 4¹/₂-hour trips daily at 9 A.M. and 2:30 P.M. The tide may cause variations in some departure times; passengers may want to call ahead. Weekday afternoon trips are busiest.
Fare:	Rates vary with season and time of day; range is from $10 to $20 per person, with discounts for children, senior citizens, and groups. Reservations advised. Discount coupons for trips are available at all lodging facilities on Cape Cod.

Departure: Trips leave from Barnstable Harbor, just 3 miles from Hyannis. Take Exit 6 off the mid-Cape highway (Route 6) and make a right turn onto Route 132. At the first traffic light, turn left and follow for 3 miles, straight to the harbor.

Naturalist: Yes

"We are the only whale watch located in the mid-Cape harbor and the only one which departs from Barnstable and Provincetown," notes general manager Linda Miller. "Our crew is always friendly and in uniform, and our galley staff offers complete food and beverage service."

South Yarmouth, Massachusetts

Butcher Boy Sportfishing
120 Driftwood Lane, South Yarmouth, MA 02664,
(508) 398–5676

Whales: Humpback, finback, minke, right

Season: June 1 through October 1

Boats: One, the 46-foot *Butcher Boy*; 10 passengers

Trips: One trip daily, by charter only. Weekends are busiest.

Fare: Fees range from $400 to $600 for a 6-hour trip. Reservations required.

Departure: Trips leave from Packett's Landing, next to the Bass River Bridge in South Yarmouth.

Naturalist: No

"We are the alternative to the noisy, crowded, and often uncomfortable whale-watching boats," says owner Jonathan Evans. "We cater to private parties. The *Butcher Boy* is the ideal boat for a group of people who wish to ride in utmost comfort and get as close to the whales as possible."

Provincetown, Massachusetts

Cape Cod Cruises
58 Seven Hills Road, Plymouth, MA 02360; (508) 747–2400

Whales:	Humpback, finback, minke, right, Atlantic white-sided dolphin
Season:	May through October
Boats:	One, the 100-foot *Cape Cod Clipper*; 250 passengers
Trips:	One 4-hour trip daily departs at midday from Provincetown. Weekends are busiest.
Fare:	Adults, $17; children under 12, $13. Reservations advised.
Departure:	The cruise originates in Plymouth, the whale watch departs from Fisherman's Wharf in Provincetown, at the foot of Standish Street.
Naturalist:	Naturalist on board

"We are unique in that we pick up passengers from Plymouth as well as Provincetown," notes president Stan Tavares. "We give large groups with variable interests an option when their trip originates in Plymouth. Part of a group can get off in Provincetown, to shop or go to the beach, and the remaining passengers may stay aboard for a whale watch."

Cape Cod Whale Watcher Cruises

P.O. Box 254, Barnstable, MA 02630; (508) 362–6088

Whales:	Humpback, finback, minke, right
Season:	April through early November
Boats:	One boat; 150 passengers
Trips:	Three 3¹/₂-hour trips daily at 9 A.M., 1 P.M., and 5 P.M. The midweek afternoon trip is busiest.
Fare:	Rates vary with season and time of day; range is from $10 to $20 per person, with discounts for children, senior citizens, and groups. Reservations advised. Discount coupons for trips are available at all lodging facilities on Cape Cod.
Departure:	Trips leave from MacMillan Wharf in Provincetown, at the foot of Standish Street.
Naturalist:	Naturalist on board

"We are the proud owners of the newest and fastest vessel in these waters, built in May of 1989 and specifically built for whale watching," says general manager Linda Miller. "We can also provide groups with transportation if necessary, and our sales staff is available to assist with travel plans."

Dolphin Fleet of Provincetown

MacMillan Wharf, Provincetown, MA 02657;
(800) 826–9300 (in Massachusetts), (508) 255–3857

Whales:	Humpback, fin, minke, right
Season:	April 15 through October
Boats:	Three boats; 147 passengers each

Trips:	Nine 4-hour trips daily, beginning at 8:30 A.M. and scheduled throughout the day until sunset. Tuesday afternoon is busiest.
Fare:	Adults, $15; senior citizens, $13; children, $13; under 7, free. AAA members receive a discount. Reservations advised.
Departure:	Trips leave from MacMillan Wharf, at the foot of Standish Street.
Naturalist:	Naturalist on board from Provincetown's Center for Coastal Studies

Owner and Captain Albert J. Avellar, once referred to as "the patron saint of whale watching," notes, "We are in our third generation in our study of whales—we know the reproductive rate, etc. The scientists from the Center for Coastal Studies make ours educational trips."

On some summer weekends, the *Dolphin VII* makes special all-day whale watches. Write for information.

Portuguese Princess Whale Watch

P.O. Box 1469, MacMillan Wharf, Provincetown, MA 02657; (800) 442–3188 (in Massachusetts), (508) 487–2651

Whales:	Humpback, finback, minke, right, Atlantic white-sided dolphin
Season:	April through November
Boats:	Two boats; each has room for 270 passengers but carries only 150 to avoid crowding
Trips:	Three to six 4-hour trips daily, according to demand. Trips are in the morning, at midday, in the afternoon, and at sunset. In April, May, and early June, weekends

	are busiest; in summer weekends are slow and discounts are available. Tuesdays, Wednesdays, and Thursdays are busiest during the summer.
Fare:	Fares range from $12 to $18, depending on the day and time. Reservations required during peak season.
Departure:	Trips leave from MacMillan Wharf, at the foot of Standish Street in Provincetown.
Naturalist:	Naturalist on board

"We serve homemade foods, including Portuguese specialties, and offer folk music on most trips," notes owner Suzanne Carter. "We donate money to many whale conservation organizations, but we don't solicit money from customers during the trips. And we guarantee whale sightings."

The Portuguese Princess also owns and operates the Whale Watchers General Store at 309 Commercial Street in Provincetown.

Provincetown Whale Watch Inc.

MacMillan Pier, Provincetown, MA 02657; (800) 992–9333 (in Massachusetts), (508) 487–1582

Whales:	Humpback, finback, minke, right
Season:	Mid-May through mid-November
Boats:	One boat, the *Ranger V*; 415 passengers
Trips:	Three 3½-hour trips daily at 9 A.M., 1 P.M., and 5 P.M. The midday trip on Tuesdays, Wednesdays, and Thursdays is the busiest.
Fare:	Off-season rates (May through June and September through November): adults, $12; senior citizens, $10; children under 12, $8. In-season rates (July and August): adults, $15; senior citizens, $13; children, $10; children under 7 always ride free. Discounts for

AAA members. Guests at the Top Mast Motel in Truro also receive a discount coupon.

Departure: Trips leave from MacMillan Wharf, at the foot of Standish Street in Provincetown.

Naturalist: Naturalist on board

Co-owner Helen Costa says, "Your captain, Gerald Costa, brings something to your trip that few others can offer—a lifetime of experience on the sea and a rich family history, dating back to the early days of American whaling."

Nantucket, Massachusetts

Nantucket Whale Watch
Straight Wharf, Nantucket, MA 02554;
(800) 322–0013 (in the northeast), (508) 283–0313

Whales:	Humpback, fin, minke
Season:	Mid-July to mid-September
Boats:	Two boats, the 70-foot *Yankee Clipper* and the 100-foot *Yankee Spirit*
Trips:	One 7-hour trip from 9:30 A.M. to 4:40 P.M. on Tuesdays, Wednesdays, and Thursdays.
Fare:	Adults, $35; children, $18. Reservations advised.
Departure:	Trips leave from the Hy-Line dock on Straight Wharf in downtown Nantucket.
Naturalist:	Naturalist on board

The Nantucket Whale Watch was started by the Yankee Fleet (out of Gloucester) and Seafarers Expeditions to provide cruises to the Great South Channel near Nantucket Shoals.

"These full-day excursions will allow you to appreciate the grace and beauty of the whales, dolphins, and seabirds of Nantucket's waters on a first-hand basis while contributing to ongoing marine studies," a representative from the Nantucket Whale Watch said.

Waterford, Connecticut

Captain John's Sport Fishing Center
15 First Street, Waterford, CT 06385; (203) 443–7259

Whales:	Fin, minke, humpback
Season:	Memorial Day to Labor Day
Boats:	The 100-foot *Sunbeam Express*; 149 passengers
Trips:	One 6-hour trip on Thursdays and Sundays only. Sunday is the busier day.
Fare:	Adults, $30; senior citizens, $27; children under 12, $20. Group rates available. Reservations advised.
Departure:	Trips leave from Captain John's in Waterford. Take I–95 to Route 161; get off at Exit 74 and head for Route 156. Captain John's is at the Niantic River Bridge.
Naturalist:	Yes

Owner Robert Wadsworth notes that the *Sunbeam Express* is Connecticut's first whale-watch boat. The boat is available for private charter trips, and bald eagle and harbor seal trips are available during the winter months. "The whole family can enjoy a relaxing trip aboard the *Sunbeam Express*, watching nature's wildlife in its natural surroundings."

Montauk, New York

Okeanos Whale Watch Cruises

Okeanos Ocean Research Foundation Inc., 216 East Montauk Highway, P.O. Box 776, Hampton Bays, NY 11946; (516) 728–4522

Whales:	Fin, minke, humpback, pilot; occasional right, sperm
Season:	May through September
Boats:	One, the 90-foot *Finback II*; 150 passengers
Trips:	One or two 4½-hour trips daily. Schedule varies according to season and demand. Reservations advised.
Fare:	Adults, $25; children ages 5 through 13, $15. Senior citizens get a 10 percent discount. Trip not recommended for children under 5. Reservations advised.
Departure:	Trips depart from the Montauk Viking Dock out of Montauk, Long Island, New York. Take the Long Island Expressway to Exit 70 (Manorville); go south on Route 111 to Route 27 (Sunrise Highway). Take Route 27 east all the way to Montauk. Upon entering Montauk business district, turn left at traffic circle with flagpole onto Edgemere Street, which becomes Flamingo Avenue. Continue to Montauk fishing fleet on right side. Look for Viking Fleet dock and OKEANOS WHALE WATCH sign.
Naturalist:	Naturalist is either a biologist or an educator.

The Okeanos Ocean Research Foundation is a nonprofit organization primarily interested in research and secondarily in educating the public about marine life. All proceeds from whale watches provide funding for the organization's programs.

"Our on-board team of researchers collect data on a variety of research topics, and we have a large volunteer team on every cruise to assist with everything from data compilation to boat maintenance," notes a spokesman. "It's a unique concept!"

Museums, Aquariums, and Science Centers

Connecticut

The Maritime Center at Norwalk
10 North Water Street, South Norwalk, CT 06854;
(203) 852–0700

Built in and around a restored nineteenth-century factory building on five acres of waterfront, the Maritime Center at Norwalk
encompasses the ecology and the history of Long Island Sound.
More than 175 different species of marine life, including tiny
brine shrimp and 10-foot sharks, are on display in a score of
aquariums.

Summer hours at the Center (from June 15 through Labor
Day) are from 10 A.M. to 6 P.M. In winter, the Center is open from
10 A.M. to 5 P.M. Closed Thanksgiving, Christmas, and New Year's
Day. Admission to Aquarium and the Maritime Hall or to the
IMAX Theater is $5.50. Combined admission is $9.50. Discounts
for senior citizens and children.

Each year, the Maritime Center at Norwalk schedules two
three-day whale-watch trips off Cape Cod and a nine-day trip to
Baja with an established tour operator. For information, contact
the Center.

Mystic Marinelife Aquarium
55 Coogan Boulevard, Mystic, CT 06355; (203) 536–3323

More than 6,000 sea life specimens, including beluga whales, are
displayed in forty-nine living exhibits in the Mystic Marinelife

Aquarium. Seal Island, a 2.5-acre outdoor exhibit, shows the natural habitats of seals and sea lions. Dolphin and sea lion shows daily.

From June 30 through Labor Day, the Aquarium is open 9 A.M. to 5:30 P.M.; the rest of the year, 9 A.M. to 4:30 P.M. Closed Thanksgiving, Christmas, and New Year's Day. Admission is $7 for adults, $4 for children 5 through 17, and $6 for senior citizens.

Maine

Natural History Museum
College of the Atlantic, Eden Street, Route 3, Bar Harbor, ME 04609; (207) 288–5015

This small museum is part of the College of the Atlantic and features displays of Mount Desert Island flora and fauna. Daily participatory programs include assembling a 20-foot whale skeleton.

The Natural History Museum is open daily 9 A.M. to 4 P.M., mid-June to Labor Day. Admission is free.

The Maine Whalewatch, out of Northeast Harbor, is sponsored by Allied Whale, an affiliate of the College of the Atlantic. See the listing under Northeast Harbor for details.

Maryland

National Aquarium in Baltimore
Pier 3, 501 East Pratt Street, Baltimore, MD 21202; (301) 576–3800

The main building of the National Aquarium is a seven-level building where more than 5,000 salt- and freshwater species are on display. Special exhibits include a South American tropical rain forest, an outdoor 7,000-gallon rock pool, and a 220,000-gallon ocean tank that houses sharks, rays, and large fish. The Marine Mammal Pavilion, which opened in June 1990, is primarily dedicated to whales and includes a life-size model of Scylla, a known humpback who lives in the Atlantic Ocean.

Admission is $7.75 for adults; $6 for students, senior citizens, and active military; $4.75 for children ages 3 to 11. Children under 3 are free.

Massachusetts

Museum of Comparative Zoology

Harvard University, 26 Oxford Street, Cambridge, MA 02138; (617) 495-3045

The Museum of Comparative Zoology is one of four natural history museums affiliated with Harvard University. Permanent exhibits include several skeletons of marine mammals, including a right whale and a narwhal.

The museum is open from 9 A.M. to 4:30 P.M. Monday through Saturday and from 1 to 4:30 P.M. on Sunday. It is closed New Year's Day, July 4, and Christmas Day. Admission is $3 for adults, $2 for senior citizens and students, and $1 for children 15 and younger. Admission is free from 9 to 11 A.M. on Saturday.

Periodically, the Museum of Comparative Zoology schedules extensive natural history expeditions, some of which include whale watching, with established tour operators.

New England Aquarium

Central Wharf, Boston, MA 02119; (671) 973-5200

More than seventy exhibits, with new displays each year, continue to delight visitors to the New England Aquarium on Boston's historic waterfront. The 187,000-gallon ocean tank extends from floor to ceiling, and huge sea turtles, sharks, and moray eels swim alongside as you descend the spiral ramp around the tank. Bottlenose dolphins and California sea lions perform daily aboard *Discovery*, a floating marine mammal pavilion.

From July 1 through Labor Day, the Aquarium is open 9 A.M. to 6 P.M. Monday, Tuesday, and Friday; 9 A.M. to 8 P.M. Wednesday and Thursday; 9 A.M. to 7 P.M. Saturday, Sunday and holidays. From Labor Day to June 30, open 9 A.M. to 5 P.M. Monday, Tuesday, Wednesday, and Friday; 9 A.M. to 8 P.M. Thursday; and 9 A.M. to 6 P.M. Saturday, Sunday, and holidays. Closed Thanksgiving and Christmas; open at noon on New Year's Day. Admission is $7 for adults, $3.50 for children 3 to 15, $6 for senior citizens. Slight discount on Thursday afternoons and Wednesdays during the summer.

The New England Aquarium operates whale watches on its own boat. See listing under Boston, Massachusetts.

Peabody Museum of Salem
East India Square, Salem, MA 01970; (508) 745–1876

Among the many treasures at the Peabody Museum are exhibits on the natural resources, environment, and marine ecology of Essex County. Exhibits include birds, reptiles, fish, plants, mammals, and pond life. Special programs for children include classes on whale biology and Yankee whaling.

The Peabody Museum is open 10 A.M. to 5 P.M. Monday through Saturday; until 9 P.M. Thursday, and noon to 5 P.M. Sunday. Admission is $4 for adults; $3 for senior citizens and students; $1.50 for children 6 to 16.

New Bedford Whaling Museum
18 Johnny Cake Hill, New Bedford, MA 02740; (617) 997–0046

This charming museum is the largest in the United States that tells the story of whaling in the age of sail. Exhibits include a skeleton of a humpback whale, a whale mural painted by Richard Ellis, and a half-scale replica of a whaling ship. A twenty-two-minute film featuring a whaling expedition is shown from June through September.

The Whaling Museum is open 9 A.M. to 5 P.M. Monday through Saturday and 1 to 5 P.M. on Sunday. In July and August Sunday hours are 11 A.M. to 5 P.M. Closed Thanksgiving, Christmas, and New Year's Day. Admission is $3.50 for adults, $3 for senior citizens, $2.50 for children 6 through 14.

New York

American Museum of Natural History
Central Park West at 79th Street, New York, NY 10024;
(212) 769–5100

Said to be the largest museum of its kind, the American Museum of Natural History offers forty exhibit halls and numerous special display areas, with more than thirty-six million artifacts and specimens. The Hall of Ocean Life includes a 94-foot model of a diving whale.

The American Museum of Natural History is open 10 A.M. to 5:45 P.M. Monday, Tuesday, Thursday, and Sunday and 10 A.M. to 9 P.M. Wednesday, Friday, and Saturday. Closed Thanksgiving and Christmas. Suggested admission is $4 for adults, $2 for children. Admission is free after 5 p.m. on Friday and Saturday evenings.

The museum schedules an annual three-day whale watch off Cape Cod in May. The chartered trip includes a visit to the Mystic Aquarium. For more information, contact the museum's Department of Education.

The Pacific Northwest

The Pacific Northwest

Whale watchers in Washington enjoy two seasons, in two different areas. Westport, on the Pacific Coast, boasts several tour operators who take whale watchers to see the annual migration of the gray whales. April and May are considered the best months; the weather has calmed sufficiently, and the whales swim more slowly as they head north to the Bering and Chukchi seas. The summer months, especially June and July, find whale watchers in search of three large populations of orcas and an abundance of minkes off the San Juan Islands.

Trips in the San Juan Islands, which depart from three cities, are available for one, two, three, or four days, on excursion boats, sailboats, and sea kayaks. Beginners are welcome on the kayak trips, which include instructions on maneuvering the craft. One tour operator notes, "Kayaking among whales is quite a thrill."

Oregon celebrates the annual migration of the gray whales and also welcomes those sperm whales, orcas, and humpbacks that are occasionally seen in the area. Like their colleagues on the Washington coast, whale-watch tour operators in Oregon all are at the mercy of the weather. Depoe Bay has the only "inside" whale watching, within the protection of the bay; because of this geological advantage, Depoe Bay bills itself as "The Whale-Watching Capital of the Oregon Coast." Trips are also available in four other cities.

Gray whales traveling south reach Oregon early in December and are gone by mid-February. Whale watching peaks early in January. Heading north on the return trip, adult males and some females pass by Oregon from early March through mid-April; females with calves can be seen from early May through mid-June.

Even when the cold, rainy weather keeps the boats in their harbors, the state of Oregon has whale watchers in mind. Volunteers trained at the Extension Service at Oregon State University stand at lookout points at sixteen locations along the Oregon coast. On duty from 11 A.M. to 2 P.M., December 26 through January 1, the volunteers point out the passing whales and answer questions about the migration.

The lookout points, marked with signs that read WHALE WATCHING SPOKEN HERE, include North Head, Fort Stevens State Park, Ecola State Park, Neahkahnie Mountain, Cape Meares State Park, Cape Lookout State Park, "D" River State Wayside, Boller Bay Wayside, Depoe Bay seawall, Rocky Creek Wayside, Cape Foulweather, Cape Perpetua overlook, Sea Lion Caves turnout, Umpqua Lighthouse State Park, Shore Acres State Park, and Harris Beach State Park.

TOURISM INFORMATION

Oregon

Economic Development Department
Tourism Division
595 Cottage Street N.E., Salem, OR 97310
(800) 547–7842 (outside Oregon)
(800) 543–8838 (inside Oregon)

Oregon Coast Association
P.O. Box 670, Newport, OR 97365
(800) 982–6278

Washington

Department of Trade and Economic Development
Tourism Development Division
101 General Administration Building, AX-13, Olympia,
WA 98504
(206) 753–5600

Westport-Grayland Chamber of Commerce
1200 North Montesano Street, P.O. Box 306, Westport,
WA 98595
(800) 345–6223

Bellingham, Washington

Island Mariner Cruises
#5 Harbor Esplanade, Bellingham, WA 98225; (206) 734–8866

Whales:	Orca, minke
Season:	May through September
Boats:	Two boats; 110 and 149 passengers
Trips:	Offered on an irregular basis throughout the summer, primarily in June and July. Weekends are the busiest times.
Fare:	A 90-mile cruise costs $35 per person, with $6 extra for lunch. Reservations advised.
Departure:	Trips leave from Squalicum Harbor in Bellingham. From Interstate 5, take the Meridian Street exit (Exit 256) and drive south for 0.5 miles. Turn right on Squalicum Way and drive 1.8 miles. Turn right on Coho Way and drive 2 blocks, to the Esplanade Building. The office is at the far east end.
Naturalist:	Naturalist is on board, and the boats are equipped with hydrophones (underwater microphones) so that passengers may listen to the whales.

"We are the only company offering whale-watching cruises in the San Juan Islands that have a departure point on the mainland," co-director Terry Buzzard writes. "Our company regularly provides cruises for the National Audubon Society, National Wildlife Federation, Pacific Science Center and Greenpeace Northwest."

Friday Harbor, Washington

Biological Journeys
1696 Ocean Drive, McKinleyville, CA 95521; (800) 548–7555,
(707) 839–0178

Whales:	Orca
Season:	June
Boats:	The 50-foot *Delphinus*; 40 passengers, who live on the boat
Trips:	Five- and eight-day trips in the San Juan Islands. Trips leave from Friday Harbor.
Fare:	Five-day trips cost $895 per person and conclude in Friday Harbor. The eight-day trip costs $2,095 and concludes in Port McNeill.
Departure:	Trips leave from Friday Harbor.
Naturalist:	Naturalist accompanies all trips.

"Puget Sound's orcas are world-famous, and these trips take us deep into the realm of three family pods, totaling approximately eighty whales," note co-owners Ron LeValley and Ronn Storro-Patterson. "You'll get to know individual orcas and you'll also thrill to their sounds through hydrophones hooked into *Delphinus'* speaker system."

Northwest Outdoor Center
2100 Westlake Avenue North, Seattle, WA 98109;
(206) 281–9694

Whales:	Orca
Season:	June through August

Boats:	Kayaks
Trips:	Two- and three-day trips in the San Juan Islands. Participants camp overnight. Saturday is the busiest departure day.
Fare:	Prices range from $110 to $175. Reservations required.
Departure:	Trips leave from Smallpox Bay on San Juan Island. Proceed west from Friday Harbor to San Juan County Park.
Naturalist:	Naturalist accompanies trips.

The Northwest Outdoor Center was founded by five "paddling enthusiasts/maniacs" in 1980. Co-founder Bill Stewart notes, "We use small nonmotorized craft to view the whales."

 Classes, longer trips, and Christmas caroling by kayak are also available.

Ocean Research and Conservation Association (O.R.C.A.)
720 Olive Way, Suite 900, Seattle, WA 98101; (206) 382–6722

Whales:	Orca, minke, harbor porpoise
Season:	May through September
Boats:	One boat; 33 passengers
Trips:	One 3-hour trip from 12:30 to 3:30 P.M. each weekday and on Sundays. The Sunday trip is the most popular.
Fare:	Adults, $35; children: ages 12 through 17, $25; under 12, $20. Reservations required.
Departure:	Trips leave from Friday Harbor on San Juan Island.
Naturalist:	Yes

"The San Juan Island trips are more of an all-around natural history trip as we cannot guarantee orcas on each and every trip. We look at eagles, seals, seabirds, porpoises, and other whales as well as the beautiful scenery. Still, our capability for finding orcas is probably second to none," writes Chuck Flaherty, director of O.R.C.A. field trips.

Resource Institute

6532 Phinney Avenue North, #B, Seattle, WA 98103;
(206) 784–6762

Whales:	Orca, minke, sometimes humpback
Season:	April through October
Boats:	The 65-foot wooden schooner *Crusader;* 12 passengers
Trips:	Several trips, lasting from three to seven days, are offered, including one to southeast Alaska. The San Juan Island trips go in search of orcas and minkes, humpbacks are seen in Alaska. Participants live on board.
Fare:	Trips cost about $100 to $125 per day. Reservations required.
Departure:	Trips depart from Friday Harbor in Washington and from Sitka, Petersburg, Juneau, and Ketchikan in Alaska.
Naturalist:	Naturalist aboard

"Seminars along the way (from the San Juan Islands to Alaska) range in subject matter, including natural history, marine biology, woodcarving, photography, psychology, poetry, philosophy, conservation, etc. Groups live on board as we travel and study," says Jonathan White, trip operator.

San Juan Kayak Expeditions Inc.
3090 Roche Harbor Road, Friday Harbor, WA 98250;
(206) 378–4436

Whales:	Orca, minke, harbor porpoise
Season:	Late May through September 30
Boats:	Kayaks that hold two people each
Trips:	Two-, three-, and four-day trips available. Participants camp overnight. Weekends are busiest.
Fare:	Prices range from $135 for the two-day trip to $245 for the four-day trip. Reservations required.
Departure:	Trips leave from Friday Harbor, with transportation to the launch point.
Naturalist:	Naturalist accompanies trips.

Guide and founder Tim Thomsen notes, "Kayaking among whales is quite a thrill."

Sea Quest Expeditions
Zoetic Research, P.O. Box 2424, Friday Harbor, WA 98250;
(206) 378–5767

Whales:	Orca, minke, harbor porpoise
Season:	May through October (June is peak season for orcas, with July and August a close second)
Boats:	Small motorized vessels
Trips:	Five-hour nature cruises in the San Juan Islands, available by charter only.
Fare:	$39 per person, with a minimum of two people and a maximum of six people. Reservations required.

Where the Whales Are

Departure:	Trips leave from Friday Harbor. Transportation to the launch site, which varies according to the tide, is provided.
Naturalist:	Skipper serves as naturalist.

"Our trips are very personalized and flexible as far as scheduling goes," says Mark Lewis, executive director of Sea Quest Expeditions. "When compared with the larger for-profit vessels operating in the San Juans, our approach is much more intimate. Our smaller groups are allowed a much higher degree of interaction with the skipper, who is a trained field biologist."

Sea Quest Expeditions also offers research trips that qualify for college credit and will design custom trips.

(Note: For Sea Quest kayak trips, see next entry.)

Sea Quest Expeditions

Zoetic Research, P.O. Box 2424, Friday Harbor, WA 98250; (206) 378–5767

Whales:	Orca, minke, harbor porpoise
Season:	May through October
Boats:	Sea kayaks
Trips:	One-, two-, three-, and four-day kayak trips in the San Juan Islands. Participants camp overnight.
Fare:	Depending on the length of the trip, fares range from $45 to $229 per person, including meals. Reservations required.
Departure:	Trips leave from the Whale Museum in Friday Harbor. Transportation is provided to the launch site, which varies according to the tides.
Naturalist:	A research associate from the Whale Museum serves as naturalist.

Mark Lewis, executive director of Sea Quest Expeditions, notes, "On numerous occasions, we have found our flotilla of kayaks completely infiltrated by orcas! We have never felt threatened during these exciting encounters. In fact, the whales seem very careful about their movements when in close proximity to kayaks. We have even had participants be able to reach out and touch a wild orca that spy-hopped next to the kayak!" Lewis says that beginners are welcome—90 percent of the participants have never been in a kayak before.

Sea Quest Expeditions also offers research trips that qualify for college credit and will design custom trips.

Shearwater Adventures

P.O. Box 787, Eastsound, WA 98245; (206) 376–4699

Whales:	Orca, minke, harbor porpoise
Season:	April through October
Boats:	Sea kayaks
Trips:	One 6-hour trip daily at 10 A.M.
Fare:	$49 per person. Reservations required.
Departure:	Trips leave from the Whale Museum in Friday Harbor. Transportation to launch site provided.
Naturalist:	Trips are accompanied by a naturalist.

"We use sea kayaks, so we have less impact on the whales, plus we are in a craft that is less separate from the water environment than a motorboat," says a spokesman at Shearwater Adventures. "Because we do not always see orcas, we integrate the natural history of Puget Sound as a whole, including marine mammals, birds, flora and fauna. But it sure is a special and unique occasion to be in the presence of whales."

Western Prince Cruises

P.O. Box 418, Port of Friday Harbor, Friday Harbor, WA 98250;
(206) 378–5315

Whales:	Orca, minke, harbor porpoise
Season:	Early May through the end of September
Boats:	The *Western Prince;* 33 passengers
Trips:	One 4-hour trip daily at 1 P.M. Saturday is the busiest day.
Fare:	Adults, $35; children: 12 through 17, $25; 11 and younger, $20. Reservations advised though not required.
Departure:	Trips leave from the Port of Friday Harbor, 80 miles northwest of Seattle on I–5 and via the San Juan ferry from Anacortes.
Naturalist:	Naturalist on board

"The San Juan Islands are the only place in the United States where you can reliably see killer whales (orcas) in the wild," note owners Bob and Jean Van Leuven. "Because we operate on 'inland' waters which are usually calm during our summer season, seasickness is not a problem."

Anacortes, Washington

Discovery Charters

P.O. Box 636, Anacortes, WA 98221; (206) 293–4248

Whales:	Orca, minke
Season:	May through September

Boats:	One boat; 46 passengers
Trips:	One 7- to 8-hour trip daily; usually departs at 9 A.M. Weekends are the most crowded. Occasional two-day trips are available and include a night in Friday Harbor.
Fare:	Individual fares: adults, $31; children under 12, $23. Group tours: $23 per person per day. Motel fee extra for two-day trips. Prices include lunch. Reservations required.
Departure:	Trips leave from Cap Sante marina in Anacortes. From Commercial Avenue (the main street), turn right on Eleventh Street. Cross the railroad tracks and go into the Cap Sante marina parking lot.
Naturalist:	Knowledgeable skipper serves as narrator.

"All our trips are nature tours. We regularly see tufted puffins, bald eagles, harbor seals, seabirds, California sea lions, river otters, and porpoises as well as whales," tour operator Jess Starnes says. "And lunch is always rated as outstanding!" On the two-day trips, participants stay overnight in Friday Harbor, on San Juan Island, and tour the Whale Museum there.

Seattle Aquarium
Pier 59, Waterfront Park, Seattle, WA 98101; (206) 386–4300

Whales:	Orca
Season:	June through August
Boats:	One boat; 30 passengers
Trips:	Seven 9-hour trips from mid-July through the end of August. Trips are scheduled for Saturdays or Sundays at 9:30 A.M.
Fare:	Adults, $45; children, $40. Reservations required. Cost

	includes pretrip lecture scheduled for a day or two before each cruise.
Departure:	Trips leave from Cap Sante marina in Anacortes. From Commercial Avenue (the main street), turn right on Eleventh Street. Cross the railroad tracks and go into the Cap Sante marina parking lot.
Naturalist:	Naturalist aboard

"The Seattle Aquarium offers boat trips for the general public to observe whales during two seasons of the year," says Leo J. Shaw, marine education specialist at the Aquarium. "During March and April, the Aquarium offers gray whale–watching trips from Westport, Washington, on weekends. During the months of June, July, and August, we offer cruises in the San Juan Islands of Washington state to search for the local killer whales."

Westport, Washington

Deep Sea Charters
Across from Float 6, Box 1115, Westport, WA 98595; (206) 268–9300

Whales:	Gray
Season:	March through May
Boats:	Nine boats; 6 to 20 passengers
Trips:	Several 2$\frac{1}{2}$-hour trips scheduled daily according to the tide.
Fare:	$25 per person. Family and school rates available. Reservations required. Deep Sea Charters and several local motels offer a $32.25 package deal that includes a night's lodging and a whale watch.

Departure:	Trips leave from the dock off Westhaven Drive, north east of the Old Coast Guard Station and Westport Museum.
Naturalist:	No

Owner Ken Bowe notes, "Before we leave the dock, we have an educational discussion about the gray whale and what you can expect." Illustrated informational brochures are also available.

Ocean Research and Conservation Association (O.R.C.A.)
720 Olive Way, Suite 900, Seattle, WA 98101; (206) 382–6722

Whales:	Gray
Season:	March and April
Boats:	Six boats; 25 passengers each
Trips:	Departure times vary with the tide, but trips run daily. Saturdays are busiest.
Fare:	Adults, $22; children under 16, $18.50. Reservations required.
Departure:	Trips leave from the Westport dock, at the foot of Dock Street at Westhaven Drive.
Naturalist:	Skippers serve as naturalists.

"Gray whale trips are virtually assured of locating the animals," O.R.C.A. director Chuck Flaherty writes. "Trips where whales aren't seen are normally given rain checks for another trip. The water can be rough on gray whale trips, and we advise participants to take precautions against seasickness."

From time to time, O.R.C.A. also offers its members special extended nature trips. Write for more information.

Seattle Aquarium

Pier 59, Waterfront Park, Seattle, WA 98101; (206) 386–4300

Whales:	Gray
Season:	Mid-March through the end of April
Boats:	Several small fishing boats; maximum of 100 passengers altogether
Trips:	Three-hour trips are offered on Saturdays or Sundays.
Fare:	Adults, $25; children, $17. Reservations required. Fee includes pretrip educational program scheduled a few days in advance.
Departure:	Trips leave from Westport dock, at the foot of Dock Street at Westhaven Drive.
Naturalist:	Naturalist on board from the Aquarium staff

The Seattle Aquarium offers boat trips for the general public to observe whales during two seasons of the year: from Westport during March and April, to observe gray whales, and from Anacortes in June, July, and August, to search for orcas in the San Juan Islands.

"The Seattle Aquarium does not display whales, dolphins, or porpoises," notes Leo J. Shaw, marine education specialist. "Our marine mammals on display are harbor seals, northern fur seals, and sea otters."

Snider's Rainbow Charters Inc.

P.O. Box 585, Westport, WA 98595; (206) 268–9182

Whales:	Gray
Season:	March through May
Boats:	Two boats; 55 passengers each
Trips:	Two 2¹/₂-hour trips daily, one at 10 A.M. and one at 2 P.M.

Fare: Adults, $20; children: ages 6 to 12, $10; under 6, free. Reservations advised.

Departure: Trips leave from Dock 14 at the Westport dock, at the foot of Dock Street and Westhaven Drive. Turn left at the docks and look for the last office on the left.

Naturalist: No

Snider's Rainbow Charters has been in businesssince 1967, notes Margie Snider.

Westport Whale Watch
Ocean Charters Inc., 2315 W. Westhaven Drive,
P.O. Box 548, Westport, WA 98595;
(800) 562–0105 (in season), (206) 268–9144

Whales: Gray, sometimes orca

Season: March 1 through early May

Boats: Five boats, all 50 feet or longer; 14 to 28 passengers each

Trips: One 2-hour trip daily at 10 A.M. on weekdays; two trips at 10 A.M. and 2 P.M. on Saturdays and Sundays. (Times may vary with the tides.) Saturday is the busiest day.

Fare: Adults, $23; senior citizens, $20; children 12 and under, $13.50; $20 per person for groups of four or more. Reservations required.

Departure: Trips leave from Float 6 at the Westport Marina. In the dock area, turn left at the blinking light. Look for the only two-story building on the block.

Naturalist: No

Where the Whales Are

"Westport Whale Watch was the pioneer in establishing whale-watch tours out of Westport in 1979," notes Sue Geary, booking agent and "all around general flunky." "Our tour includes a seminar, presented by knowledgeable narrators, to familiarize you with the history, migration, and social habits of the gray whales."

Whales Ahoy
Salmon Charters Inc., P.O. Box 545, 2329 Westhaven Drive, Westport, WA 98595; (206) 268–9150

Whales:	Gray, occasional orca and pilot
Season:	Mid-March through mid-May
Boats:	Seven boats; 12 to 36 passengers each
Trips:	One 2½-hour trip daily at 9:30 A.M. on weekdays; two on weekends, at 9:30 A.M. and 1 or 1:30 P.M., depending on the tide. Saturday is the busiest day.
Fare:	Adults, $22; senior citizens over 60, $19; children 12 and under, $13. Group rates available. Reservations advised.
Departure:	Trips leave from Float 8 at the Westport Marina. All roads in Westport lead to the water. When you reach the sea, turn left and go about 1 block to Whales Ahoy office.
Naturalist:	Marine biologist John Smith narrates trips.

"Our naturalist makes our trips somewhat unique and very interesting," said Captain B. G. Brown. "Dr. Smith answers questions and gives highlights during the trip, and he also puts on a slide show and holds a discussion before the trip."

Brown added that it's not unusual to see 200 to 250 whales in a 2½-hour period during March and April.

Garibaldi, Oregon

Troller Deep Sea Fishing Charters

P.O. Box 452, 604 Mooring Basin Road, Garibaldi, OR 97118;
(503) 322–3796

Whales:	Gray
Season:	February through April
Boats:	Eight boats; 140 passengers altogether
Trips:	Two 2¹/₂-hour trips on weekdays and three on week-ends, scheduled whenever the ocean permits. Saturday is the busiest day.
Fare:	$15 per person. Reservations required.
Departure:	Trips leave from the Garibaldi boat basin, just off Highway 101.
Naturalist:	No

Lawrence S. Vandecoevering, the owner of Troller Deep Sea Fishing Charters, has been in business since 1961. His pelagic bird trips are as popular as his whale-watch trips.

Depoe Bay, Oregon

Dockside Charters

P.O. Box 1308, 270 Southeast Coast Guard Place, Depoe Bay,
OR 97341; (503) 765–2545

Whales:	Gray
Season:	December 26 "until the whales leave"
Boats:	Two boats; 30 passengers each
Trips:	Trips scheduled every hour from 10 A.M. until dark. Saturday is the busiest day.

Fare:	Adults, $7 an hour; children 12 and younger, $5 an hour. Reservations advised during holidays.
Departure:	Trips leave from the town harbor. Off Highway 101, turn east at Bay Street (the only stoplight in town) and follow the road past the Coast Guard station. Dock is 100 feet from the parking lot.
Naturalist:	No

Owner James M. Tate says that Depoe Bay is the "whale-watching capital of Oregon" because the whales come closer to the coast than anywhere else and because some whales spend all spring, summer, and fall in the area. "That provides us with great whale-watching cruises the year round. Overall, we want people to feel safe, good, and happy. That's what we're about."

Enterprise
P.O. Box 575, Depoe Bay, OR 97341; (503) 765–2245

Whales:	Gray
Season:	December through April
Boats:	One boat; 30 passengers
Trips:	Trips scheduled from 9 A.M. until dark, according to demand and the tide. Weekends are the busiest days.
Fare:	Adults, $8 per hour; children: ages 7 to 12, $5 per hour; 7 and younger, free. Reservations advised.
Departure:	Trips leave from the town harbor. Off highway 101, turn east at Bay Street (the only stoplight in town) and follow the road past the Coast Guard station. Dock is 100 feet from the parking lot.
Naturalist:	No

"Depoe Bay is the World's Smallest Harbor, and whales come in close to shore," says Mary de Belloy, who with her husband, Dave, owns the *Enterprise.* "We have seen whales feeding, mating, breaching, spyhopping, and cows with their calves. The north migration, in the spring, is the best time, because the whales are slower."

Tradewinds Charters
P.O. Box 123, Depoe Bay, OR 97341; (503) 765–2345

Whales:	Gray
Season:	All year
Boats:	Twelve boats; 180 passengers altogether
Trips:	Nine trips daily; some 1-hour and some 2-hour. Hourly trips leave from 9 A.M. until dark. The 2-hour trips leave at 11 A.M. and 1 P.M. Hourly trips on week ends are the most crowded.
Fare:	Adults, $7 an hour; children: ages 7 to 12, $5 an hour; 6 and younger, free. Group rates available. Reservations advised. Custom packages are available through several local motels; write for more information.
Departure:	Trips leave from the town harbor. Off Highway 101, turn east at Bay Street (the only stoplight in town) and follow the road past the Coast Guard station. Dock is 100 feet from the parking lot.
Naturalist:	Sometimes

"Our crews are extremely friendly and make each trip a fun experience," owner Rich Allyn notes. "We have clean, modern vessels, and if a naturalist is not aboard, each of our crew is extremely knowledgeable and provides a very good talk about the whales."

Newport, Oregon

South Beach Charters
P.O. Box 1446, Newport, OR 97365; (503) 867–7200

Whales:	Gray
Season:	November through June
Boats:	Four boats; 6 to 28 passengers each
Trips:	One 2-hour trip daily at 1:30 P.M. (A second trip may be added, according to demand.) Saturday is the busiest day.
Fare:	$16 per person. Reservations required.
Departure:	Trips leave from the South Beach Marina, on the south side of Yaquina Bay in Newport.
Naturalist:	No

Owners Russell and Marilyn Sisley work with the Hatfield Marine Science Center.

Newport Sportfishing
1000 Southeast Bay Boulevard, Newport, OR 97365; (503) 265–7558

Whales:	Gray
Season:	December 1 through May 1
Boats:	Seven boats; 30 passengers each
Trips:	One 2-hour trip daily at 10 A.M.; two 2-hour trips on weekends, at 10 A.M. and 1 P.M. The Saturday morning trip is the most popular.

Fare:	Adults, $20; children under 12, $10. Reservations required.
Departure:	Trips leave from the Embarcadero Marina, on Bay Boulevard.
Naturalist:	Yes

"Location and friendly people," are what make Newport Sportfishing special, according to owner Art Burk. He works with the Oregon Natural Resources Council.

Charleston, Oregon

Betty Kay Charters
P.O. Box 5020, Charleston, OR 97420; (503) 888–9021

Whales:	Gray
Season:	November, December, March, April, May
Boats:	Two boats; 18 passengers each
Trips:	Trips are offered according to demand and the tide. Weekends are the busiest.
Fare:	$20 per person for a 3-hour trip. Minimum of 10 people. Reservations required.
Departure:	Trips leave from the Charleston boat basin, 8 miles west of Coos Bay. Driving west, cross the Charleston Bridge, turn right toward the small boat basin, and follow the signs.
Naturalist:	No

Where the Whales Are

Ken Gardner, skipper and owner of Betty Kay Charters, has been going to sea since the early 1970s. In addition to whale watching, Gardner offers salmon- and bottom-fishing expeditions.

Bob's Sportfishing
P.O. Box 5018, 7960 Kingfisher Drive, Charleston, OR 97420; (503) 888–4241

Whales:	Gray
Season:	December through March
Boats:	One boat, the *Miss Carol*; 13 passengers
Trips:	Trips are scheduled according to demand and the tide.
Fare:	$20 per person for a 3-hour trip. Reservations required.
Departure:	Trips leave from Charleston small boat basin. Follow the signs from Coos Bay/North Bend to Charleston; park at the small boat basin at the east end of the Charleston Bridge, near the Coast Guard Station.
Naturalist:	No

"The crew is very helpful and friendly," note owners Dick and Donna Harrington. "Our 36-foot charter boat is only used for up to thirteen passengers, which gives everyone plenty of room and seating."

Charleston Charters

P.O. Box 5032, 5100 Cape Arago Highway, Charleston,
OR 97420; (503) 888–4846

Whales:	Gray
Season:	November, December, February, March, April
Boats:	Three boats; 30 passengers altogether
Trips:	Trips are scheduled on demand and according to the tide. Saturday is the busiest day.
Fare:	$20 per person for a 3-hour trip. Minimum of 10 people. Group rates available.
Departure:	Trips leave from Charleston small boat basin. Follow the signs from Coos Bay/North Bend to Charleston; park at the small boat basin at the east end of the Charleston Bridge, near the Coast Guard Station.
Naturalist:	No

"The best whale-watch trips are in spring, during the northerly migration with the new calves," says a spokesman for Charleston Charters. "We cater to individuals and small groups."

Brookings, Oregon

Leta J Charters

97748 North Bank, Chetco River Road, Brookings, OR 97415;
(503) 469–6964

Whales:	Gray
Season:	November, December, March, April, and May
Boats:	One, the *Leta J*; 15 passengers

Where the Whales Are

Trips:	Two 3-hour trips daily, scheduled according to demand and the tide. Saturday is the busiest day.
Fare:	$20 per person. Reservations required.
Departure:	Trips leave from the dock behind the Wharfside Seafood Restaurant, at the top of the boat ramp. Take Highway 101 to the Chetco River Road.
Naturalist:	No

Skipper Fred Stutsman has been in business since 1963 and notes that Brookings is one of the safest departure points on the Oregon coast.

Museums, Aquariums, and Science Centers

Oregon

Oregon State University
Mark O. Hatfield Marine Science Center, 2030 South Marine Science Drive, Newport, OR 97365; (503) 867–0100

Aquarium tanks and interpretive exhibits draw nearly half a million people each year to the Science Center, where visitors may observe and touch sea creatures. Special exhibits include sculptures of seven different whales, with accompanying text in Braille, and the skeleton of a minke whale. Special school programs are also available. The public area is open daily, 10 A.M. to 4 P.M.; summer hours are 9:30 A.M. to 6 P.M. Admission is free

The Extension Service of Oregon State University also trains volunteers who are posted along the Oregon coast from December 26 through January 1 at sites from Astoria to Brookings. Signs at the staffed lookouts (see list page 81) read WHALE WATCHING SPOKEN HERE, and volunteers are available from 11 A.M. to 2 P.M., rain or shine. They hand out educational materials and answer questions for the more than 6,000 people who visit the lookouts each year.

Rogue-Pacific Interpretive Center
510 Colvin Street, Gold Beach, OR 97444; (503) 247–2732

The Center sponsors one- and two-day workshops, guided field trips, how-to demonstrations, nature slide shows, and children's programs.

Washington

Seattle Aquarium
Pier 59, Waterfront Park, Seattle, WA 98101; (206) 386–4320

The Seattle Aquarium features exhibits on sea life, a Touch Tank, a salt marsh, and the Underwater Dome, where visitors may see salmon, sharks, octopus, and numerous other marine marvels that live in Puget Sound. In addition to permanent and special exhibits, the Aquarium also offers tours, classes, and lecture series.

Summer hours are 10 A.M. to 7 P.M. daily; from Labor Day to Memorial Day, hours are 10 A.M. to 5 P.M. daily. Admission is $3.25 for adults, $1.50 for teenagers and senior citizens. Children 6 to 12, 75 cents; under 6, free.

The Whale Museum
62 First Street North, Friday Harbor, WA 98250; (206) 378–4710

A research and development institution as well as a museum, the Whale Museum collects and disseminates information on the marine environment, with special emphasis on whales, dolphins, and porpoises. Programs include exhibits, workshops, field courses in whale biology, a teaching curriculum, lab work, and educational programs as well as whale-watch trips.

The Whale Museum is open seven days a week, 10 A.M. to 5 P.M. Memorial Day weekend through September and 11 A.M. to 4 P.M. October through May. Admission is $2.50 for adults, $2 for senior citizens and students; children under 12, $1; under 5, free. Group rates are available.

California

EUREKA

NORTHERN CALIFORNIA

FORT BRAGG

POINT ARENA

SANTA CRUZ

SAUSALITO
BERKELEY
SAN FRANCISCO
HALF MOON BAY

MONTEREY

MORRO BAY

SOUTHERN CALIFORNIA

SANTA BARBARA

VENTURA
OXNARD

REDONDO BEACH
LONG BEACH

SAN PEDRO
NEWPORT BEACH
BALBOA

DANA POINT

OCEANSIDE

SAN DIEGO

California

You may choose from more than fifty whale-watch trip operators off the coast of California. In southern California, competition is lively in areas where six or more trip operators vie for passengers. In northern California, where the tides and the weather are less consistent than in the southern part of the state, whale watching is less popular but entirely possible.

If you plan to be in California sometime during the annual gray whale migration, between late December and April, you will have no trouble booking a whale-watch trip in most coastal towns. Yet surprisingly few companies offer trips from June to October, when blue whales, orcas, and humpbacks are in the area. If you plan to be in California then, call or write to ask about "off-season" whale-watch trips or private charters.

Many of the trip operators on the California coast are primarily sportfishing charter companies that turn their attention to whale watching during the early months of the year. Their commitment to customer service has kept them in business for fifteen or twenty years or even longer, and most of them strive to provide enjoyable, educational whale-watch trips.

Because it's so unusual not to see gray whales during the annual migration, many trip operators guarantee sightings and offer a "whale check" for a free trip in the unlikely event that whales are nowhere to be found.

TOURISM INFORMATION

California Office of Tourism
1121 L Street, Suite 103, Sacramento, CA 95814
(800) TO–CALIF

Eureka, California

Celtic Charter Service
5105 Woodland Way, Eureka, CA 95501; (707) 442–7580

Whales:	Gray, occasional humpback
Season:	April
Boats:	One boat, the *Celtic*; 48 passengers
Trips:	Four 2-hour trips annually during the Sequoia Park Zoological Society Celebration of Whales (held at the end of March and in early April); also occasional private charters.
Fare:	The Celebration of Whales cruises cost $30 for non-members and $25 for members of the Zoological Society. Private whale-watch charters are $650. Reservations are required.
Departure:	Trips leave from the Woodley Island Marina, Dock D, in Eureka. From Highway 101, turn onto the Samoa Bridge (255). Make the next right to the marina and watch for Slip D.
Naturalist:	Naturalist aboard for some Sequoia Park Zoological Society trips

Owner and skipper Phil Glenn says, "Eureka is a small, somewhat isolated town, and so public whale watching is usually unprofitable, except during the annual festival. However, we will do whale watching for groups, on private charters."

Fort Bragg, California

Captain Jack

P.O. Box 1002, Fort Bragg, CA 95437; (707) 964–4550

Whales:	Gray
Season:	December 31 through April 15
Boats:	One boat, the *Trek II*
Trips:	Afternoon trips on some weekdays, according to demand. One trip on Saturdays and one on Sundays, at 1 P.M. Up to four whale-watch trips a day during the Mendocino–Fort Bragg Whale Festival in March. All trips are 1¹/₂ to 2 hours long. Generally, Saturday is the busiest day.
Fare:	Adults, $20; children, $15. Reservations required. Guests at the Trade Winds Motel receive discount coupons for Captain Jack whale watches.
Departure:	Trips leave from Sportsman's Dock on the Noyo River, at the end of North Harbor Drive, which is on the north side of the river under the green bridge.
Naturalist:	No naturalist on board

Owner Jack Schults notes, "The *Trek II* is high in the bow, so you can look right down on the whales—great for photographers. Not only will you have a perfect view of the whales, but also a fantastic panorama of the rugged Mendocino coastline."

Lady Irma II

P.O. Box 103, Fort Bragg, CA 95437; (707) 964–3854

Whales:	Gray, occasional orca, humpback, finback
Season:	January 1 through April 15
Boats:	Two boats; 40 passengers each

Trips:	One 2-hour trip daily at 2 P.M. Saturday is the busiest day.
Fare:	Adults, $20; childern under 12, $14.
Departure:	Trips leave from the Wharf Restaurant on the Noyo River. As you travel north on Highway 2, make the first right after the Noyo River Bridge.
Naturalist:	No naturalist on board

"There is a whale festival in this area that starts in Mendocino the second weekend in March and ends in Fort Bragg the following weekend. On those weekends, we run four whale-watch trips a day. A wine tasting, whale run, and arts and crafts shows are all part of the festival, and it draws quite a crowd," says owner Rick Thornton.

Misty II Charters
P.O. Box 223, Fort Bragg, CA 95437; (707) 964–7161

Whales:	Gray
Season:	November and December; March and April
Boats:	One boat; 26 passengers
Trips:	Two trips every weekday; five trips on Saturdays and Sundays. Departure times vary, but all trips are 2 hours long. Saturday is busiest day.
Fare:	$20 per person. Reservations advised.
Departure:	Trips leave from Sportsman's Dock on the Noyo River, at the end of North Harbor Drive, which is on the north side of the river under the green bridge.
Naturalist:	No naturalist aboard

Charlie and Peggy Johnson specialize in personal attention. "We're family owned and operated, and we like what we do. And we love whales!"

111

Point Arena, California

Second Semester Charters
P.O. Box 383, Point Arena, CA 95468; (707) 882–2440

Whales:	Gray
Season:	Late November through late April
Boats:	One boat; 6 passengers
Trips:	Trips are scheduled according to demand, for any length of time. Saturday is the busiest day.
Fare:	$27 per person for 2 hours.
Departure:	Trips leave from the Point Arena Pier. From the south end of town, turn left on Iversen Road and follow to the pier.
Naturalist:	No

Owner Patrick Bellew says, "We offer personalized service that's as close to going to sea with a friend as you can get. Also, we're just five minutes from the pier to the whale migration path."

Bellew grew up in a suburb of St. Louis, close to my home, and he is proof that there is Life After St. Louis—on the ocean.

Sausalito, California

Allen Barry Boat Company
1001 Bridgeway, Suite 533, Sausalito, CA 94965; (415) 332–7329

Whales:	Gray
Season:	December 1 through February 28

Boats:	Two: a 40-foot power yacht and a 40-foot sailing yacht; 6 passengers each
Trips:	One trip daily, by charter only. Weekends are the busiest days.
Fare:	The power boat is available for $360 a day. The sailing yacht costs $50 a person, with a minimum of $200 a day. Reservations required.
Departure:	The yachts are berthed in two different harbors in Sausalito.
Naturalist:	No

"Generally, the yachts are chartered by groups who determine the day's agenda," says owner Allen Barry. "Guests generally pack their own food and drinks but we will provision the boat to the guests' specifications at cost of the provisions plus a 15 percent fee."

Berkeley, California

Dolphin Charters
1007 Leneve Place, El Cerrito, CA 94530; (415) 527–9622

Whales:	Gray in winter, humpback and blue in summer
Season:	January through May
Boats:	The 50-foot *Delphinus*; 44 passengers
Trips:	Selected day-long trips on weekends (not in February) to Point Reyes, to San Francisco Bay, and to the Farallon Islands. Saturday is the busiest day.
Fare:	Trips range from $35 to $59. Reservations advised.
Departure:	Trips leave from the Berkeley marina, at the foot of University Avenue, just off I–80.
Naturalist:	Yes

Where the Whales Are

Dolphin Charters and its sister company, Biological Journeys, specialize in whale-watch trips worldwide. "We have had nearly 100 percent success in seeing gray whales on trips to Point Reyes in January and March," says owner and marine biologist Ronn Storro-Patterson. The Farallon Islands cruises provide an opportunity to see a variety of whale species, including blue and humpback, as well as sharks, pinnipeds (seals, sea lions, walruses, etc.), and other sea life.

San Francisco, Sausalito, and Bodega Bay, California

Footloose Forays
P.O.Box 1179, Point Reyes Station, CA 94965; (415) 663–9206

Whales:	Gray in winter and spring; blue and humpback in summer and fall
Season:	Year round
Boats:	Two boats, about 50 passengers each; one whale watch conducted from shore.
Trips:	Trips scheduled at various times in winter and spring to see gray whales and in summer and fall to see blue whales and humpbacks. Summer trips to the Farallon Islands are the most popular.
Fare:	Range is from $20 to $45 per person, depending on length of trip. Reservations required.
Departure:	Depending on destination, trips leave from San Francisco, Sausalito, and Bodega Bay.
Naturalist:	Yes

Owner Michael Ellis is a well-versed naturalist, and he accompanies every trip. Ellis also writes a nature column for the Point Reyes newspaper.

San Francisco, California

Oceanic Society Expeditions
Fort Mason Center, Building E, San Francisco, CA 94123; (415) 474–3385

Whales:	Gray
Season:	December 26 through mid-April
Boats:	The 85-foot *Ranger;* 80 passengers
Trips:	Every Friday, Saturday, Sunday, and Monday at 9:30 A.M.; also selected weekdays at 9:30 A.M. Trips are 6½ hours long.
Fare:	On weekends, adults, $42; children 10 through 15 and senior citizens 60 or older, $38. On weekdays, adults, $38; children 10 through 15 and senior citizens 60 or older, $34. No one under 10 permitted on the boat. Group rates available. Reservations required.
Departure:	Trips leave from San Francisco Yacht Harbor/Marina Green.
Naturalist:	Naturalist on board from Oceanic Society

Oceanic Society Expeditions also sponsors eight-hour trips to the Farallon Islands on selected dates from June through mid-November. Blue and humpback whales are occasionally spotted on these trips, which cost $50 per person. Write for more information.

Half Moon Bay, California

Huck Finn Sportfishing
P.O. Box 1432, El Granada, CA 94018; (415) 726–7133

Whales:	Gray
Season:	Mid-December through April
Boats:	Three; *Hull Cat*, 30 passengers and *Red Baron* and *Queen of Hearts,* 46 passengers each
Trips:	Trips by request only on weekdays; two or three on Saturdays and Sundays at 8 A.M., 11 A.M., and 2 P.M. All trips are 2 1/2 hours long. Saturday afternoon trips are the most popular.
Fare:	$15 per person. Reservations advised.
Departure:	Trips leave from Pillar Point Harbor at Half Moon Bay, 25 miles south of San Francisco on Highway 1 or 4 miles north of Half Moon Bay on Highway 1.
Naturalist:	No naturalist on board

"Our primary income is from fishing, but whale watching is something that is a thrill for both my husband, Bill, and me. If the whales were here all the time, we could easily do it every day," says co-owner Peggy Beckett.

"We do provide written information on the whales for passengers to take home, books to look at on board, a running commentary on what we are looking for and seeing, and whale certificates for those days we are successful."

Oceanic Society Expeditions

Fort Mason Center, Building E, San Francisco, CA 94123
(415) 474–3385

Whales:	Gray
Season:	December 26 through mid-April
Boats:	The 70-foot *Rain Song II;* carries 68 passengers
Trips:	Selected weekdays at 1:30 P.M.; Saturdays and Sundays at 10 A.M. and 1:30 P.M. Trips are 2¼ hours long.
Fare:	On weekdays, adults, $26; children 5 through 15 and senior citizens over 60, $23. On weekends, adults, $28; children 5 through 15 and senior citizens over 60, $24. No one under 5 permitted on the boat. Group rates available. Reservations required.
Departure:	Trips leave from Pillar Point Harbor in Half Moon Bay.
Naturalist:	Naturalists on board from Oceanic Society Expeditions

Oceanic Society Expeditions was founded in 1973 to create educational world-wide nature programs. The organization's whale-watch program strives to increase public awareness of the importance of protecting our fragile marine environment.

Santa Cruz, California

Pacific Yachting

Santa Cruz Yacht Harbor, 333 Lake Avenue, Santa Cruz, CA 95062; (408) 476–2370

Whales:	Gray
Season:	Mid-December through mid-February
Boats:	Ten luxury sailing yachts; 6 passengers each

Trips: All yachts available for skippered whale-watch char-
            ters or "bareboat" (unskippered) sailing seven days a
            week. Weekends are busiest.

Fare: Two-, 3-, 4- and 6-hour skippered charters range in
            price from $30 per person to $400 for six people.
            Reservations required.

Departure: Trips leave from the Santa Cruz Harbor, near the
            Crow's Nest Restaurant.

Naturalist: No naturalist on board

"We have a fleet of ten luxury sailing yachts, with auxiliary diesel engines, sleeping quarters for six, as well as all cooking appliances and bathing conveniences," says owner Marc Kraft.

Rain Song Sportfishing

P.O. Box 369, Capitola, CA 95010; (408) 462–3553

Whales: Gray in winter; blue and humpback in summer and fall

Season: January through April; July through October

Boats: Two boats; 70 and 49 passengers

Trips: One or two trips, depending on demand, every Satur-
            day and Sunday from January through April. From
            July through October, trips depart at 9 A.M. and
            return at 3 P.M. Saturdays are the busiest days.

Fare: For trips seeking grays: adults, $16; children, $14.
            Summer and fall trips cost $39 per person. Reserva-
            tions required.

Departure: Trips leave from Santa Cruz Yacht Harbor, 20 miles
            south of San Jose on Highway 17.

Naturalist: Naturalist on board

Co-owner Brian Richards notes that these trips take place on "the newest fleet in California."

Stagnaro Fishing Trips
Box 7007, Santa Cruz, CA 95061; (408) 425–7003

Whales:	Gray
Season:	December through April
Boats:	Two boats; 49 and 60 passengers
Trips:	Trips on request by private charter on weekdays; two 3-hour trips on Saturdays and Sundays at 10 A.M. and 2:30 P.M. Saturday is the busiest day.
Fare:	Adults, $16; children under 12, $12. Reservations advised, but not required.
Departure:	Trips leave from Santa Cruz Wharf, at the foot of Washington Street on Beach Street.
Naturalist:	No naturalist on board

"Set off with us for a morning or afternoon trip on the waters of Monterey Bay to enjoy sightings of one of the greatest wonders of our coast, the gray whale," says owner Jeff Goyert.

Monterey, California

Chris' Fishing Trips
48 Fisherman's Wharf, Monterey, CA 93940; (408) 375–5951

Whales:	Gray in winter; blue, minke, orca in summer and fall
Season:	December 25 through late March

Where the Whales Are

Boats:	Four boats; 49 to 75 passengers each
Trips:	Weekday trips are scheduled according to demand. Four trips are scheduled on Saturdays and four on Sundays, at 9 A.M. 11 A.M., 1 P.M., and 3 P.M. Most trips are 1½ to 2 hours long. When the naturalist is on board, trips last 3 hours. The most popular trip is at 1 P.M. on Saturdays.
Fare:	Adults, $12; children, $6. Reservations advised but not required.
Departure:	Trips leave from Fisherman's Wharf in Monterey, just off the Pacific Grove/Del Monte exit off Highway 1, going south.
Naturalist:	Some weekend trips are accompanied by naturalists, and then fare is $1 or $2 more.

Todd Arcoleo, an office staff member, says, "Enjoy an outing with family and friends on Monterey Bay with the gray whales."

Monterey Sport Fishing

96 Old Fisherman's Wharf #1; Monterey, CA 93940;
(408) 372–2203

Princess Monterey Cruises

96 Old Fisherman's Wharf, Monterey, CA 93940; (408) 372–2628

Whales:	Gray, humpback, and blue
Season:	Mid-December through March for gray whales; August through October for humpback and blue
Boats:	Two boats; 50 and 80 passengers
Trips:	Four trips daily at 9 A.M., 11 A.M., 1 P.M., and 3 P.M. Additional 7 A.M. trip on Saturdays and Sundays. Trips are 1½ to 2 hours long. The early weekend trips are the most popular.

Fare:	December through February 15: adults, $12; children under 12, $6. February 15 through March: adults, $15; children, $8. August through October: $20 per person. Group rates available. Reservations required. Discount coupons for whale watches given to guests at Double-tree Hotel, Gosby House Inn, Hyatt Regency, Monterey Plaza, and the Sheraton Monterey.
Departure:	Trips leave from Monterey's Fisherman's Wharf, just off the Pacific Grove/Del Monte exit off Highway 1, going south.
Naturalist:	Naturalist from the American Cetacean Society

"Our boats provide excellent opportunities for close-up viewing of one of the world's largest animals in a special and diverse habitat," owner Benji Shake says.

Randy's Fishing Trips
66 Fisherman's Wharf #1, Monterey, CA 93940; (408) 372–7440

Whales:	Gray; occasionally orca, blue
Season:	January and February
Boats:	Four boats; 45, 48, 48, and 68 passengers
Trips:	Three trips each weekday, according to demand. Departure times vary. Four trips on Saturday and four trips on Sunday, at 8:30 A.M., 10:30 A.M., 12:30 P.M., and 2:30 P.M. All trips last about 2 hours. The busiest day is Saturday.
Fare:	On weekdays: adults, $12; children 12 and younger, $8. On weekends: adults, $15; children, $8.
Departure:	Trips leave from Monterey's Fisherman's Wharf, just off the Pacific Grove/Del Monte exit off Highway 1, going south.

Naturalist: Crew members narrate trips on weekdays; a naturalist is on board every weekend.

Owners Peter Bruno and John Lupo, in recognition of the "immeasurable assistance the Society for the Protection of Cruelty to Animals offers our sea life," donate 50 cents for each passenger on the naturalist cruises.

Shearwater Journeys
P.O. Box 1145, Soquel, CA 95073; (408) 688–1990

Whales:	Gray, blue, fin, humpback, orca, minke
Season:	Whale watches all year
Boats:	Four boats; 50 to 60 passengers each
Trips:	Gray whale trips in January (selected dates). Trips to see blue whales are scheduled from August to October. Weekends are the busiest time.
Fare:	Half-day and full-day whale watches in January range from $15 to $40 per person. One- and two-day trips from August through October range from $40 to $140. Group rates available. Reservations required.
Departure:	Most trips leave from Fisherman's Wharf in Monterey, just off the Pacific Grove/Del Monte exit off Highway 1, going south. Some leave from San Diego or Bodega Bay.
Naturalist:	One naturalist from the American Cetacean Society is on board for every ten passengers.

Owner Debra Love Shearwater notes, "We specialize in seabird trips. The best time of the year is August through October, which is also the best time for seeing blues and humpbacks. In 1988, on every trip from August through October, we saw blue whales, and as many as five species of dolphins in one day."

Morro Bay, California

Virg's Sportfishing & Whale Watching
1215 Embarcadero, Morro Bay, CA 93422; (805) 772–1222

Whales:	Gray
Season:	Mid-December through March 31
Boats:	Six boats; 35 to 75 passengers each
Trips:	One or two trips, according to demand, on weekdays. Two trips on Saturdays and two on Sundays at 11 A.M. and 2 P.M. Trips are 2 to 2¹/₂ hours long. The busiest day is Saturday.
Fare:	Adults, $14; children under 13, $8. Discounts for groups. Reservations required.
Departure:	Trips leave from the dock, across from Pacific Gas and Electric.
Naturalist:	Naturalist on some trips

"Sail alongside the gray whale on its way to its winter quarters, and learn about the whales from the experts," says a spokesman from Virg's Sportfishing. "Our knowledgeable sea captains narrate each cruise. Bring your camera!"

Santa Barbara, California

Capt. Don's Coastal Cruises
P.O. Box 1134, Summerland, CA 93067; (805) 969–5217

Whales:	Gray
Season:	Mid-February to mid-April
Boats:	Two boats; 49 passengers each

Where the Whales Are

Trips:	Three 2½- to 3-hour trips daily at 9 A.M., noon, and 3 P.M. Weekends are busiest.
Fare:	Adults, $18; senior citizens, $16; children 12 and under, $12. Reservations required.
Departure:	Trips leave from Stearn's Wharf, at the base of State Street in Santa Barbara.
Naturalist:	Captain serves as naturalist.

Captain Donald L. Hedden notes, "Over 22,000 gray whales migrate through the Santa Barbara Channel during our season, within 5 miles from shore."

SEA Landing Sportfishing
1321 Los Alamos Place, Santa Barbara, CA 93109;
(805) 965–1985

Whales:	Gray, common dolphin, Pacific white-sided dolphin
Season:	December 15 through April 30
Boats:	The 88-foot *Condor*; 125 passengers
Trips:	From December 15 through February 15, the *Condor* makes 9-hour whale-watch trips on Sundays and selected other dates to the Channel Islands. From February 15 through April 30, three 2½-hour trips are offered daily (except Wednesday) at 9 A.M., noon, and 3 P.M. The most popular trip is on Saturday morning.
Fare:	Day-long trips: adults, $60; children, $30; price includes a barbecue lunch and a trip by skiff inside the Painted Cave at Santa Cruz Island. The 2½-hour trips: adults, $18, children 12 and younger, $9. Group rates available for schools on weekdays. Reservations required. The Harbor View Inn offers guests discount coupons for trips on the *Condor*.

Departure: Trips leave from SEA Landing in the Santa Barbara Harbor.

Naturalist: Crew members serve as naturalists.

From July through December, Captain Fred Benko also runs one-and two-day trips on the *Condor* in search of humpbacks, orcas, minkes, and blue whales. Call or write for schedule and costs.

Ventura, California

Island Packers
1867 Spinnaker Drive, Ventura, CA 93001; (805) 642–1393

Whales: Gray, minke

Season: December 26 through March 31

Boats: Four boats; 25, 48, 48, and 100 passengers

Trips: One or two trips on weekdays; two on Saturdays and two on Sundays. According to demand, trips are offered at 9:30 A.M., 11 A.M., or 1:30 P.M. Saturday is the busiest day.

Fare: Half-day excursions: adults, $20; children, $14. Anacapa Island whale-watch trips: adults, $35; children, $22 Whale-watch trips to Santa Cruz Island: adults, $40; children, $30. Reservations required. The Doubletree Hotel in Ventura offers guests discount coupons for Island Packers whale watches.

Departure: Trips leave from Ventura Harbor. Take the Seaward off-ramp south on Harbor Boulevard and turn right on Spinnaker Drive in the Ventura Harbor.

Naturalist: Crew members, most of whom have degrees in environmental science or biology, serve as naturalists.

"Island Packers is a family-owned and -operated business," notes owner William Mark Connally, the son of the founder. "We are the concessionaire to the Channel Islands National Park and provide transportation to the park and interpretive services for the National Park Service."

Oxnard, California

Captain Dave's Waterfront Cruises
1434 Fathom Street, Oxnard, CA 93035; (805) 984–0030

Whales:	Gray
Season:	January 1 to March 30
Boats:	One boat; 23 passengers
Trips:	Three or four trips each week, according to demand. Trips leave at 9 A.M. and 1 P.M. and last about 3 hours. The busiest day is Saturday.
Fare:	Adults, $25; children, $18. Reservations required.
Departure:	Trips leave from Channel Islands Harbor. From the 101 Freeway, take the Victoria Avenue exit. Follow the sign for the Channel Islands Harbor, about 7 miles south on the right.
Naturalist:	No

Captain Dave Willhite is proud of his high-quality boat and the knowledge he's gained since the 1960s of the Channel Islands and their wildlife.

Cisco's Sportfishing
4151 South Victoria Avenue, Oxnard, CA 93035;
(800) 323–BOAT (outside California), (800) 322–FISH
(in California), (805) 985–8511

Whales:	Gray
Season:	January 1 through April 1
Boats:	One fishing boat; 70 passengers
Trips:	Two 3-hour trips daily at 9 A.M. and 1 P.M. Weekends are the busiest time.
Fare:	Adults, $20; senior citizens, $15; children under 11, $12. Reservations advised.
Departure:	Trips leave from Captain Jack's Landing. From the 101 Freeway, take Victoria Avenue exit. Follow the sign for Channel Islands Harbor, about 7 miles south on the right.
Naturalist:	Naturalist on board

Each Cisco's trip uses one or another of owner Nick Dikoya's fleet of fourteen fishing vessels.

Redondo Beach, California

Redondo Sport Fishing
223 North Harbor Drive, Redondo Beach, CA 90277;
(213) 372–3566

Whales:	Gray, orca, pilot
Season:	December 26 through April 1
Boats:	The *Voyager;* 125 passengers

Where the Whales Are

Trips:	Two 3-hour trips daily: 10 A.M. and 1:30 P.M. on weekdays, 9:30 A.M. and 1:30 P.M. on Saturdays and Sundays. Saturday is the busiest day.
Fare:	Adults, $10, children under 12, $7.50. Group rates available.
Departure:	Trips leave from the Redondo Sport Fishing Pier. From the 405 Freeway, go west on 190th Street to Harbor Drive and then turn south. Pier is across from the Sheraton Hotel.
Naturalist:	Naturalist from the Cabrillo Marine Museum/American Cetacean Society

Owner Terry Turk says, "The *Voyager* is a double-deck excursion boat designed specifically for whale watching, with ample seating for all passengers. This is not a fishing boat, which often has limited seating. Also, we are just minutes from the open ocean, which increases our whale-watching time."

San Pedro, California

L.A. Harbor Sportfishing
1150 Nagoya Way, Berth 79, San Pedro, CA 90731;
(213) 547–9916

Whales:	Gray
Season:	December 26 through March 31
Boats:	Eight boats; 100 passengers each

Trips: Two trips on weekdays at 11 A.M. and 2 P.M.; three
trips on Saturdays and Sundays at 9 and 11:30 A.M.
and 2 P.M. Trips last about 2¹/₂ hours. The 11:30 A.M.
trip on Saturdays is the most popular.

Fare: Adults, $10; children ages 1 to 12; $7. Group rates
available for 25 or more. Reservations are not
required, but are advised.

Departure: Trips leave from L.A. Harbor Sportfishing dock, near
the Ports O'Call Village at 6th Street and Harbor.

Naturalist: The captain serves as naturalist.

Skipper's 22nd Street Landing

141 West 22nd Street, San Pedro, CA 90731; (213) 832–8304

Whales: Gray

Season: January through March

Boats: Three boats; 150 passengers each

Trips: Two trips on weekdays at 10 A.M. and 1 P.M.; three to
five trips every Saturday and Sunday at 9 and 11:30 A.M.
and 2 P.M. and sometimes at 10 A.M. and 1 P.M.,
depending on demand. Trips last about 2¹/₂ hours.
Saturday morning is the busiest time.

Fare: Weekdays: adults, $10; children under 12 and senior
citizens over 62, $7. Weekends: adults, $11; children
and senior citizens, $8. Reservations required.

Departure: Trips leave from the new Cabrillo Marina. Take the
Harbor Freeway south to the end; go to 22nd Street
and turn left; drive five blocks.

Where the Whales Are

Naturalist: Naturalist on board from Cabrillo Marine Museum/ American Cetacean Society

"Come on down and visit with the greatest creatures on the earth as they make their way to the breeding grounds off Mexico's coast," says manager Dorothy H. Cummins.

Spirit Cruises and Whale Watch

Ports O'Call, Berth 75, San Pedro, CA 90731; (213) 831–1073

Whales:	Gray
Season:	December 26 through mid-April
Boats:	Three boats; 49, 100, and 150 passengers
Trips:	One trip on weekdays at 11 A.M.; two trips on Saturdays at 11 A.M. and 2 P.M.; three trips on Sundays at 9 A.M., noon, and 2 P.M. Trips last about 2 hours. The Sunday midday trip is the most popular.
Fare:	Adults, $12.50; children ages 2 through 12, $7.50. Reservations required. With advance reservations, you get a discount on weekday trips.
Departure:	Trips leave from Ports O'Call and Long Beach; call for directions.
Naturalist:	Naturalist on board

Owner Jayme S. Wilson says, "We use sailing ships and motor yachts—the nicest boats in southern California. Guaranteed whale sightings or you get a free pass for another trip!"

Long Beach, California

Belmont Pier Sportfishing
Ocean Avenue and 39th Place, Long Beach, CA 90803;
(213) 434–6781

Whales:	Gray
Season:	December through April
Boats:	Three boats; one, 109 passengers; two, 125 passengers each
Trips:	One trip every weekday at 10 A.M.; two trips Saturdays and Sundays at 9 A.M. and 1 P.M. All trips last 3 hours. Weekends are busiest.
Fare:	Weekdays: adults, $7; children 12 and under, $5. Weekends: adults, $9; children, $7. Group rates are available. Reservations required.
Departure:	Trips leave from Belmont Pier at Ocean Boulevard and Termino.
Naturalist:	Naturalist from the Cabrillo Marine Museum/American Cetacean Society

Whale-watch coordinator June Ithurralde notes, "Friendly crew and staff coordinator are on hand at all times to assure your trip is a success." The narrator talks about the migration of the gray whales and their behavior and hands out whale-watch certificates to passengers at the end of each trip.

Catalina Cruises
P.O. Box 1948, San Pedro, CA 90733; (213) 436–5006

Whales:	Gray
Season:	December 26 through early April

Where the Whales Are

Boats:	Five boats; 700-passenger capacity each, but whale-watch cruises are limited to 450 passengers
Trips:	Weekday schedule varies according to whale traffic. Two 3-hour trips on Saturdays and Sundays at 10 A.M. and 1:30 P.M. Saturday morning trips are the most popular.
Fare:	Adults, $12; senior citizens 55 and older, $11; children: ages 5 through 11, $10; under 5, $3. Group rates available. Reservations are required.
Departure:	Trips leave from the Catalina Landing, 320 Golden Shore Drive in downtown Long Beach, at the south end of the Long Beach Freeway 710.
Naturalist:	Naturalist from Cabrillo Marine Museum/American Cetacean Society

Manager Terry Koenig says, "We have the largest whale-watching vessels on the West Coast, and the most comfortable, too, with three levels of outside viewing and two spacious interior cabins with large windows."

Long Beach Sportfishing
555 Pico Avenue, Long Beach, CA 90802; (213) 432–8993

Whales:	Gray, pilot, occasional orca
Season:	December 26 through early April
Boats:	Five boats; 497 passengers total
Trips:	Two 2½-hour trips daily at 10 a.m. and 1 p.m. The morning trip is the most popular.
Fare:	Adults, $9.50; children ages 2 to 15 and senior citizens; $6.50. Group rates available. Reservations required.

Departure: Trips leave from Berth 55 at the Long Beach marina.
Take the 710 Freeway south to the off-ramp at 7th
Avenue and Pico. The marina is just across from the
ramp.

Naturalist: Captains serve as naturalists.

Between them, owners Veronica Nangano and Don Ashley have
nearly two decades in the sportfishing business. "All our captains
have been running whale watches for years and have extensive
knowledge of gray whales' physical and biological features, of their
migration habits and feeding habits," Nangano says.

Shoreline Village Cruises
429 Shoreline Village Drive, Suite N, Long Beach, CA 90802;
(213) 495–5884

Whales: Gray

Season: December 26 through mid-April

Boats: Two boats, a 50-foot cruise boat and a 90-foot sailing
ship; 49 and 103 passengers respectively

Trips: Weekdays, one trip at 11 A.M.; Saturday, two trips at
11 A.M. and 2 P.M.; Sunday, four trips at 9 and 11 A.M.,
noon, and 2:45 P.M. Trips are about 2 1/2 hours long.
The Sunday midday trip is the busiest.

Fare: Adults, $12.50; children ages 2 to 12, $7.50. Twenty
percent discount on weekday trips. Reservations
required.

Departure: Trips leave from Long Beach and San Pedro, depending on which trip you book. Call for details and directions.

Naturalist: Captain serves as naturalist.

Staff member Kristin Wilson notes, "We guarantee a whale sighting. And we use charter boats with seating for everyone, not old fishing boats."

Star Party Cruises
140 Marina Drive, Long Beach, CA 90803; (213) 428–3782

Whales:	Gray
Season:	January through mid-April
Boats:	One 65-foot boat; 109 passengers
Trips:	Two 2¹/₂-hour trips daily at 10 A.M. and 1 P.M. Weekends are the busiest.
Fare:	Adults, $11; senior citizens, $10; children, $8. Reservations required.
Departure:	Trips leave from Seaport Village in Long Beach.
Naturalist:	Naturalist on board from the Cabrillo Marine Museum/American Cetacean Society

Newport Beach, California

Newport Landing Sportfishing
309 Palm, Suite F, Balboa, CA 92661; (714) 675–0550

Whales:	Gray, minke, several species of dolphin
Season:	December 26 through early April
Boats:	Three boats; 116, 48, and 45 passengers
Trips:	Two trips each weekday at 10 A.M. and 1 P.M.; three trips on Saturdays and Sundays at 9 A.M., noon, and

2:30 P.M. All trips last 2 to 2½ hours. Weekend mid-day trips are busiest.

Fare: Adults, $10; senior citizens, $6; children 12 and younger, $6, on weekdays. Group rates for schools, churches, and community groups. Reservations advised. Newport Beach Meridian Hotel guests receive discounts on Newport Landing Sportfishing whale watches.

Departure: Trips leave from Newport Landing Sportfishing dock between Adams and Palm Street, just off Balboa Boulevard.

Naturalist: Skipper serves as naturalist.

"Since the gray whale can be readily found within a few miles off the coast, a simple cruise of a few hours lets thousands of people view not only the whales in their natural habitat, but also many species of resident marine animals, such as the common dolphin, bottlenose dolphin, sea lions, birds, and occasionally killer whales and sharks," says staff member George Eddy.

Balboa, California

Catalina Passenger Service

Balboa Pavilion, 400 Main Street, Balboa, CA 92661; (714) 673–5245

Whales: Gray, occasional minke and blue

Season: January through mid-March

Boats: One luxury catamaran; 400 passengers

Trips: One 2- to 3-hour trip at 10 A.M. on Monday, Tuesday, and Wednesday.

Fare:	Adults, $10; children 12 and under, $6. Group rates and senior citizen rates available. Reservations required.
Departure:	Trips leave from Balboa Pavilion, on the Pacific Coast Highway and Balboa Boulevard. Take the 55 Freeway south to Newport Boulevard; follow to Main Street and turn left.
Naturalist:	Naturalist from the American Cetacean Society

Betsy Sturgeon from Catalina Passenger Service notes that passengers ride on a luxury catamaran with three decks, inside and outside seating, a bar, and a snack bar.

Davey's Locker Sportfishing

400 Main Street, Balboa, CA 92661; (714) 673–1434

Whales:	Gray; Pacific white-sided dolphin
Season:	December 26 through April 1
Boats:	Five boats; 149 passengers total
Trips:	Weekdays, two trips at 10 A.M. and 1 P.M. Saturdays and Sundays, three trips at 9 A.M., noon, and 2:30 P.M. All trips are 2¹/₂ hours long. Weekends are the busiest times.
Fare:	Adults, $10, children, $6. Special school rates available. Reservations required.
Departure:	Trips leave from Balboa Pavilion, on the Pacific Coast Highway and Balboa Boulevard. Take the 55 Freeway south to Newport Boulevard; follow to Main Street and turn left.
Naturalist:	Naturalist from the American Cetacean Society

Manager Eddie DiRuscio also runs Para-Sailing Newport. (Para-sailing is riding a parachute that is towed aloft behind a power boat.)

DiRuscio offers "direct flights"—you take off and land directly from the boat—and he says you never get wet. He says that riders often spot whales.

American Cetacean Society
Orange County Whalewatch, 400 Main Street, Balboa, CA 92661; (714) 675–9881

Whales:	Gray, minke, blue, sperm, Pacific white-sided dolphin
Season:	December 26 through late March or mid-April
Boats:	Three boats; 119, 148, and 350 passengers
Trips:	Weekdays, two trips at 10 A.M. and 1 P.M.; Saturdays and Sundays, three trips at 9 A.M., noon, and 2:30 P.M. All trips last 2¹/₂ hours. Weekend noon trips are the busiest.
Fare:	Adults, $10; children 12 and younger, $6. Reservations advised.
Departure:	Trips leave from Balboa Pavilion, on the Pacific Coast Highway and Balboa Boulevard. Take the 55 Freeway south to Newport Boulevard; follow to Main Street and turn left.
Naturalist:	Naturalist from the American Cetacean Society

The American Cetacean Society promotes education, conservation, and research related to marine mammals and their habitat. According to staff member Ridgely Montrosa Keeley, the Orange County chapter supports those activities and makes the public aware of them through special programs.

Dana Point, California

Dana Wharf Sportfishing
34675 Golden Lantern, Dana Point, CA 92629; (714) 496–5794

Whales:	Gray
Season:	December 26 through March 31
Boats:	Ten boats; 6 to 99 passengers each
Trips:	Weekdays, three trips at 10 A.M., noon, and 2 P.M.; Saturdays and Sundays, five trips at 8 A.M., 10 A.M., noon, 2 P.M., and 4 P.M. Nine trips daily during the annual February–March Dana Point Festival of Whales, which includes educational programs and cultural events as well as whale-watch trips. All trips last 2 hours. Early morning trips on Saturdays are the busiest.
Fare:	Adults, $10; senior citizens, $6; children 12 and under, $6 on weekdays. Reservations required. Discounts on whale-watch trips are available for guests at Dana Point Resort, the Ritz-Carlton, Dana Point Inn, and Best Western Marina Inn.
Departure:	Trips leave from the Dana Wharf Docks in Dana Point Harbor. From the Pacific Coast Highway, follow Golden Lantern down to the water.
Naturalist:	Yes

The Dana Point Festival of Whales is held each year in February and March to celebrate the arrival of the gray whales. Jody Tyson, general manager of Dana Wharf Sportfishing, notes, "Emphasis is placed on the local marine environment, but the whales are the center of attention."

Thompson Voyages
P.O. Box 217, Laguna Beach, CA 92652; (714) 497–1055

Whales:	Gray
Season:	January through early April
Boats:	One 65-foot boat; 30 passengers
Trips:	Two 2-hour trips on Saturdays and Sundays at 9 A.M. and 1 P.M.
Fare:	$20 per person. Reservations advised.
Departure:	Trips leave from the Dana Wharf Docks in Dana Point Harbor. From the Pacific Coast Highway, follow Golden Lantern down to the water.
Naturalist:	Yes

Owner Doug Thompson, who also serves as the naturalist, is a marine wildlife expert, photojournalist, filmmaker, writer, and lecturer who has been in the whale-watching business since the 1960s.

"On all of our trips, we stress the interrelationships of the coastal and marine environments, how it all works together and what happens when changes occur," Thompson said. "And we have fun!"

Oceanside, California

Helgren's Sportfishing
315 Harbor Drive South, Oceanside, CA 92054; (619) 722–2133

Whales:	Gray
Season:	December 26 through April 1
Boats:	Two boats; 125 and 135 passengers
Trips:	Weekdays, two trips at 10 A.M. and 1 P.M.; Saturdays and Sundays, three trips at 9 A.M., 11:30 A.M. and 2 P.M.

All trips are 2 hours long. Saturday midday trip is the busiest.

Fare: Adults, $10; senior citizens, $8; children, $7. Reservations required.

Departure: Trips leave from Oceanside Harbor. Take Harbor Drive exit off the San Diego Freeway; follow to the boat harbor.

Naturalist: Captain narrates trips.

Helgren's has been a family-owned business since 1979. All information provided during the captain's narration is from Dr. Raymond Gilmore at the American Cetacean Society.

San Diego, California

Bagheera Sailing Adventures
P.O. Box 6058, San Diego, CA 92106; (619) 223–8808

Whales: Gray

Season: Mid-December through mid-March

Boats: The *Bagheera*; holds 49 passengers

Trips: One trip every Wednesday, Thursday, and Friday, 1 to 4 P.M.; two trips on Saturday, 9 A.M. to noon and 1 to 4 P.M.; one trip Sunday, 9 A.M. to noon. Saturday is the busiest day.

Fare: Adults, $25; children, $15; under 5, free. Reservations required.

Departure: Trips leave from H&M Landing. Take North Harbor Drive along San Diego Bay to Point Loma, turn left on Scott Street, then left on Emerson to H&M Landing.

Naturalist: No naturalist on board

Susan Curtis, office manager, says, "Our vessel is a restored 1924 Alden schooner, a racing class schooner of yesteryear. Her black hull coincides with her name, *Bagheera,* which means Black Panther, from Rudyard Kipling's *The Jungle Book.*"

"Whale check" issued for another trip if no whales are sighted.

Classic Sailing Adventures
1380 Harbor Island Drive, San Diego, CA 92101;
(619) 542–0646

Whales:	Gray
Season:	December 15 through March 15
Boats:	The 35-foot cutter *Mariposa*; 6 passengers
Trips:	Two trips daily, 8:30 A.M. to 12:30 P.M. and 1 to 5 P.M. Weekend afternoon trips are the most popular.
Fare:	$35 per person. Price includes beverages and snacks. Lunch is also available. Reservations required. Sheraton guests receive discounts on Classic Sailing Adventures whale-watch trips.
Departure:	Trips leave from Sheraton Harbor Island East Hotel, across the street from the San Diego Airport.
Naturalist:	No naturalist on board

Captain Roger Anderson says, "As we take only six passengers on each excursion, there is a more personalized experience for everyone on board. If wind permits, we sail as much as possible. Passengers may participate in the sailing or just go along for the spectacular view."

Where the Whales Are

H&M Landing
2803 Emerson Street, San Diego, CA 92106; (619) 222–1144

Whales:	Gray
Season:	December 15 through March 15
Boats:	Twenty boats; 6 to 100 passengers; limited passenger loads on whale watches
Trips:	Two 3-hour trips daily at 10 A.M. and 1:30 P.M. The busiest day is Saturday.
Fare:	Adults, $12; senior citizens; $10; children: ages 13 through 17, $10; 12 and under, $8. Reservations required.
Departure:	Trips leave from San Diego Bay, on Emerson, which is off Rosecrans, just before Shelter Island Drive.
Naturalist:	Narrative provided by staff

"We guarantee whale sightings or you get a free reride," notes Katrina Coleman, general manager. "We are friendly, and we run every day unless weather prohibits."

Harbor Sailboats
2040 Harbor Island Drive, Suite 118, San Diego, CA 92101;
(800) 854–6625

Whales:	Gray
Season:	December 15 through March 15
Boats:	Thirty sailboats; 6 passengers each
Trips:	One trip on weekdays, 11 A.M. to 3 P.M.; many trips on Saturdays and Sundays. Weekends are busiest time.
Fare:	$45 per person. Price includes lunch and soft drinks. Reservations recommended, especially on weekends.

Departure:	Trips leave from Harbor Island West Marina, 2040 Harbor Island Drive, overlooking San Diego Bay.
Naturalist:	Captain serves as narrator.

Owner Tom Hirsh says that thanks to two decades in business, "We have been able to customize trips exactly to suit the desires of the clients. Since sailing is a quiet way to view the whales, we can get a little closer without as much risk of disturbing them or their young. We will also tailor a private whale-watching cruise with or without deluxe catering."

Invader Cruises Inc.
1066 North Harbor Drive, San Diego, CA 92101;
(800) 445–4FUN (nationwide), (800) 262–4FUN (in California),
(619) 234–8687

Whales:	Gray
Season:	Mid-December to mid-March
Boats:	The 151-foot *Invader;* 300 passengers
Trips:	Two 3¹/₂-hour trips daily at 9:30 A.M. and 1:30 P.M. The busiest day is Saturday.
Fare:	Adults, $12.50; children ages 3 through 12 and senior citizens over 55, $8.50. Reservations advised.
Departure:	Trips leave from the B Street Pier, at the foot of Broadway just off Harbor Drive, in downtown San Diego.
Naturalist:	All trips narrated

The *Invader* is a schooner that was built in 1905 and starred in *Robinson Crusoe* with Douglas Fairbanks. A video documentary film on whales is part of the trip. Guaranteed whale sightings.

Islandia Sportfishing

1551 West Mission Bay Drive, San Diego, CA 92109;
(619) 222–1164

Whales:	Gray, finback, Pacific white-sided dolphin
Season:	Mid-December through late March
Boats:	The 85-foot *Dolphin*; 147 passengers
Trips:	Weekdays, two trips at 10 A.M. and 1 P.M.; Saturdays and Sundays, three trips at 9 A.M., 11:30 A.M., and 2 P.M. All trips last 2 to 3 hours. Saturday midday trips are the busiest.
Fare:	Adults, $12; senior citizens and children; $8. Guaranteed sighting or ride again free. Group rates are available. Reservations advised but not required. The Islandia-Hyatt Hotel offers guests a discount coupon for Islandia Sportfishing whale watches.
Departure:	Trips leave from the marina dock by the Islandia-Hyatt Hotel, just off West Mission Bay Drive.
Naturalist:	Naturalist on board

Tim J. Voaklander, one of the *Dolphin*'s three captains, notes that he and his cocaptains have a total of three decades of experience running whale-watch trips. "Symbolically, whales represent great spiritual truths. No wonder whale watching brings peace and tranquillity."

Orion Charters Inc.

3842 Liggett Drive, San Diego, CA 92106; (619) 574–7504

Whales:	Gray
Season:	December 15 through March 31
Boats:	The 64-foot sailing yacht *Orion*; 16 passengers

Trips: Five trips daily on weekdays; two on Saturdays and Sundays. Group charters only. Weekend days are the busiest.

Fare: Group charters $225 per hour, with a minimum of 3¹/₂-hour trips for whale watching. Reservations required.

Departure: Trips leave from Sheraton Harbor Island East Hotel marina, just across the street from the San Diego International Airport.

Naturalist: The owner, who holds a degree in oceanography with a special emphasis on marine biology, serves as naturalist.

"Whale watching is a special experience aboard a sailing vessel—quiet, smooth," notes Captain Keith Korporaal. "We quite literally sail alongside the wonderful creatures."

San Diego Harbor Excursion
570 North Harbor Drive, San Diego, CA 92101; (619) 234–4111

Whales: Gray; occasional fin, orca, pilot, blue

Season: December 26 through the end of March

Boats: Two boats, the 65-foot *Morning Star* and a smaller 45-foot private charter boat; 103 and 25 passengers respectively

Trips: Two 3-hour trips daily at 10 A.M. and 2 P.M. The most popular day is Saturday.

Fare: Adults, $12.50; senior citizens 55 and older, $8.50; children 12 and under, $7. Reservations required only for large groups.

Departure: Trips leave from San Diego Harbor Excursions, at the foot of Broadway on the waterfront.

Where the Whales Are

Naturalist:	Captain serves as naturalist.

Ben Griffith, the owner and captain of the *Morning Star*, has been in the sportfishing business since 1960. "We completely narrate the whale-watch trips, including information on the harbor and the history of San Diego. We also show a gray whale video on the return trip," he said. "I personally try to see that one and all enjoy themselves. We're run more like a family operation than a large company operation."

An open-ended rain check is issued if no whales are sighted.

San Diego Natural History Museum
Balboa Park, P.O. Box 1390, San Diego, CA 92112;
(619) 232–3821

Whales:	Gray; occasionally fin, blue, orca, humpback
Season:	December through mid-March
Boats:	One boat, the *New Seaforth;* 149 passengers
Trips:	Two 2-hour trips on seven Saturdays and two Sundays in December and January, at 11:30 A.M. and 2 P.M. The busiest day is Saturday.
Fare:	Museum members: adults, $10; children under 12, $8. Nonmembers: adults, $12; children, $10. Reservations required.
Departure:	Trips leave from Seaforth Landing at 1717 Quivira Road in Mission Bay. From the east and south, take I–8 west to the Sports Arena Boulevard turnoff. Exit right and follow the TO WEST MISSION BAY signs to the cloverleaf. Exit on West Mission Bay Drive, turn left at Quivira Road.
	From the north, take I–5 to Sea World Drive exit.

Pass Sea World and follow the To West Mission Bay signs to the cloverleaf. Then repeat as above.

Naturalist: Naturalist from the San Diego Natural History Museum on board

"Dr. Raymond Gilmore, a former museum staff member, began the first whale-watching program in southern California," notes Laura Nichols, chairwoman of the museum's education department. The museum also offers a nine-day whale-watch trip to Baja California. Write for more information.

Seaforth Sportfishing Corp.

1717 Quivira Road, San Diego, CA 92109; (619) 224–3383

Whales: Gray

Season: December through mid-March

Boats: Three boats; 105, 118, and 149 passengers

Trips: Two 2¹/₂-hour trips on weekdays at 10 A.M. and 1 P.M. Three trips on Saturdays, Sundays, and holidays at 9 A.M., 11:30 A.M., and 2 P.M. Weekends are busiest days.

Fare: Adults, $12; children, senior citizens, and military, $8. Group rates available. Reservations advised.

Departure: Trips leave from Seaforth Landing at 1717 Quivira Road in Mission Bay. From the east and south, take I–8 west to the Sports Arena Boulevard turnoff. Exit right and follow the To West Mission Bay signs to the cloverleaf. Exit on West Mission Bay Drive, turn left at Quivira Road.

From the north, take I–5 to Sea World Drive exit. Pass Sea World and follow the To West Mission Bay signs to the cloverleaf. Then repeat as above.

Naturalist: Yes

Where the Whales Are

"We invite you to journey with us and experience these magnificent creatures in their natural habitats," notes an employee at Seaforth Sportfishing. "Guaranteed whale sighting, or ride again free!"

Museums, Aquariums, and Science Centers

Cabrillo Marine Museum

3720 Stephen White Drive, San Pedro, CA 90731;
(213) 548–7562

The Cabrillo Marine Museum has more than thirty aquariums and exhibits, which provide a close-up look at a wide variety of sea creatures. Among the exhibits is one on the migration of the gray whales. Recreational and educational programs are available.

Open noon to 5 P.M. Tuesday through Friday; 10 A.M. to 5 P.M. Saturday and Sunday. Closed on Mondays, except on holidays.

California Academy of Sciences

Golden Gate Park, San Francisco, CA 94118; (415) 221–5100

The Academy is a natural history museum, aquarium, and planetarium all rolled into one. Classes on marine mammals, including whales, are held periodically for adults and children, and a gray whale skeleton is on display in Cowell Hall. For information on adult education classes, call (415) 750–7100.

Open daily 10 A.M. to 5 P.M.; extended hours in the summer. Adults, $3; students and senior citizens, $1.50; children ages 6 through 12, 75 cents. Admission is free on first Wednesday of each month.

Lawrence Hall of Science

University of California, One Centennial Drive, Berkeley,
CA 94720; (415) 642–5133

The Lawrence Hall of Science is a public museum that often features exhibits on whales and other marine life. A marine biology program for children is offered in the summer and fall, and special school programs are also available. Open 10 A.M. to 4:30 P.M. Monday through Friday, 10 A.M. to 5 P.M. on weekends. Closed New Year's Day, Easter, Thanksgiving, and Christmas. Admission varies from $1 to $4, depending on the exhibit.

An annual whale-watch trip is scheduled with an established tour operator during the gray whale migration. The day-long trip includes a visit to the Monterey Bay Aquarium. For more information write to Ted Robertson at the Lawrence Hall of Science.

Long Marine Laboratory
100 Shaffer Road, Santa Cruz, CA 95060; (408) 459–2883

Long Marine Labratory serves as the marine and instructional facility of the University of California. Exhibits include an 85-foot skeleton of a blue whale, tidepool animals in touch tanks, an aquarium, and displays related to current research.

Open 1 to 4 P.M. Tuesday through Sunday; closed on Mondays and holidays. Docent-led tours are available.

Monterey Bay Aquarium
886 Cannery Row, Monterey, CA 93940; (408) 648–4888

More than 6,500 marine creatures are housed in the Aquarium. Special features are several undersea habitats, including a three-story kelp forest and a 90-foot-long exhibit of Monterey Bay habitats. From the public entrance, a parade of life-size marine mammals, including a 43-foot gray whale and her 22-foot calf, wends its way overhead into the Marine Mammals gallery.

Open daily from 10 A.M. to 6 P.M. Adults, $8; students and senior citizens, $5.75; children, $3.50. Free shuttle runs from downtown.

Orange County Museum of Natural History and Science
2627 Vista del Oro, Newport Beach, CA 92660; (714) 640–7120

The museum houses a large fossil collection of marine mammal specimens. Open Tuesday through Saturday 10 A.M. to 5 P.M.; Sunday noon to 5 P.M. Adults, $2; children, $1; members free.

San Diego Natural History Museum
Balboa Park, San Diego, CA 91112; (619) 232–3821

Exhibits on marine life, shells, desert ecology, and the Foucault pendulum are on display. Open 10 A.M. to 4:30 P.M. seven days a week. Adults, $5; children 6 through 18, $1; children 5 and younger, free. Free admission once a month. For dates call (619) 239–0512.

The museum sponsors whale watches; see listing under San Diego.

Santa Barbara Museum of Natural History
2559 Puesta del Sol Road, Santa Barbara, CA 93105; (805) 682–4711

Marine life exhibits include a 70-foot skeleton of a blue whale and several marine life displays. A research laboratory, library, observatory, and planetarium are on the museum grounds.

Open 9 A.M. to 5 P.M. weekdays; 10 A.M. to 5 P.M. Sunday and holidays. Closed Thanksgiving, Christmas, and New Year's. Free guided tours every Sunday. Admission $3 for adults, $1.50 for children under 12.

A model of a gray whale is on display at the Sea Center, #211 Stearns Wharf, which is affiliated with the Santa Barbara Museum of Natural History. The Sea Center is open every day from 10 A.M. to 5 P.M. Adults, $1.50; children 17 and under, $1.

Where the Whales Are

Scripps Aquarium

Scripps Institution of Oceanography, 8602 LaJolla Shores Drive, LaJolla, CA 92093; (619) 534–6933

In addition to displays of oceanic wonders, the Scripps Aquarium sponsors occasional whale-watch cruises, snorkel and scuba expeditions, tidepooling trips, and classes for children and adults. Write for a brochure and calendar of events.

Open daily 9 A.M. to 5 P.M. Donation.

National Parks
and Marine Sanctuaries

Gulf of the Farallones National Marine Sanctuary
National Oceanic and Atmospheric Administration, GGNRA,
Fort Mason, San Francisco, CA 94123; (415) 556–3509

The Gulf of the Farallones National Marine Sanctuary encompasses
948 square nautical miles of water off the California coastline
north of San Francisco. Designated in 1981, the sanctuary con-
sists of an offshore marine region of the Gulf of the Farallones
and the nearshore waters of Bodega Bay, Tomales Bay, Drakes
Bay, Bolinas Bay, Estero San Antonio, Estero de Americano,
Duxbury Reef, and Bolinas Lagoon. Write for a free brochure and
map of the area.

Point Reyes National Seashore
Point Reyes, CA 94956; (415) 663–1092

The Point Reyes National Seashore, about 50 miles north of San
Francisco, has a rich cultural and natural heritage to explore.
Visitors centers, hiking trails, exhibits, and stationary whale
watching from several points are all available in the 73,000-acre
recreational area. From December 30 through February, free
shuttle bus service for whale watchers is provided between
Drakes Beach and the Point Reyes Lighthouse, one of the best
observation spots. Informal lectures on whale watching are also
scheduled, with educational materials provided. Write for a free
brochure, map, and calendar of events.

Channel Islands National Park
1901 Spinnaker Drive, Ventura, CA 93001; (805) 644–8262

Channel Islands National Marine Sanctuary
735 State Street, Santa Barbara, CA 93101; (805) 966–7107

Five of the eight Channel Islands make up Channel Islands National Park. The islands are Anacapa, Santa Cruz, Santa Rosa, San Miguel, and Santa Barbara plus 125,000 acres of submerged lands. The Marine Sanctuary encompasses 1,252 square nautical miles of near-shore and offshore waters. Boat trips, diving, fishing, visits to the Sea Center, and wildlife watching are all available. Write for a free map and brochures about island life, ecology, and activities.

Monuments

Cabrillo National Monument
P.O. Box 6670, San Diego, CA 92106; (619) 557–5450

The Cabrillo National Monument is located at the southern end of Point Loma, within the city limits of San Diego. Whale Watch Weekend, held annually in January, includes informal lectures and presentations and displays as well as opportunities to sight the migrating gray whales from a sheltered overlook. Educational materials about whales are available all year.

Open every day, 9 A.M. to 5:15 P.M.; extended hours in summer. $3 per vehicle.

Hawaii

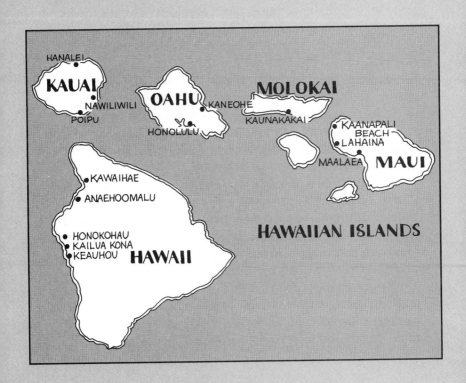

HANALEI

KAUAI

- NAWILIWILI

POIPU

OAHU KANEOHE

HONOLULU

MOLOKAI

KAUNAKAKAI

- KAANAPALI
  BEACH
- LAHAINA

MAALAEA **MAUI**

- KAWAIHAE

- ANAEHOOMALU

HAWAIIAN ISLANDS

- HONOKOHAU
- KAILUA KONA
- KEAUHOU **HAWAII**

Hawaii

Lahaina, on the island of Maui, was once the capital of the American Pacific whaling fleet. Today whale-watch tour boats stand in the harbor, waiting to carry passengers to see the whales that swim in Hawaiian waters each year from December to April.

Just a few years ago, the only whale-watch tours in the Hawaiian Islands operated out of Lahaina, though some sport-fishing boats based on other islands were available for private charter. Today, wherever you succumb to the seductive languor of Hawaii, you can book passage on a whale-watch trip. Excursion boats, sailboats, and inflatable rafts are all available, with departure points from Kauai, Maui, Molokai, Oahu, and the "Big Island," Hawaii. (Can Lanai be far behind?)

The attraction is primarily humpback whales, which come to Hawaii each year to mate and give birth. Some areas are so replete with mothers and calves that they have been dubbed "nurseries" and declared sanctuaries. In addition to the frolicsome humpbacks, pilot whales, bottlenose dolphins, and other smaller cetaceans are frequently seen in Hawaiian waters.

If you miss the boat, so to speak, and happen to be lying on a beach on the northwestern coast of Maui at the right time of year, you may think that you see whales breaching along the shore of Lanai. It's probably more than just a Mai Tai–induced illusion.

TOURISM INFORMATION

Hawaii Visitors Bureau
2270 Kalakaua Avenue, Suite 801, Honolulu, HI 96813
(808) 923–1811

Hanalei, Nawiliwili, and Poipu, Kauai

Fantasy Island Boat Tours
P.O. Box 10, Hanalei, Kauai, HI 96714; (808) 826–1111

Whales:	Humpback, pilot, sperm
Season:	December until April or May
Boats:	Four boats; 6, 16, 20, and 43 passengers
Trips:	Two 3½-hour trips daily at 9 A.M. and 2 P.M. Busiest days are Tuesday, Wednesday, and Thursday.
Fare:	Adults, $65; children: 7 to 12, $42.50; 2 to 7, $35. Hourly and group rates also available. Underwater cameras, lunch, beverages, and snorkel gear are all included. Reservations advised.
Departure:	Boats leave from Hanalei Bay, Nawiliwili Harbor, and Poipu. Stop by the Fantasy Island Boat Tours office, three blocks past Ching Young Shopping Village.
Naturalist:	No naturalist on board

"Our trips are rafting adventures along the NaPali Coast that include whale watching and snorkeling, as well as the spectacular scenery of this north shore area of Kauai, the Garden Island," says staff member Suzanne Perry. "Also, tours can be designed especially for individual groups. And because we have boats leaving from all sides of the island, you never have to drive more than twenty minutes to board a boat for a whale-watch tour."

Hanalei, Kauai

Hanalei Sea Tours

P.O. Box 1437, Hanalei, Kauai, HI 96714; (800) 733–7997;
(808) 826–7254

Whales:	Humpback
Season:	December to April
Boats:	Eight boats; rigid-hull inflatable rafts, 15 passengers; power-driven catamarans, 16 passengers
Trips:	Trips for 2¹/₂, 4, and 5 hours daily, with morning and afternoon departures.
Fare:	$50 per person for 2¹/₂-hour trip, including beverage; $65 for half day on raft; $75 for half day on catamaran, including light lunch; $95 for 5-hour trip, including lunch. Children $20 less on all trips. Group rates available. Reservations required.
Departure:	Boats leave from Hanalei Bay. Meet at Hanalei Sea Tours office, the second building on the left after the first one-lane bridge in Hanalei, next to the Hanalei Museum.
Naturalist:	Captain serves as naturalist.

"Hanalei Sea Tours operates year round offering scenic cruises of the beautiful NaPali coastline," says Donna Herold, general manager. "During these adventures, we enjoy viewing marine life, including dolphins, sea turtles, and the humpback whales in season.

"NaPali is our objective—to get our passengers out to explore the majestic cliffs that are so rich in Hawaiian history, cruise through sea caves and lava tubes, and experience seeing marine life in their natural habitat."

Paradise Adventure Cruises
P.O. Box 1379, Hanalei, Kauai, HI 96714; (808) 826–9999

Whales:	Humpback
Season:	January to end of May
Boats:	Two boats; 6 passengers each
Trips:	Two 4¹/₂-hour trips daily at 8 A.M. and 1 P.M. Charters available. Busiest days are Monday through Thursday.
Fare:	Adults, $75; children 12 and younger, $60. Reservations required.
Departure:	Boats leave from Hanalei Bay. Meet at Paradise Adventure Cruises office, at Ching Young Shopping Village.
Naturalist:	Captain serves as naturalist.

"The first humpbacks arrive at Kauai during December in very small numbers," says owner Byron Fears. "As January matures we see a substantial increase in the numbers. During the past three years the humpback population in the waters surrounding Kauai has increased in epic proportions—to our happiness.

"During January through April we spot whales almost every trip, but of course we cannot guarantee that we will find them. There appears to be a lot of birthing taking place in the coastal waters of the NaPali Coast, and often we spot frolicking calves checking us out with great curiosity."

Nawiliwili, Kauai

Captain Zodiac Raft Expeditions
P.O. Box 456, Hanalei, Kauai, HI 96714; (800) 422–7824, (808) 826–9371

Whales:	Humpback
Season:	January to mid-April

Where the Whales Are

Boats:	Rigid-hull inflatable rafts; 16 passengers each
Trips:	At least two 3¹/₂-hour trips daily at 8:50 A.M. and 12:50 P.M. Trips include snorkeling off coral reefs. Wednesday is busiest day.
Fare:	Adults, $65; children 2 to 11, $45. Beverages, brunch or lunch, and snorkel gear provided. Reservations advised.
Departure:	Boats leave from Nawiliwili Harbor. Check in at the Captain Zodiac office on Highway 56, just past the Shellhouse Restaurant and before the Ching Young Shopping Village.
Naturalist:	No naturalist on board

"We use 23-foot Zodiac rafts popularized by Jacques Cousteau," says owner Clarence H. Greff Jr. "We are the pioneer rafting company in Hawaii, having started the rafting tour business here in 1976. We have three locations in Hawaii—Kauai, Maui, and the Big Island—and we are the largest rafting company in the islands."

Kaneohe and Honolulu, Oahu

Honolulu Sailing Company
45-995 Wailele Road, #49, Kaneohe, Oahu, HI 96744;
(808) 235–8264

Whales:	Humpback, pilot
Season:	June to May
Boats:	Two boats; 8 passengers each
Trips:	Two half-day trips at 8 A.M. and 1 P.M. One all-day trip at 9 A.M. Overnight trips available also. Weekends are the busiest times.

Fare:	$50 per person for half day, $90 for full day, $260 for overnight (two days). Reservations required.
Departure:	Boats leave from the West Beach Marina at Kaneohe Bay and from Honolulu Harbor.
Naturalist:	No naturalist on board

"We have been observing humpback whales on our cruises longer than anyone," says Mike Mickelwait, one of the captains. "Quiet sailboats are much better for not disturbing whales."

Honolulu, Oahu

Nature Expeditions International
474 Willamette, P.O. Box 11496, Eugene, OR 97440;
(503) 484–6529

Whales:	Humpback
Season:	December through April
Boats:	Motor/sailer; 11 to 16 passengers
Trips:	Three 15-day trips exploring the Hawaiian Islands.
Fare:	$1,990 per person, double occupancy; $350 extra for single occupancy; $580 airfare from San Francisco; $200 extra if tour group fewer than 11 people. Fare includes transportation after arrival, helicopter flight, ship charters, transfers, first-class accommodations, park fees, service and handling charges, tips, and guides.
Departure:	Trip originates in Honolulu.
Naturalist:	At least one biologist accompanies each trip.

"The Hawaiian Islands, isolated in the mid-Pacific, thousands of miles from their nearest neighbors, present a living museum of geol-

ogy and island biology found nowhere else on earth," president
David Roderick says.

"On this expedition to explore Kauai, Oahu, Maui, and the `Big
Island' of Hawaii, we will study the marine life, native and intro-
duced plants and animals, active volcanoes, tropical birds, and past
and present cultures. In addition, the history of whaling and obser-
vations of the humpback whale in its Hawaiian calving grounds are
of special interest."

Pacific Whale Foundation
101 North Kihei Road, Suite 25, Kihei, Maui, HI 96753;
(800) WHALE–11, (808) 947–9971

Whales:	Humpback
Season:	November to May
Boats:	One boat, *Navatek I;* 400 passengers
Trips:	One 3¹/₂-hour cruise daily at 7:30 A.M.
Fare:	Adults, $45; children ages 3 to 12; $23. Reservations required. Whale sighting guaranteed; see a whale or get a coupon for a free trip.
Departure:	Boat leaves from Honolulu Pier No. 2 or No. 9.
Naturalist:	Naturalists on board have marine field research experience.

"We are a marine research, education, and conservation organization, says Dr. Paul Forestell, director of research and education. "Our
interest in taking you out whale watching is to educate you experientially about the marine environment so you become more aware
of what's at stake and more conscientious about the impact of both
your own actions and those going on in your own backyard.

"The ocean is not a vast endless resource, and experiencing the wonder of these great mammals motivates people actually to change their own behaviors that are detrimental to them."

Southern Cross Charters

1750 Kalakaua, Suite 3-525, Honolulu, HI 96826;
(808) 946–6785

Whales:	Humpback
Season:	December 1 to March 31
Boats:	One 72-foot schooner, *Red Witch*; 49 passengers
Trips:	By charter only
Fare:	$19 per person (based on 49 people) for 3-hour trip. Reservations required. Saturday and Sunday are busiest days.
Departure:	Ship sails from Slip X in the Kewalo Marine Basin, next to Fisherman's Wharf Restaurant in Honolulu.
Naturalist:	No naturalist on board

"Our 72-foot schooner is a replica of a nineteenth-century trading schooner—very romantic and sea kindly," says Gordon R. Howard, owner and captain.

"Our usual charter is three hours, but we can accommodate any length of time. This is a hands-on charter, with passengers helping to raise and lower sails and steering the boat. The whales, porpoises, and sea turtles that play alongside the *Red Witch* could very easily become your new friends."

Kaunakakai, Molokai

Whistling Swan Charters
P.O. Box 1350, Kaunakakai, Molokai, HI 96748; (907) 892–6899

Whales:	Humpback
Season:	Mid-December to mid-April
Boats:	One sailboat; 6 passengers
Trips:	Seven-day interisland sailing trips. Participants live on board. Also private "bareboat" (unskippered) charters.
Fare:	$895 per person for the 7-day trips; private charters, $2,950 per week.
Departure:	Boat leaves from east side of the wharf, 1/4 mile from Kaunakakai.
Naturalist:	Naturalist accompanies each trip.

"We offer interisland sailing charters on a luxury yacht," says owner Karen Hills. "Whales frequently breach or surface within 100 feet of our vessel as we quietly glide through the island waters of Maui, Lanai, and Molokai.

"Guests sleeping on board may experience the thrill of hearing the whales singing at night, as the sound resonates through the hull in quiet, out-of-the-way anchorages. While dining under the stars in our open cockpit, we can hear the whales blowing nearby."

Kaanapali Beach, Maui

Captain Nemo's Ocean Emporium
150 Dickenson Street, Lahaina, Maui, HI 96761;
(800) 367–8088, (808) 661–5555

Whales:	Humpback
Season:	Late December to mid-April
Boats:	One boat, a 58-foot catamaran, *Seasmoke*; 40 passengers
Trips:	One 2-hour sunset cruise at 3:45 P.M. Monday through Saturday.
Fare:	Adults, $32; children under 12, $22. Fare includes snacks, drinks, and a pair of lightweight binoculars. Reservations required.
Departure:	Boat leaves from Whalers Village at Kaanapali Beach. Meet on the beach in front of El Crab Catcher Restaurant, right by Whaler's Village.
Naturalist:	Naturalist accompanies each trip.

"What makes our trip special? It's first class," says manager Hank McDermott. "The crew waits on the customers hand and foot. We take care of their every need. We're helpful, friendly. Our repeat business speaks for itself.

"Plus the boat—the *Seasmoke*—is a Transpac winner, a 58-foot catamaran with a history. And we really sail."

Lahaina, Maui

Captain Zodiac Raft Expeditions
P.O. Box 1776, Lahaina, Maui, HI 96767; (808) 667–5351 or 667–5862

Whales:	Humpback
Season:	December to late April
Boats:	Rigid-hull inflatable rafts; 15 passengers each
Trips:	Five trips daily: 2¹/₂-hour trips at 8 A.M., 11 A.M., and 2 P.M.; 3¹/₂-hour trips at 8:30 A.M. and 12:30 P.M.

Snorkeling included on 3¹/₂-hour trips. Monday is busiest day.

Fare: The 2¹/₂-hour trips: adults, $46; children ages 2 to 11, $36. The 3¹/₂-hour trips: adults, $55; children, $42. Cold juices, snacks, and snorkel gear, when appropriate, provided. Reservations advised.

Departure: Boats leave from Mala Wharf in Lahaina, about one block south of the Cannery Shopping Center.

Naturalist: No naturalist on board

"We use 23-foot Zodiac rafts popularized by Jacques Cousteau," says owner Clarence F. Greff Jr. "We are the pioneer rafting company in Hawaii, having started the rafting tour business here in 1976. We have three locations in Hawaii—Kauai, Maui, and the Big Island—and we are the largest rafting company in the islands."

Island Marine Activity

505 Front Street, #225, Lahaina, Maui, HI 96761;
(800) 833–5800 (from mainland), (800) 533–6899 (from Oahu), (808) 661–8397

Whales: Humpback

Season: Mid-December to May

Boats: Three vessels, *Maui Princess*, *Leilani*, and *Lin Wa*; 348 passengers total

Trips: Four 2¹/₄-hour trips daily at 8 A.M., 10:30 A.M., 1 P.M., and 3:30 P.M.

Fare: Adults, $25; children ages 3 to 12, $12.50; infants, free. Portion of fare goes to Maui Whale Aid, a private foundation established to fund whale research and education in Hawaii. Reservations advised.

Departure: Boats leave from Slip 3 in Lahaina Harbor, just across the street from the banyan tree and the Pioneer Inn.

Naturalist: Naturalist accompanies each trip.

"Every year, between Christmas and Easter, the waters surrounding Maui, Molokai, and Lanai become the vacation playground for thousands of tourists and about 400 North Pacific humpback whales," says Betty Purcell of Island Marine Activity. "During this four-month period, the habits, antics, and awesomeness of these creatures fascinate researchers and delight the casual whale watcher.

"Our offshore cruises focus on getting our passengers as close as possible to these huge mammals while remaining within the spirit and letter of current federal whale protection regulations. Each cruise is fully narrated by whale researchers to answer questions and explain witnessed behavior patterns."

Sightings are guaranteed. "If a cruise is 'skunked,' passengers may take another cruise at no charge."

Ocean Riders
P.O. Box 12523, Lahaina, Maui, HI 96761; (808) 661–0220

Whales:	Humpback
Season:	December through April
Boats:	Two rigid-hull inflatable rafts; 13 and 18 passengers
Trips:	Daily, four 2-hour trips for whale watching at 8:30 A.M., 10:45 A.M., 1 P.M., and 3:30 P.M.; one 3-hour trip at 7:30 A.M. for whale watching and snorkeling.
Fare:	Adults, $40; children, $25. Add $10 for the snorkeling trip. Includes beverage, light snack, snorkeling equipment, and snorkeling instruction. Reservations required.
Departure:	Boats leave from Mala Wharf in Lahaina. Turn off Front Street near the Safeway, cannery, and JESUS IS COMING sign.
Naturalist:	No

"The humpback's song has been described as unique, ever-changing, and eerily haunting," says a spokeswoman from Ocean Riders. "We give you the opportunity to listen in on this underwater communication via hydrophone; and as an added extra, tapes of live recordings taken on board are available for you to take home."

Scotch Mist Sailing Charters
P.O. Box 831, Lahaina, Maui, HI 96767; (808) 661–0386

Whales:	Humpback
Season:	December to May
Boats:	One sailing yacht, *Scotch Mist II*; 23 passengers
Trips:	Three 2 1/2-hour trips daily at 9:30 A.M., 1 P.M., and 4:30 P.M.
Fare:	Adults, $30; children under 12, $20. Beer, wine, and soft drinks included. Reservations required. Charters available.
Departure:	Boat leaves from Slip 9 in Lahaina Harbor, just off Front Street by the Pioneer Inn.
Naturalist:	No naturalist on board

"Slip into whale country and see the humpbacks up close from the deck of a private yacht," says staff member Leslie Ferguson.

The *Scotch Mist II* was first to finish in the 1982 Victoria-to-Maui Yacht Race. It is available to visitors for sailing, snorkeling, champagne sunset cruises, moonlight sails, and whale watching in season.

Seabern Yachts
P.O. Box 1022, Lahaina, Maui, HI 96767; (808) 661–8110

Whales:	Humpback
Season:	January 1 to mid-April

Boats: Two 42-foot sailboats; 6 passengers each

Trips: Two 2-hour trips a day at 9:30 A.M. and 4:15 P.M.
            Longer sailing and snorkeling trips also available.

Fare: $30 per person for a 2-hour whale-watching trip. Private charter, $90 an hour, two-hour minimum.

Departure: Boats leave from Slips 63 and 64 in Lahaina Harbor just off Front Street by Banyan Tree Square.

Naturalist: Captain serves as naturalist.

"We offer free color whale-watching brochures which provide a wealth of information about the humpback whales, and each of our yachts is equipped with binoculars for the use of our passengers," says co-owner Doug Gray.

"We also love to sail; so as long as there is wind we will be under sail. By sailing, we believe, we are less of an intrusion in the humpbacks' environment."

Windjammer Cruises
505 Front Street, Suite 229, Lahaina, Maui, HI 96761;
(808) 661–0220

Whales: Humpback

Season: Mid-November through April

Boats: Glass-bottom boat, *Coral See*; 100 passengers

Trips: Two 2¹/₂-hour cruises daily at 9 A.M. and noon.

Fare: Adults, $25; children: ages 3 to 12, $12.50; under 3, free.

Departure: Boat leaves from Slip 1 in Lahaina Harbor, just off Front Street, near the banyan tree.

Naturalist: Yes

"Help the whales by whale watching on a vessel that supports education and research on Hawaii's humpback whale," says a spokesman for Windjammer Cruises. Money from T-shirts sold on board supports a whale research project.

Maalaea and Lahaina, Maui

Pacific Whale Foundation
101 North Kihei Road, Suite 25, Kihei, Maui, HI 96753;
(800) WHALE–11, (808) 879–8811

Whales:	Humpback
Season:	November to May
Boats:	Two boats, *Whale One,* a 53-foot motor yacht, and *Whale II,* a 50-foot sailing yacht; 49 and 24 passengers respectively
Trips:	Three 2 1/2-hour motor cruises daily at 11 A.M., 1:30 P.M., and 4:15 P.M. Three 3-hour sails daily at 8 A.M., noon, and 3:30 P.M.
Fare:	Motor cruises: adults, $25; children ages 3 to 12, $12. Sailing trips: adults, $30; children, $15. Children under 3, free. Reservations required.
Departure:	*Whale One* leaves from Slip 52 in Maalaea Bay. Take Route 30 to Route 31 (Kihei Road). Turn into Kealia Beach Plaza and come to the Pacific Whale Foundation headquarters. *Whale II* leaves from Slip 11 in Lahaina Harbor, just off Front Street by the Pioneer Inn.
Naturalist:	Naturalists on board have marine field research experience.

"We are a marine research, education, and conservation organization," says Dr. Paul Forestell, director of research and education. "Our interest in taking you out whale watching is to educate you experientially about the marine environment so you become more aware of what's at stake and more conscientious about the impact of both your own actions and those going on in your own backyard.

"The ocean is not a vast endless resource, and experiencing the wonder of these great mammals motivates people actually to change their own behaviors that are detrimental to them."

Maalaea, Maui

Trilogy Excursions
P.O. Box 1121, Lahaina, Maui, HI 96761; (800) 874–2666, (808) 661–4743

Whales:	Humpback
Season:	Mid-December to mid-April
Boats:	One boat; 36 passengers
Trips:	One 2-hour trip each Saturday and Sunday at 1:30 P.M. Whale sighting guaranteed or next trip is free.
Fare:	Adults, $35; children 3 to 12, $17.50. Reservations required.
Departure:	Boat leaves from Slip 99 at Maalaea Harbor, right by Buzz's Steak House.
Naturalist:	Naturalist on board

"Our afternoon whale watch provides one of the most unique ocean experiences anywhere in the world," says a member of "the sailing Coon family," the owners. "With several hundred calving and breeding humpback whales wintering off Maui's south shore, opportunities for close encounters of the best kind are almost guaranteed.

"We always guarantee you a whale of a good time. And if for some reason we aren't able to sight those 'gentle giants,' your next Trilogy 'Whale of a Sail' is free!"

Kawaihae, Hawaii; Kaunakakai, Molokai; and Kaneohe, Oahu

Hawaii Bluewater Sailing

P.O. Box 1813, Honokaa, Hawaii, HI 96727; (808) 326–1986

Whales:	Humpback
Season:	November to May
Boats:	Three boats; 6 passengers each
Trips:	Six-day sailing trips around the "Big Island" of Hawaii and seven-day trips among the islands of Oahu, Molokai, Lanai, and Maui. Participants live on board. Shorter trips may be negotiated.
Fare:	$150 per person per day includes meals, whale watching, snorkeling, body surfing, and cruising. Reservations required.
Departure:	Boats leave from Kawaihae, Hawaii; Kaunakakai, Molokai; and Kaneohe Bay, Oahu.
Naturalist:	No

"Until April the humpback whales will be arriving in Hawaii for the mating season. Sailing is the perfect way to enjoy this yearly migration," notes Captain Bill Chambers.

"The anchorages range from the peaceful out-of-the-way harbor of Halelono, Molokai, to such active resort areas as Kaanapali, Maui. The beaches are some of the finest in the world, the waters clear and warm for snorkeling and body surfing, and the scenery—pure Hawaii."

Chambers says his trips are among the few interisland adventures available in Hawaii.

Anaehoomalu, Hawaii

Ocean Sports Waikoloa
P.O. Box 5000, Kohala Coast, Hawaii, HI 96743;
(808) 885–5555

Whales:	Humpback, pilot
Season:	Mid-December to the end of April
Boats:	Three boats; 6, 20, and 36 passengers
Trips:	Three trips daily. Three-hour snorkel and whale watch at 8:30 A.M.; 1¹/₂-hour sail at 1:30 P.M.; sunset whale watch at 4 P.M. Saturday is busiest day.
Fare:	Early trip: adults, $45; children under 12, $30. Midday trip: adults, $19; children, $15. Sunset trip: adults, $35; children, $25. Reservations advised.
Departure:	Boat leaves from Anaehoomalu Bay Beach, in front of the Royal Waikoloa Hotel.
Naturalist:	No naturalist on board

"Ocean Sports' approach to whale watching is unique in that the captains and crews are as excited and enthusiastic about seeing these gentle creatures as are our guests, and all have a genuinely good time," says Rick Conners.

"Some groups are treated to an unofficial initiation as honorary crew members as they learn our whaling song:"

> Yo ho, yo ho, a sailor's life for me!
> Yo ho, yo ho, a sailor's life for me!
> We sail this ship upon the sea
> in search of humpback whales.
> We see them breach,
> We see them splash,
> We see them wave their tales!
> Oh . . . ooooh, yo ho, yo ho, a sailor's life for me!

Honokohau, Kailua, and Keauhou, Hawaii

Captain Zodiac Raft Expeditions

P.O. Box 5612, Kailua-Kona, Hawaii, HI 96745; (808) 329–3199

Whales:	Humpback
Season:	January to mid-April
Boats:	Rigid-hull inflatable rafts; 16 passengers each
Trips:	Two 4-hour trips daily at 8 A.M. and 1 P.M. Trips may involve exploring the coast, snorkeling, visiting sights on land, and whale watching in season. Wednesday is busiest day.
Fare:	Adults, $50; children ages 2 to 11, $40, for half-day trip. Beverage, brunch or lunch, and snorkel gear provided. Reservations advised.
Departure:	Boats leave from Honokohau Harbor, Kailua Pier, and Keauhou Pier.
Naturalist:	No naturalist on board

"We use 23-foot Zodiac rafts popularized by Jacques Cousteau," says owner Clarence F. Greff Jr. "We are the pioneer rafting company in Hawaii, having started the rafting tour business here in 1978. We have three locations in Hawaii—Kauai, Maui, and the Big Island—and we are the largest rafting company in the islands."

Kailua-Kona, Hawaii

Oceanic Society Expeditions
Fort Mason Center, Building E, San Francisco, CA 94123;
(415) 441–1106

Whales:	Humpback, pilot
Season:	January through April
Boats:	One 41-foot ketch, *Pacific Pearl*; 6 passengers
Trips:	Five-day trips, living on board and sailing along the west coast of the Big Island between Kawaihae and Kealakekua Bay.
Fare:	$895 per person. Price includes meals, accommodations, guides. Reservations required.
Departure:	Trip begins upon arrival at Keahole Airport in Kailua-Kona.
Naturalist:	Two on board; one is a behavioral biologist; the other has a degree in marine resource development.

"Under the expert guidance of our naturalists, we collect baseline data on humpback whales as part of an ongoing research project for the North Gulf Oceanic Society. Research techniques include photoidentification of individual humpback whales and collecting recordings of their songs," says an Oceanic Society spokeswoman.

"Because of the water clarity here, the island of Hawaii's mild blue waters offer a variety of corals not found on older islands in the Hawaiian chain. We will be snorkeling amid intricate coral and lava formations and encountering a variety of tropical fish and myriad exotic sea creatures."

Oceanic Society has been conducting natural history tours since 1973.

Pacific Whale Foundation
101 North Kihei Road, Suite 25, Kihei, Maui, HI 96753;
(800) WHALE–11, (808) 329–3522

Whales:	Humpback, pilot, sperm
Season:	November to May
Boats:	One boat, *Hawaiian Princess* or *Captain Cook*; 140 passengers
Trips:	One 3-hour trip daily, except Tuesday, at 10 A.M. On Wednesday departure is at 2 P.M.
Fare:	Adults, $30; children: ages 3 to 12, $15; under 3, free. Reservations required. Guaranteed whale sighting; see a whale or get a coupon for a free trip.
Departure:	Boat leaves from Kailua-Kona Pier.
Naturalist:	Naturalists on board have marine field research experience.

"We are a marine research, education, and conservation organization," says Dr. Paul Forestell, director of research and education. "Our interest in taking you out whale watching is to educate you experientially about the marine environment so you become more aware of what's at stake and more conscientious about the impact of both your own actions and those going on in your own backyard.

"The ocean is not a vast endless resource, and experiencing the wonder of these great mammals motivates people actually to change their own behaviors that are detrimental to them."

Museums

Whalers Village Museum

2435 Kaanapali Parkway, G-8, Lahaina, Maui, HI 96761;
(808) 661–5992

The museum's whale pavilion features the skeleton of a 40-foot sperm whale and includes exhibits about more than seventy species of whales and the history of the whaling industry in Hawaii. The museum is in the Whalers Village Shopping Complex. Take the elevator or stairs to the Third Level of Building G.

Hours are 9:30 A.M. to 10 P.M. daily. Admission is free.

Alaska

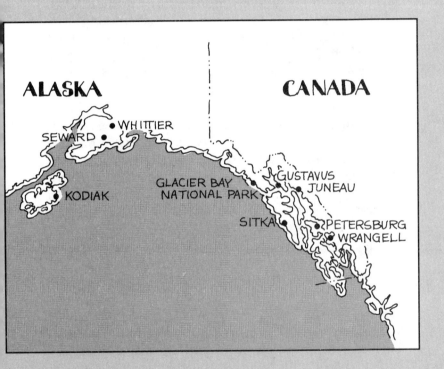

Alaska

Alaska—"The Great Land"—has its share of great whales. Humpback, fin, gray whales, and orcas all swim off Alaskan shores. Still, the whale-watch industry is developing relatively slowly, although the many, many sportfishing charters and wilderness lodges have always considered sighting whales a normal occurrence. Until recently, the citizens of the forty-ninth state may simply have taken whales for granted. Some people in Sitka can sit on their porches and watch whales all year round, and nearby whales continually delight the residents of Admiralty Island.

The little town of Gustavus, just outside of the glorious Glacier Bay National Park and Preserve, probably offers the most whale-watch tours in Alaska. Trips also originate in Juneau, Kodiak, Whittier, Seward, Sitka, Wrangell, and Petersburg. Extended tours listed on pages 182 and 184 visit several destinations in southeast and south-central Alaska, and most originate from points outside Alaska.

Some of the best serendipitous whale watching takes place aboard the Alaska State ferries that operate in southeast and south-central Alaska. The U.S. Forest Service provides Forest Interpreters on board to conduct programs on whales, marine mammals, and the special features of the Chugach and Tongass National Forests. All programs are free to ferry passengers. Cruiseship passengers who keep a careful watch also may see whales.

The scenery in Alaska is so magnificent that you're guaranteed a breathtaking backdrop for any whale sightings.

TOURISM INFORMATION

Alaska Tourism Marketing Council
P.O. Box E-501, Juneau, AK 99811
(907) 465–2010

Prince William Sound Tourism Coalition
P.O. Box 1477, Valdez, AK 99686
(907) 835–2984

Alaska Marine Highway
P.O. Box R, Juneau, AK 99811
(800) 642–0066,
(907) 465–3941 (in Canada)

Various Destinations in Alaska

Biological Journeys

1696 Ocean Drive, McKinleyville, CA 95521; (800) 548–7555, (707) 839–0178

Whales:	Orca, humpback, minke, gray, depending on trip
Season:	Late May to mid-October
Boats:	The 50-foot *Delphinus*; 12 passengers in three double staterooms, a four-person berth, and two single berths.
Trips:	Three-day to two-week cruises on various routes in southeastern Alaska, exploring areas such as Robson Bight, Misty Fjords National Monument, Frederick Sound, Glacier Bay, Icy Strait, and Queen Charlotte Islands. Participants live aboard the *Delphinus*.
Fare:	Range is from $395 for 3 days along the outer coast to $2,195 for 13 days on the Inside Passage. Price includes instruction, meals, accommodations, and transportation during the program. Reservations required.
Departure:	Boat departs from various ports in Alaska and British Columbia, depending on the trip.
Naturalist:	Naturalist accompanies each trip.

"Are you inquisitive? Do you love nature? Do you dream of an unrivaled adventure?" ask Ronn Storro-Patterson and Ron LeValley. "Biological Journeys' natural history vacations are designed just for you. We provide a penetrating view of the world. Delight you with uncommon experiences. Enrich your understanding. Reawaken the sense of wonder and excitement you felt as a child!"

Ronn Storro-Patterson is one of the world's leading authorities on whales, and Ron LeValley is a world-renowned ornithological expert. "Our trips are so refreshingly different, we feel remiss in merely calling them wilderness cruises. We invite you to reach out and touch nature. You travel in safety aboard a comfortable cruise vessel, in harmony with nature and at nature's own pace."

Sea Safaris

International Oceanographic Foundation, P.O. Box 499900, Miami, FL 33149; (305) 361–4697

Whales:	Humpback, orca
Season:	July
Boats:	The 152-foot *Sea Lion*; 70 passengers in 37 outside cabins
Trips:	One annual 10-day trip to Southeast Alaska, which includes the Misty Fjords, Prince of Wales Island, Agate Beach, Petersburg, Admiralty Island, Muir Glacier, Glacier Bay National Park, and Point Adolphus. Participants live on the boat. Trip concludes in Sitka.
Fare:	$2,620 to $3,850 per person, depending on cabin size and location. Participants must be members of the International Oceanographic Foundation ($18 a year). Fare does not include airfare, alcoholic beverages, or tips. Reservations required.
Departure:	Trip leaves from Prince Rupert, British Columbia.
Naturalist:	Naturalists affiliated with the IOF accompany the trip.

"We immerse ourselves in the natural beauty of southeast Alaska," said a spokeswoman for the IOF Sea Safaris. "Staff members who have an in-depth knowledge of Alaska lead the travelers from forest to shoreline to witness bears, eagles, whales, and other wildlife, and a scientist is on hand to enhance the natural history experience."

The International Oceanographic Foundation publishes *Sea Frontiers* in collaboration with the University of Miami Rosenstiel School of Marine and Atmospheric Science.

Nature Expeditions International

474 Willamette, P.O. Box 11496, Eugene, OR 97440;
(503) 484–6529

Whales:	Humpback, orca
Season:	June through August
Boats:	A catamaran and other motor vessels for whale watching
Trips:	Several 15-day tours of Alaska, exploring Sitka, Glacier Bay, Juneau, Kenai Peninsula, Kenai Fjords, Denali National Park, Anchorage, and Fairbanks.
Fare:	$2,990 per person, land fee for double occupancy; $865 airfare for flights during tour. $400 extra for single occupancy; $300 extra if group drops below 11 participants. Fare includes land and sea transportation, transfers, accommodations, entrance fees, service, handling charges, tips, instruction, and guides; also all meals, except in Sitka, Juneau, Anchorage, and Fairbanks. Reservations required.
Departure:	Trips begin in Seattle.
Naturalist:	At least one scientist accompanies each trip.

"Lofty mountains, mammoth glaciers, millions of salmon, and enormous bears—it is difficult to describe Alaska in anything less than superlatives," says a representative from Nature Expeditions International.

"Our wildlife expedition is specially designed for the first-time visitor who wishes to enjoy the variety of wildlife and magnificent scenery that Alaska has to offer as well as an introduction to the history and contemporary society of Alaska through brief visits to four cities."

Kodiak, Alaska

Hungry Fishermen Charters
P.O. Box 2699, Kodiak, AK 99615; (907) 486–5579

Whales:	Gray, humpback, orca
Season:	May to November
Boats:	One boat, the 28-foot *Virgo*; 6 passengers
Trips:	Half- or full-day trips, by charter only.
Fare:	$85 per person for a 4-hour trip, $150 for 8-hour trip. Minimum of four passengers.
Departure:	Boat leaves from St. Herman's Boat Harbor on Near Island, just across the bridge from Kodiak.
Naturalist:	Skipper serves as narrator.

Captain Dick Diemer and his wife, Nancy, promise sea lions, otters, seals, and assorted exotic birds on their nature charters, as well as the occasional whale. "It's hard to pinpoint an exact time and place here, but we do see whales, especially in the summer months," Dick Diemer says.

Kodiak Nautical Discoveries
P.O. Box 95, Kodiak, AK 99615; (907) 486–5234

Whales:	Gray, humpback, orca
Season:	May to November
Boats:	One boat, *Sea Surgeon*; 6 passengers
Trips:	One trip daily at 8 A.M.
Fare:	$150 per person for 8-hour trip.

Where the Whales Are

Departure: Boat leaves from Slip 52 in the main boat harbor in Kodiak, on Marine Way at Shelikof Street.

Naturalist: Skipper narrates trip.

Ron Brockman, the skipper, was born and raised on Kodiak Island. He has operated a charter boat in Kodiak waters for over twenty years, has fished commercially and taught outdoor courses at the Kodiak College, and holds a degree in biology from Alaska Methodist University.

    Brockman is a semiretired orthopedic surgeon and a captain in the Naval Reserve. Brockman's partner, Tom Stick, is a former dentist who spent many months off the coasts of Alaska and Siberia in a U.S. Navy nuclear submarine. Off the boat, Stick guides hunts and has managed a fishing lodge.

Kodiak Western Charters
P.O. Box 4123, Kodiak, AK 99615; (907) 486–2200

Whales:	Fin, humpback, minke, sei, orca, gray
Season:	April 1 to January 15
Boats:	One boat, *Ten Bears*; 6 passengers
Trips:	Single full-day trips from April 1 to September 30. Multiday charters from April 1 to January 15.
Fare:	$135 per person per day April 1 to July 31; $150 August 1 to September 30. Multiday charter, $1,500 a day.
Departure:	Boat departs from St. Herman's Boat Harbor on Near Island, just across the bridge from Kodiak.
Naturalist:	Naturalist on board

"About the middle of March, the gray whales will pass by Kodiak Island on their way north to the Bering Sea," says owner Eric Stirrup.

"June will see the arrival of the fin whales, which spend about two months around the northeast corner of the island.

"It seems that the humpbacks never stay very long, for we will see them briefly in July and briefly in September. As for the smaller species, minke whales can be seen sporadically throughout the year. Killer (orca) whales are also frequently seen and they seem to be increasingly common."

Seward, Alaska

Kenai Coastal Tours
P.O. Box 104783, Anchorage, AK 99510;
(907) 277–2131 (Anchorage), (907) 224–7114 (Seward)

Whales:	Orca, humpback
Season:	Mid-May to September
Boats:	One 82-foot vessel, *Kenai Coast*; 130 passengers
Trips:	One 7-hour trip daily at 11 A.M.
Fare:	Adults, $87; children ages 2 to 12, $36. Lunch included Group rates, early season prices available. Reservations required.
Departure:	Boat leaves from Seward Boat Harbor; the office is on the boardwalk. Via highway, Seward is 125 miles south of Anchorage. You can also get there by train, bus, or plane.
Naturalist:	No

The Chiswell Islands, in Kenai Fjords National Park, are a designated marine wildlife refuge. "As the *Kenai Coast* cruises the rugged coastline, you'll see large seabird rookeries and up to 1,000 vocal sea lions in one of the largest concentrations of marine wildlife anywhere," a spokesman says.

Where the Whales Are

"On many cruises we also see humpback or killer whales, as well as playful porpoise and sea otters. Mountain goats and bald eagles are often sighted along the shoreline. At the `Glacier of the Day,' look for harbor seals near the ice floes."

Mariah Charters

3812 Katmai Circle, Anchorage, AK 99517; (907) 243–1238

Whales:	Orca, humpback, gray, minke, fin
Season:	April 15 to September 30
Boats:	Two boats; 20 passengers each
Trips:	One trip a day, 8 A.M. to 5:30 P.M. Saturday is busiest day. Overnight charters available.
Fare:	Adults, $70; children 12 and younger, $35. Reservations advised.
Departure:	Boat leaves from Slip D6 in the Seward Boat Harbor. Office is next to Harbormaster's building. Via highway, Seward is 125 miles south of Anchorage. You can also get there by train, bus, or plane.
Naturalist:	No naturalist on board

"Let us show you a unique natural setting in and around Kenai Fjords National Park and the Chiswell Islands National Wildlife Refuge," says owner/operator John Sheedy. "Both offer unsurpassed opportunities for close-up viewing of whales; a large sea lion colony; over fifty species of birds; huge concentrations of puffins, kittiwakes, and murres; and numerous bald eagles. We visit an active tidewater glacier, up close and personal! And we limit the number of passengers so everyone has room, equal viewing opportunity, and more personalized service."

Whittier, Alaska

Alaskan Wilderness Sailing Safaris
P.O. Box 1313, Valdez, AK 99686; (907) 835–5175

Whales:	Orca, humpback, minke, fin
Season:	June 1 to September 1
Boats:	Five boats; two with 4-passenger capacity, three with 5-passenger capacity
Trips:	Week-long trips begin on Friday, end on Thursday.
Fare:	$850 per person. Price includes meals and nightly lodging. Reservations required.
Departure:	Boats leave from Whittier harbor. There is no road access to Whittier, but the Alaska Railroad makes the 60-mile trip from Anchorage.
Naturalist:	Yes

Owners Nancy and James Lethcoe say their trips afford an outstanding opportunity "to observe numerous species of whales and other marine mammals." They also note that the area offers spectacular scenery.

Prince William Sound Charters
P.O. Box 91227, Anchorage, AK 99509; (907) 344–3632

Whales:	Orca, humpback; occasionally minke, fin, blue
Season:	May 1 to September 30
Boats:	One motor yacht, *Silver Spider*; 6 passengers
Trips:	One-day or multiday charters; passengers live on board.

Where the Whales Are

Fare: Charter, $695 for one day; overnight trips, $895 for first night, $695 for each additional night. Six guests maximum. Reservations required.

Departure: Boat leaves from Whittier dock. There is no road access to Whittier, but the Alaska Railroad makes the 60-mile trip from Anchorage.

Naturalist: Skipper, first mate serve as naturalists.

"The whale-watching trips we offer are targeted toward small private groups, usually four or fewer, that are looking for a full-service executive trip," say Will and Tracy Eason, skipper and first mate, respectively.

"For whale watching, we suggest a several-day trip, which allows us to travel to the various areas of Prince William Sound where the whales are most likely to be located."

Sinbad Charters
3605 Artic, #2157, Anchorage, AK 99503; (907) 248–4768

Whales: Gray, orca, humpback, pilot

Season: Late May to September 1

Boats: One boat; 6 passengers

Trips: Custom trips on demand.

Fare: $100 per person for a 12-hour day; 20 percent discount for seniors. Lunch included. Reservations required.

Departure: Boat leaves from berth D-24 in Whittier. There is no road access to Whittier, but the Alaska Railroad makes the 60-mile trip from Anchorage.

Naturalist: Captain serves as naturalist.

Captain Eldon Gallear notes that he has been in Alaska since 1948. He takes passengers to see whales around Perry Island, Nellie Jaun, and Port Wells. Overnight bed-and-breakfast cruises are also available.

Glacier Bay, Alaska

Glacier Bay Lodge, Inc.
523 Pine Street, Suite 203, Seattle, WA 98101; (800) 622–2042, (206) 623–7110 or 623–2417

Whales:	Humpback, orca, minke
Season:	Late May to mid-September
Boats:	One boat, *Spirit of Adventure;* 300 passengers
Trips:	One trip daily, 7 A.M. to 4 P.M.
Fare:	Adults, $142; children 11 and younger, half fare. Lunch included. Reservations required.
Departure:	Whale-watching trips leave from the lodge's dock in Bartlett Cove, Glacier Bay National Park, which is accessible by plane or ferry. Packages are available that include flight to Bartlett Cove, flight and lodging, or flight and multiday cruise.
Naturalist:	National Park Service naturalist on board

Glacier Bay Lodge, Inc., is the concessionaire at Glacier Bay National Park in southeastern Alaska, about 60 miles northwest of Juneau. Bert Norby, director of marketing, says that the park is famous for whale watching. "It is the dream trip for nature photographers and those who love to see wildlife, including whales."

Norby adds, "Glacier Bay is also famous for its glaciers, with over one hundred alpine glaciers and with sixteen tidewater glaciers calving icebergs into the picturesque fjords."

Gustavus, Alaska

Fairweather Fishing and Guide Service
June–August:
P.O. Box 164, Gustavus, AK 99826; (907) 697–2335
September–May:
40220 Kent Street, Homer, AK 99603; (907) 235–6209

Whales:	Humpback, minke, orca
Season:	May 30 to September 15
Boats:	Two boats, *Tomten* and *Gusto;* 6 passengers each
Trips:	One trip a day on demand, 7 A.M. to 3:30 P.M.
Fare:	$90 per person for half day; $160 for full day, which includes lunch. Reservations required. For information on a package offer, contact Gustavus Inn, General Delivery, Gustavus, AK 99826.
Departure:	Boats leave from the dock in Gustavus, which is accessible by boat or by air.
Naturalist:	Yes

Says skipper Wayne Clark, "We have chartered trips with National Geographic, Audubon, National Wildlife, and International Wildlife organizations. The boat trip is a short twenty-minute ride to an area that has had whale numbers consistent from May to September—anywhere from six to twelve humpbacks feeding right up against the shoreline. Eagles, seals, porpoises, and sea lions, also!"

Clark also works as a rural bush teacher in the area.

Glacier Bay Puffin Charters

P.O. Box 3, Gustavus, AK 99826; (907) 789–9787
(October 1–April 30) or 697–2260 (May 1–September 30)

Whales:	Humpback
Season:	May 15 to September 15
Boats:	One boat, *Professor Puffin*; 4 passengers
Trips:	One or two 4-hour trips a day at 7 A.M. and 1 P.M.; one 8 1/2-hour trip at 7 A.M.; or by custom charter.
Fare:	Adults, $144 for a full-day trip, $72 for half day. (Full-day trips preferred.) Children 6 and younger, free. Reservations advised. Packages available at Puffin's Bed and Breakfast, same address as above.
Departure:	Boat leaves from Gustavus's dock. Gustavus is accessible only by plane or boat.
Naturalist:	Captain serves as naturalist.

Chuck Schroth, the owners' son and the captain, "has been raised on the waters of Icy Strait and has gained naturalist expertise from observing, reading, and working under a marine biologist for five years."

Sandy Schroth adds, "What is really special about Chuck's approach is his genuine consideration for unobtrusively approaching the whales. He seems to have a special sense for where they will pop up. Each whale has its own markings and personality. Chuck knows them all."

Glacier Bay—Your Way!

P.O. Box 5, Gustavus, AK 99826; (907) 697–2288

Whales:	Orca, humpback
Season:	May 1 to September 30
Boats:	Two boats, *Pacific* and *Chelsea Sunset*; 6 passengers each
Trips:	Full- or half-day charters daily at 7:30 A.M. and 1 P.M. Overnight charters also available. Packages available at Glacier Bay Country Inn, at the above address.
Fare:	$160 for full day (about 8 hours), $90 for half day (about 4 hours). Reservations advised.
Departure:	Boats leave from dock in Gustavus. Access to Gustavus is by boat or plane.
Naturalist:	Captain serves as naturalist.

"Our area offers fantastic whale watching for humpbacks and orcas," says co-owner Annie Unrein. "We depart from the Gustavus dock and watch whales at nearby Point Adolphus, a rich feeding ground.

"We've put together a number of tour options, but guests are not limited to these exact tour options. We want them to experience Glacier Bay in a style that suits them! Owner-built and operated, we serve a maximum of twenty guests. Our small size and superior staff assure warm, personal service to all."

Glacier Guides Inc.

Summer: P.O. Box 66, Gustavus, AK 99826; (907) 697–2252
Winter: P.O. Box 460, Santa Clara, UT 84765; (801) 628–0973

Whales:	Humpback, orca, minke
Season:	April to October
Boats:	One boat, *Alaskan Solitude*; 20 passengers

Trips:	Six-day trips, during which participants live on board, or daily charters.
Fare:	Charter cost is $13,200 for 6-day trip for up to 6 passengers, $2,200 per additional person. Daily charter, $2,200 for up to 10 passengers, $175 for each additional person. Reservations required.
Departure:	Boat leaves from the dock in Gustavus, which is accessible by ferry or plane.
Naturalist:	Guide serves as naturalist.

"Glacier Bay National Park's sixteen glaciers calving into the sea is one of nature's major spectacles," says Jimmie C. Rosenbruch, a licensed Alaska Master Guide. "Less than two hundred years ago, Glacier Bay was a great icefield. Today, ice has receded nearly 100 miles, leaving a magnificent bay full of all manner of wildlife. We cruise the calm inside waters, so don't worry about motion sickness."

Gustavus Marine Charters
P.O. Box 81, Gustavus, AK 99826; (907) 697–2233

Whales:	Humpback, orca
Season:	May 15 to September 15
Boats:	Two boats; 6 passengers each
Trips:	Single- or multiday charters.
Fare:	For party of four, $880 a day. Or $660 each for three days, two nights on board, with four-person minimum. Reservations required.
Departure:	Boats leave from the dock in Gustavus. Access to Gustavus is by plane or boat.
Naturalist:	No naturalist on board

"Cruise the icy fjords in the comfort and privacy of your own diesel-powered yacht," owner Mike Nigro says. "Enjoy photography, birding, whale watching, and tidewater glaciers, plus the finest saltwater fishing Alaska has to offer. Spend three or four days getting to know this special part of `the Great Land.'"

Spirit Walker Expeditions
P.O. Box 240, Gustavus, AK 99826; (907) 697–2266 or 697–2346

Whales:	Humpback, orca, minke, gray
Season:	May 1 to October 1
Boats:	Six 2-person kayaks
Trips:	One 4-day trip kayaking in Icy Strait and camping on Chichagof Island.
Fare:	$565 per person
Departure:	Trips leave from the dock in Gustavus, which is accessible by ferry or plane.
Naturalist:	Naturalist accompanies trip.

"Sea kayaking is probably the most exciting way to see whales," says Nathan Borson, vice president. "We have seen humpback whales on every "WHALES! Trip" we have done. We get close, without chasing or disturbing whales. There is no engine noise, so we hear the whales breathing and slapping the water clearly. There is no prop noise to interfere with our hydrophone.

"Drifting right at the surface of the water, we see other life, too—sea lions, seals, much bird life, even plankton and kelp. We get a feeling of what it's like for a whale to live here. We camp on a beach that whales swim past at night, breathing noisily."

Juneau, Alaska

Alaska Naturalist & Photography Cruise Tours
9951 Sprucewood Park, #47, Juneau, AK 99801;
(800) 252–7457, (907) 789–7429

Whales:	Humpback; occasionally minke, orca
Season:	June 1 to August 31
Boats:	Two boats; 6 and 49 passengers
Trips:	One trip daily, 8 A.M. to 5 P.M. Also 2- and 6-day cruises. Charters available.
Fare:	$175 per person for one day includes seaplane, cruise, and food; $249 for two days, one night. $1,200 a day for 12 people for six-day cruise. Children under 12, half fare. Reservations required.
Departure:	Boats leave from Marine Park dock or Aurora Boat Basin #C1 in Juneau, which is accessible by plane or ferry.
Naturalist:	Naturalist on board

"For groups who request whale watching," says Captain Howard C. Robinson, "I cruise to a special whale feeding habitat, in addition to other attractions. During the past six years, humpback whales have been at this location every trip I have gone there. I carefully approach them in a way that gives passengers good close viewing and pictures."

Robinson says he has been a naturalist and photographer for the past half century. He tells passengers about glaciers, history, Indians, and Russian culture; he locates and identifies wildlife; and he offers photography advice.

Oceanic Society Expeditions
Fort Mason Center, Building E, San Francisco, CA 94123;
(415) 441–1106

Whales:	Humpback, orca
Season:	July
Boats:	The 126-foot research vessel *Acania*; 14 participants
Trips:	One 10-day trip to study humpbacks in their feeding grounds in southeast Alaska.
Fare:	$2,490 per person. Price includes meals, guides, and accommodations in six cabins with shared facilities. Airfare not included. Reservations required.
Departure:	Trip originates in Juneau, Alaska.
Naturalist:	Marine mammal expert accompanies trip.

"This expedition combines research with wilderness exploration," says Oceanic Society Expeditions. "No special experience is required. Under the guidance of the research director, you will have the opportunity to participate in research activities such as recording humpback whale sounds, photographing animals for identification, and cataloguing. We will also discover how individual colorations are unique to each humpback, making entries of sightings in the research log."

Oceanic Society Expeditions has conducted nature trips since 1973.

Outdoor Alaska
P.O. Box 7814, Ketchikan, AK 99901; (907) 225–6044

Whales:	Humpback
Season:	June through September

Boats:	Three boats, *Misty Fjord*, *Emerald Fjord*, and *Crystal Fjord*; up to 32 passengers each
Trips:	One-day or multiday charters. One-day trips for up to 32 passengers; multiday for up to 8 passengers.
Fare:	$145 per person per day for single-day trips, $125 per day for multiday trips. Reservations required.
Departure:	Trips leave from Juneau and Petersburg, both of which are accessible by air or boat.
Naturalist:	Skipper is marine biologist.

"Admiralty Island in southeast Alaska has surrounding it one of the largest populations of humpback whales in Alaska," says native Alaskan Captain Dave Pihlman. "These whales are concentrated for convenient viewing in the inland waters of Stephens Passage and Seymour Canal."

Sitka, Alaska

Alaska Travel Adventures
9085 Glacier Highway, Suite 204, Juneau, AK 99801
(907) 789–0052

Whales:	Humpback, orca, minke
Season:	May 1 to September 30
Boats:	One catamaran; 150 passengers; portion of trip in rigid-hull inflatable rafts
Trips:	Two 4-hour trips on weekdays leave between 7 and 9 A.M. and noon and 2 P.M. One trip on Saturday and Sunday, usually between 7 and 9 A.M. The busiest day is Wednesday.

Fare:	Adults, $75; children 12 and younger, $45. Reservations advised.
Departure:	Boat leaves from Crescent Harbor Dock, next to the Visitor Center in Sitka, which is accessible by plane or ferry.
Naturalist:	Naturalist accompanies trip.

Operations manager Mark Kaelke says, "Although we are not a whale-watching tour specifically, we are always looking for opportunities to view whales. The Sitka area offers opportunities to see puffins, murres, storm petrels, sea otters, harbor seals, and sea lions as well as whales."

Kaelke says that passengers find the portion of the tour in the rafts the most memorable because "they have a guide/operator who interprets what is being seen (for example, marine invertebrates are brought in the boat). Passengers get an up-close view of all wildlife encountered during this portion of the trip."

Alaska Wyldewind Charters
617 Katlian, B-33, Sitka, AK 99835; (907) 747–5734

Whales:	Humpback; occasionally gray, orca, minke
Season:	Late April to late September
Boats:	One boat, the *Wyldewind*; 6 passengers
Trips:	Numbers and times of trips depend on demand, accessibility of whales, and captain's availability
Fare:	Boat charter is $60 for half day; $85 for full day; $96 for 24 hours, sharing purchase and preparation of food; $140 for 24 hours, including meals. Minimum two passengers. Reservations advised. Special room

rate available at Westmark Shee Atika, P.O. Box 318, Sitka, AK 99835; (907) 747–6241.

Departure: Boat leaves from Sitka, which is accessible by plane or ferry.

Naturalist: Skipper serves as naturalist.

Skipper Jerry Dzugan says, "We also combine other activities with whale watching, such as sailing, other wildlife viewing, hot springs, hiking, and exploring. We have no set schedule of arrivals/departures but plan trips around our clients' schedules, interests, and budgets.

"Our whale-watching activities for the public emphasize nonintrusive observation techniques so as to cause the least amount of stress and disturbance to marine mammals' natural behavior. The ability to sail noiselessly along while observing the rich wildlife and spectacular scenery helps create a unique experience for those who appreciate unspoiled wilderness and rich wildlife viewing."

National Audubon Society

950 Third Avenue, New York, NY 10022; (212) 546–9140

Whales: Humpback

Season: Summer

Boats: The *Sea Lion* or *Sea Bird*; 37 cabins for 70 passengers each, plus small inflatable landing craft for short expeditions

Trips: An 11-day cruise at least once a season.

Fare: $2,620 to $3,850 per person. Price includes cabin, meals, transfers, excursions, permits, tips, and taxes. Airfare not included. Reservations required.

Where the Whales Are

Departure: Group gathers in Seattle and flies to Sitka, Alaska, where the cruise begins.

Naturalist: Naturalist is Audubon research biologist.

In June 1989 the National Audubon Society sponsored its first excursion along the coast of southeast Alaska. Susan P. Martin, senior vice president, notes, "I wish I could share with you all the wonderful responses of those who sailed together. Even our seasoned, world-traveling Audubon staff guide, Chris Willie, came back with stories of unbelievable beauty and magnificent wildlife."

Steller Charters
319 Peterson Avenue, Sitka, AK 99835; (907) 747–6711

Whales: Humpback, gray, and occasionally minke

Season: Year round

Boats: One boat, *Steller J*; 6 passengers

Trips: Two 3- to 4-hour trips a day; departure flexible.

Fare: $50 per person, minimum four people. Reservations advised. For information on a package room rate, write to Westmark Shee Atika, P.O. Box 318, Sitka, AK 99835; (907) 747–6241.

Departure: Boat leaves from Crescent Harbor in downtown Sitka, which is reached by plane or ferry.

Naturalist: Captain is a naturalist.

"I am a retired high school science teacher who lives year round in Sitka," says Captain William L. Foster. "Sitka is in relatively mild southeast Alaska, and we are fortunate to have a lot of whale watching year round. Humpbacks have been seen here every month of the year.

"Our most unique humpback watching is, however, in winter! For the past ten years we have had from five to fifteen humpbacks from

November through March. Not all Alaska humpbacks go to Hawaii for the winter! Many times you don't even need a boat to see this winter group, since they feed along some of our short road system."

Wrangell, Alaska

Alaskan Star Charters

P.O. Box 2027, Wrangell, AK 99929; (907) 874–3084

Whales:	Humpback, minke, orca
Season:	Mid-April to early November
Boats:	One boat, *Star Queen*; 6 passengers
Trips:	Five-day trips April through August. Charters until November.
Fare:	$2,500 per person. Price includes double occupancy aboard, private bath, food, shore excursions. Reservations required.
Departure:	Boat leaves from Wrangell, which is accessible by plane or ferry.
Naturalist:	Naturalist on board

"These outings are designed to let guests experience the wildest areas while enjoying wine with dinner and other creature comforts," says Captain Ken Wyrick. "The day's activities can be planned to be rustic or rugged, but the boat and staff are available with comfort."

Museums

Pratt Museum
3779 Bartlett Street, Homer, AK 99603; (907) 235–8635

The Pratt Museum, run by the Homer Society of Natural History, collects, preserves, and interprets the history of the Kenai Peninsula. The whale exhibit includes a beluga skeleton, a Bering beaked whale skeleton, a minke skull, and a Cuvier's beaked whale skull.

Hours are 10 A.M. to 5 P.M. daily in summer and noon to 5 P.M. Tuesday through Sunday in winter. The museum is closed in January. Admission for nonmembers is $3 for adults, $2 for senior citizens, $1 for youths 6 to 18, and free to children under 6.

University of Alaska Museum
907 Yukon Drive, Fairbanks, AK 99775; (907) 474–7505

The mission of the museum is to collect, interpret, and teach the natural and cultural history of the circumpolar area. Included in the exhibit on whales are the skull and lower jaw of a bowhead whale and paraphernalia related to the Eskimos' whale hunting. One such item is a twelve-person umiak, a boat made of split walrus hide with waterproof stitching.

From June through August, the museum is open daily 9 A.M. to 7 P.M.; in May and September, 9 A.M. to 5 P.M.; from October through April, noon to 5 P.M. Adults, $3; seniors, $2.50; children under 12, free. No admission is charged on Fridays during the winter.

National Parks

Glacier Bay National Park and Preserve
P.O. Box 140, Gustavus, AK 99826; (907) 697–2231

Glacier Bay National Park and Preserve was completely covered by ice just two hundred years ago. Today the park has sixteen tidewater glaciers, remnants of a general ice advance—the Little Ice Age—that began four thousand years ago. Wildlife in the park and preserve, which cover 3,328,000 acres, include humpback, minke, and orca whales. Write for a free brochure and map.

Kenai Fjords National Park
National Park Service, 540 West 5th Avenue, Anchorage, AK 99501; (907) 224–3175

Glaciers, seabirds, marine mammals, and a rugged coast are thespecial features of the Kenai Fjords National Park, which covers 567,000 acres. Write for a map and brochure.

Western Canada

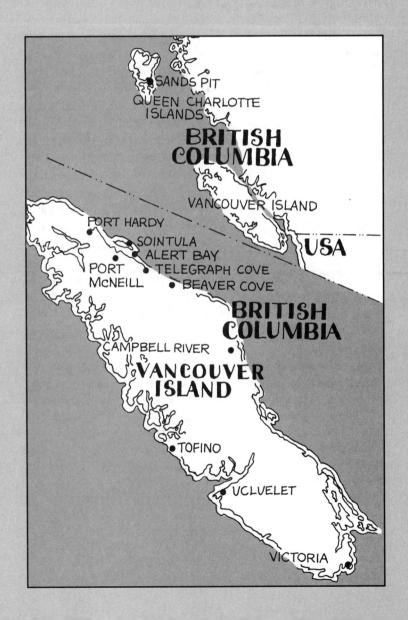

Western Canada

When it comes to whales, Canada has something for everyone. The mighty blues, rare right whales, finbacks, humpbacks, almost-mythical bowheads, grays, tusked narwhals, pilot whales, orcas, and belugas swim in the seas off both coasts, inhabit arctic waters, and populate at least two rivers. Whales are also in Canada's gulfs, bays, and sounds, and at the right time of year, you can watch the whales of your choice from shore.

British Columbia can count on gray whales in March and April; orcas and minkes in July, August, and September; and maybe some finbacks and humpbacks later in the year. In response, tour operators sponsor trips from several cities on Vancouver Island and in the Queen Charlotte Islands. Two tour operators, Bluewater Adventures and Maple Leaf Adventures (pp. 210-211), offer several extended trips departing from various locations in British Columbia to better watch Canada's whales.

Every July and August, special expeditions leave Churchill, Manitoba, to see belugas in Hudson Bay and the Churchill River. The popular belugas can also be seen off Inuvik, in the Northwest Territories, in July and August. Trips to see the tusked narwhal and the seldom-observed bowhead originate from Baffin Island.

Basically, you can count on whales wherever there are whale-watch tour operators; but given the vast coastal exposures of Canada, don't be surprised if you encounter them elsewhere, too.

TOURISM INFORMATION

British Columbia

Ministry of Tourism & Provincial Secretary
Parliament Buildings, Victoria, BC, V8V 1X4 Canada

Tourism British Columbia
Parliament Buildings, Victoria, BC, V8W 2Z2 Canada
(604) 387–1642

Manitoba

Travel Manitoba
Dept. 6020, Seventh Floor, 155 Carlton Avenue, Winnipeg, MB
R3C 3H8 Canada
800 (665–0040)

Northwest Territories

TravelArctic
Yellowknife, NWT, X1A 2L9 Canada
(800) 661–0788

Various Departure Points in Canada

Bluewater Adventures

No. 202–1676 Duranleau Street, Vancouver, British Columbia, V6H 3S4 Canada; (604) 684–4575

Whales:	Orca, gray, humpback, minke
Season:	April to October
Boats:	One 68-foot ketch, *Island Roamer*; 16 passengers on multiday live-aboard trips
Trips:	Three- to 9-day trips to the San Juan and Gulf Islands, to the Queen Charlotte Islands, or along the Inside Passage.
Fare:	Sample fares: $375 (U.S.) per person for 3 days in the San Juan and Gulf Islands; $675 for 6 days in the San Juans; $1,295 for 8 days in the Inside Passage; $1,590 for 9 days in the Queen Charlotte Islands. Reservations required.
Departure:	Trips leave from Victoria, Vancouver, Port Hardy, or Sandspit, depending on the destination.
Naturalist:	Yes

"*Island Roamer*'s crew has many years' experience running quality sailing adventures," a spokesman says. "We have operated cruises for many well-known educational institutions and were privileged to be chosen by World Wildlife of Canada to run a whale-watching trip for His Royal Highness Prince Philip.

"You can rely on our experienced crew to offer you the finest sailing adventure possible. Their knowledge of marine biology, whales, native Indian culture, birds, and ecology will make your trip as interesting and as educational as you wish."

Maple Leaf Adventures

4360 River Road, Richmond, British Columbia, V7C 1A2 Canada;
(604) 644–4343

Whales:	Orca, gray, humpback
Season:	April through September
Boats:	The 92-foot schooner *Maple Leaf;* 8 passengers
Trips:	Four-day to 2-week charters along the coast and among the Queen Charlotte and Gulf Islands.
Fare:	Rates start at $600 (Canadian) per person for bed and board. Reservations required.
Departure:	Departure from various ports, depending on destination.
Naturalist:	Naturalist often on board

"While we see whales on just about all of our trips, the best time and area is Robson Bight in early September for orcas. We often have prominent whale researchers on board and our own hydrophone," say owners Brian and Susan Falconer.

"*Maple Leaf*'s accommodations are very comfortable. The spacious main cabin is open and airy by day and at night is divided by curtains into four double 'cabins' accommodating eight guests in extra-large bunks. Our experienced crew will help you to participate in the sailing of the ship, or you may wish just to relax and enjoy the experience."

Sandspit, British Columbia

Pacific Synergies Ltd.

P.O. Box 3500-18, Whistler, British Columbia, V0N 1B0 Canada;
(604) 932–3107

Whales:	Gray, orca, humpback, minke, fin, blue
Season:	April to October

Boats:	One 71-foot ketch, *Darwin Sound*; 10 passengers in double cabins, plus 4 crew members
Trips:	Six- to 10-day trips to various destinations along the coast of British Columbia, the Queen Charlotte Islands, and Graham and Moresby islands.
Fare:	Approximately $200 (Canadian) per person per day. Price includes activities, gear, guides, fuel, meals, snacks, beverages, and wine with dinner. Reservations required.
Departure:	Boat leaves from Sandspit, Queen Charlotte Islands.
Naturalist:	Naturalist on board

"Pacific Synergies designs wilderness expeditions to remote or endangered coastal areas," owners/operators Irene and Al Whitney explain in their brochure. "We tailor our expeditions to the wishes of each group, emphasizing our abundant natural history, regional art, and anthropology.

"There is the opportunity to be off the boat for several hours each morning, afternoon, and evening to fish, kayak, or explore on shore. As a group we may wander beaches, hike into the alpine, or visit abandoned villages, and there is always opportunity to choose to be on your own."

Port Hardy, British Columbia

Oceanic Society Expeditions
Fort Mason Center, Building E, San Francisco, CA 94123; (415) 441–1106

Whales:	Orca, minke
Season:	August
Boats:	One 68-foot ketch, *Island Roamer*; 16 passengers

Trips:	One-week trip living on board and sailing in the Inside Passage off Vancouver Island.
Fare:	$1,290 (U.S.) per person. Price includes meals, accommodations, and guides. Reservations required.
Departure:	Trip begins at Port Hardy, on north Vancouver Island.
Naturalist:	Yes

"Johnstone Strait is absolutely the best place in the world to see killer whales," says Oceanic Expeditions. "Nowhere else can you expect to experience such close encounters with these majestic mammals.

"Approximately 330 individual whales have been identified in the waters off British Columbia and Washington. Pods can contain up to 50 animals. Our expedition combines whale watching with sailing and exploring the shores of an island wilderness."

Sointula, British Columbia

Wayward Wind Charters
P.O. Box 300, Sointula, British Columbia, V0N 3E0 Canada; (604) 973–6307

Whales:	Orca
Season:	Mid-June through September
Boats:	One 28-foot sailboat; 8 to 10 passengers
Trips:	One 8-hour trip daily to Robson Bight, a marine preserve set aside for orcas. Hot lunch and afternoon tea included.
Fare:	Adults, $55 (Canadian); seniors and children 5 to 12, $35. Reservations required. Bed and breakfast available in the Wayward Wind Lodge.

Departure: Trips leave from Sointula, on Malcolm Island. Regular ferry service runs from Port McNeill across Alert Bay to Sointula; the trip takes 30 minutes.

Naturalist: Skipper serves as naturalist on board.

John and Vilma Gamble say, "We feel our business is unique because of its personalized service. Depending on the group and time, a little fishing or sightseeing may be done." *Wayward Wind*'s skipper has been sailing on the Pacific since the 1970s and gladly shares his extensive knowledge.

Port McNeill, British Columbia

Ecosummer Expeditions

1516 Duranleau Street, Vancouver, British Columbia, V6H 3S4 Canada; (604) 669–7741

Whales: Orca, gray, minke

Season: Late June to late September

Boats: Six 2-person kayaks; 10 participants and 2 guides.

Trips: Eight-day trips paddling and camping along the Inside Passage off Vancouver Island.

Fare: $750 (U.S.) per person. Reservations required.

Departure: Trips start at Port McNeill.

Naturalist: Guides are naturalists.

"Although we have operated sea kayak adventures since the 1970s, the concept is still new to many people, who may have visions of paddling in the small unstable kayaks typically used for river trips," says a spokesman.

"However, in actuality, we use very stable craft especially designed for ocean environments. These boats demand no previous experience, and all persons adapt very quickly to the paddling and sailing skill required."

Founded in 1976, Ecosummer Expeditions began as an adventure company that promoted environmental education, working primarily with high school students. Founder Jim Allen was soon deluged with requests from adults who wanted activity-oriented, natural history trips, and so Ecosummer Expeditions evolved.

Northern Lights Expeditions

6141 Northeast Bothell Way, Suite 101, Seattle, WA 98155; (206) 483–6396

Whales:	Orca, minke
Season:	June to September
Boats:	Six 2-person kayaks, plus two 1-person kayaks for guides
Trips:	Kayaking and camping for 6 days along the Inside Passage.
Fare:	$650 (U.S.) per person. Price includes food, kayak, and camping gear. Minimum age 16. Reservations required.
Departure:	Trips leave from Port McNeill.
Naturalist:	Guides are naturalists.

"Participants have a chance to live on the shores of the whale's environment for a week," says trip leader David Arcese. "They can hear the whales passing in the night, close to the beach. They can paddle within a few feet of the whales because the kayaks are silent and slow-moving, thereby not causing anxiety among the whales.

"The trips are intended for people who have no experience kayaking, and the pace is relaxed."

Sea Cloud Charters

Independent Charter Boat Referrals Ltd., P.O. Box 1239, Port McNeill, British Columbia, V0N 2R0 Canada; (604) 956–3739

Whales:	Orca
Season:	July 15 to September 30
Boats:	Four vessels; up to 10 passengers
Trips:	Daily 6-hour trip to Robson Bight in Johnstone Straits; lunch included. Also a 4-hour trip at 5:30 P.M. for up to six passengers; coffee served. Hourly charters also available.
Fare:	$55 (Canadian) per person if boat is full. Charters, $55 an hour. Reservations required.
Departure:	Boats leave from Beaver Cove, just south of Port McNeill.
Naturalist:	Skipper serves as naturalist.

Owners Lois and Jonn Bertramm say, "Once the whales are spotted we cruise alongside of them watching their behavior and playful antics, providing you with wonderful photo opportunities and time to listen to the whales on an underwater microphone system.

"Please understand that we cannot guarantee whale sightings, but our success rate is over 90 percent, as our whales are very predictable."

Sea Smoke/Sail with the Whales

P.O. Box 483, Alert Bay, British Columbia, V0N 1A0 Canada;
(604) 974–5225

Whales:	Orca, minke, humpback
Season:	July to October
Boats:	*Tuan*, a 43-foot sailboat; 14 passengers
Trips:	One 7-hour trip daily to Robson Bight at 8:10 A.M. Boat stops for passengers in Alert Bay at 9:30 A.M.
Fare:	Adults, $60 (Canadian); children: 5 to 12, $50; under 5, free. Reservations required.
Departure:	Boat leaves from Port McNeill and Alert Bay.
Naturalist:	No

David and Maureen Towers say their trip is special because of their yacht—its interior is mahogany, teak, and brass—and their food, fresh fish at lunch and scones at tea time.

Also, they say, "We are quiet." Their brochure notes, "there is no engine noise, only the sounds of the whales from our hydrophones as wind, water, whales, and yacht blend together in natural harmony."

Viking West Lodge & Charter

P.O. Box 113, Port McNeill, British Columbia, V0N 2R0 Canada;
(604) 956–3431

Whales:	Orca, minke, humpback, gray
Season:	June through October
Boats:	One rigid-hull inflatable raft and a 24-foot cabin cruiser; 3 and 5 passengers respectively

Trips:	One or two trips daily to Robson Bight, leaving between 8 and 10 A.M. and returning by 5 or 7 P.M.
Fare:	Smaller boat rents for $25 (Canadian) an hour; larger for $50. Four-hour minimum. Reservations advised. Multiday packages available for lodging on board, in three-bedroom floathouse, or in hotel. Write to tour operator for details.
Departure:	From Port McNeill and Telegraph Cove
Naturalist:	Skipper serves as naturalist.

The skipper, Dennis Richards, says, "Whale watching is the neatest thing in the water, except maybe swimming with them." All passengers receive a chart, on which they may mark their route. They also may record the sounds of the whales.

Telegraph Cove, British Columbia

Stubbs Island Charters Ltd.
P.O. Box 7, Telegraph Cove, British Columbia V0N 3J0 Canada; (604) 928–3185 or 928–3117

Whales:	Orca
Season:	Late June through September
Boats:	One 60-foot cabin cruiser
Trips:	From late June to mid-July, one 5-hour trip daily to Robson Bight. From mid-July to early September, two 5-hour trips a day.
Fare:	$60 (Canadian) per person, with discounts for senior citizens and children. Daytime cruise includes lunch; evening cruise, light supper. Reservations advised.
Departure:	Trips leave from the end of the boardwalk in Telegraph Cove, south of Port McNeill.
Naturalist:	Skipper serves as naturalist.

Co-owner Anne Borrowman says, "After many seasons of whale watching, we are finding that it is an international 'sport' that has no language barrier!"

Her brochure advises: "Please remember to dress warmly and bring your camera with plenty of film."

Campbell River, British Columbia

American Cetacean Society Expeditions
P.O. Box 2639, San Pedro, CA 90731; (213) 548–6279

Whales:	Orca
Season:	Late August to early September
Boats:	One 68-foot sailing yacht, *Island Roamer*, 16 passengers
Trips:	One 7-day trip sailing and living on board.
Fare:	Members, $1,250 (U.S.) per person. Nonmembers, 10 percent more, or join ACS ($25 per family). Fare includes meals and accommodations.
Departure:	Trip starts in Campbell River, on the east coast of Vancouver Island.
Naturalist:	American Cetacean Society naturalist accompanies trip.

The American Cetacean Society has been conducting specialized trips for small groups to see whales since 1973. "ACS trips are designed for people who are interested in the world about them and want adventure with whales and nature," says a spokeswoman.

"The Campbell River supports a resident population of 140 orcas. You also will visit several Indian villages and explore the beaches and tidepools."

Tofino, British Columbia

Inter Island Excursions
P.O. Box 393, Tofino, British Columbia, V0R 2Z0 Canada;
(604) 725–3163

Whales:	Gray, orca, minke, humpback
Season:	March 1 to October 31
Boats:	Four rigid-hull inflatables; 10 passengers each; "cruiser suits" provided.
Trips:	Three 2-hour trips daily Sunday through Friday at 9 A.M., noon, and 3 P.M. Trips added at 7 A.M. and 6 P.M. on Saturday if demand warrants.
Fare:	Adults, $35 (Canadian); children under 12, $20. Reservations advised. Hotel package for $49.95 per person includes double occupancy ocean view accommodation, whale-watching tour, entrance to Maritime Museum/Whale Center, and whale information package.
Departure:	Trips leave from the Whale Center, 411 Campbell Street in Tofino.
Naturalist:	Naturalist is marine biologist.

Ocean Pacific Whale Charters Ltd.
P.O. Box 590, Tofino, British Columbia, V0R 2Z0 Canada;
(604) 725–3919

Whales:	Gray, orca, minke
Season:	March 1 to October 30
Boats:	Two rigid-hull inflatable rafts; 12 passengers each; also cabin cruiser, *Lady Selkirk*; 56 passengers

Trips:	Two to four 2-hour trips a day. Small boats go at 9:30 A.M., noon, 3 P.M., and 5:30 P.M. Large boat goes at 10 or 11 A.M. and 1:30 P.M.
Fare:	Rafts: adults, $30 (Canadian); youths, $20. Children under 6 and senior citizens not allowed on rafts. Cruiser: adults; $35; senior citizens, $33; children: 6 to 16, $20; under 6, free. Family rates available. Reservations advised. Packages offered with Weigh West Marine Resort on Tofino's waterfront.
Departure:	Boats depart from Government Wharf, at the foot of First Street, in downtown Tofino.
Naturalist:	Yes

Watching whales off Vancouver Island's west coast in a rigid-hull inflatable raft is "ideal for those who enjoy life in the fast wave," says president Jamie Bray.

"On our whale-watching cruises, you'll enjoy tall tales and local legends as we cruise past the islands and inlets that housed many a colorful character. Wild about wildlife? We've got more than whales to show you."

Ucluelet, British Columbia

Canadian Princess Resort

P.O. Box 939, Ucluelet, British Columbia, V0R 3A0 Canada; (800) 663–7090, (604) 726–7771

Whales:	Gray and occasionally orca
Season:	March 1 to September 31
Boats:	Ten boats; 18 to 22 passengers each
Trips:	Two 4-hour trips daily at 9 A.M. and 1:30 P.M. Sunday is busiest day.

Fare:	Adults, $35 (Canadian); children 12 and under, $20. Family rates available. Rates higher on weekends. Reservations advised on weekdays, required on weekends. Accommodations available at the resort's center, a 235-foot ship, *Canadian Princess*, or on the shore.
Departure:	Trips leave from Ucluelet Harbor.
Naturalist:	No

Lorena Kemps, service manager, says, "The mainstay of this resort and the reason we have so many return guests is our crew, who are the backbone of this operation. That is what makes us special. They really do care about the guests."

She adds, "The drive from Nanaimo to Ucluelet is very scenic, with lots of stops along the way. Traveling along the Pacific Rim Highway is breathtaking."

Subtidal Adventures

P.O. Box 78, Ucluelet, British Columbia, V0R 3A0 Canada; (604) 726–7336 or 726–7061

Whales:	Gray, humpback, orca
Season:	March 1 to October 31
Boats:	A 36-foot ex-rescue boat, *Dixie IV*, and a 24-foot rigid-hull inflatable raft; 24 passengers total
Trips:	Three or four trips daily of different durations to various destinations in Barkley Sound. Busiest day is Saturday during school months.
Fare:	Fares start at $29 (Canadian) for adults, $19 for children 6 to 12, and $9 for children under 6. Reservations advised; make them at the Gray Whale Deli in Ucluelet, (604) 726–7336.
Departure:	Boats depart from Ucluelet Boat Basin on Vancouver Island.

Naturalist: Skipper serves as naturalist.

"We are the oldest charter boat company here and have tailored our cruises to provide the best possible experience to our guests," says owner Brian Congdon. "Whichever cruise you choose, we know you will go home with memories to last a lifetime."

Victoria, British Columbia

Sea Coast Expeditions
1655 Ash Road, Victoria, British Columbia, V8N 2T2 Canada; (604) 477–1818

Whales:	Orca, minke
Season:	May 1 to September 30
Boats:	One rigid-hull inflatable raft; 12 passengers; full-length cruiser suits provided
Trips:	As many as three 3-hour trips daily at 9 A.M., 1 P.M., and 5 P.M. Busiest day is Saturday.
Fare:	Adults, $65 (Canadian); children under 14, $40. Guaranteed sightings, $80 and $50, respectively. Reservations advised.
Departure:	Boats depart Dock A of the Government Street floats, directly across from the Empress Hotel main entrance.
Naturalist:	Naturalist on board

"Our naturalists have expertise on whales, dolphins, porpoises, birds, seals, and sea lions. Naturalists stimulate discussion, provide some commentary, and invite questions," says owner Alex Rhodes.

"Not one of our passengers to date has experienced seasickness. The fresh air and forward motion of the boat counteract seasickness exceptionally well. Take your favorite motion sickness medicine if you have any doubts."

Inuvik, Northwest Territories

Arctic Tour Company
P.O. Box 2021, Inuvik, Northwest Territories, X0E 0T0 Canada; (403) 979–4100

Whales:	Beluga
Season:	July and August
Boats:	One boat; 6 passengers and a guide
Trips:	Several 12-hour trips down the Mackenzie River to Kendall Island. Trips conclude in Inuvik.
Fare:	$1,200 (Canadian) for six people, meals included. Reservations required.
Departure:	Boat leaves from Inuvik.
Naturalist:	Guide is native Inuit.

"The Arctic Tour Company is located in Inuvik, 150 miles north of the Arctic Circle," notes manager Kimberly Staples. "We offer a variety of tours and services within the Western Arctic year round."

The whale-watching tour includes visiting an Inuit family's subsistence whaling campground and viewing the beluga whales and scenery. The Inuit guide will share the history and stories of the area.

Baffin Island, Northwest Territories

Atlantic Marine Wildlife Tours Ltd.
227 Wright Street, Fredericton, New Brunswick, E3B 2E3 Canada; (506) 459–7325 or 459–7876

Whales:	Narwhal, bowhead, beluga
Season:	May and June
Boats:	None; see **Trips** below.
Trips:	Two 10-day trips by plane, sled, and snowmobile to Baffin Island in the Arctic Circle, with stops at Frobisher Bay, Pond Inlet, and Bylot Island. Food and lodging in hotels and tents. Trips conclude in Ottawa.
Fare:	$3,250 (U.S.) per person. Price includes airfare from Ottawa to Baffin Island, room, board, guides, tours, entertainment. Reservations required.
Departure:	Trips leave from Ottawa.
Naturalist:	Naturalist accompanies trip.

"The adjacent waters around Baffin Island and Bylot Island contain the richest profusion of marine mammals in the eastern Arctic, including concentrations of narwhal, bowhead, and beluga whales," says Dr. Eugene Lewis, president of Atlantic Marine Wildlife Tours. "There are also many harp, bearded, and ring seals along with wandering polar bears, arctic foxes, and migratory birds en route to their summer nesting grounds."

The inlets and waterways are still frozen in May and June, but there are twenty-four hours of daylight and the temperatures are above freezing.

Seafarers Expeditions

P.O. Box 691, Bangor, ME 04401; (207) 942–7942

Whales:	Narwhal, possibly bowhead
Season:	June
Boats:	None, see **Trips** below.
Trips:	One 10-day trip includes camping, living among the Inuits on Baffin Island—400 miles north of the Arctic Circle—and observing narwhals from the ice's edge. Trip concludes in Ottawa.
Fare:	$2,995 (U.S.) per person. Price includes lodging, meals, ground transportation, guides, and round-trip airfare from Ottawa. Reservations required.
Departure:	Trip starts in Ottawa.
Naturalist:	Yes

"This trip offers the opportunity to explore some of the last true wilderness in North America," says Seafarers Expeditions founder Scott Marion. "The rugged beauty of Baffin Island's north shore is punctuated by 5,000-foot mountains, glacial fjords, and massive icebergs. This expedition is timed to let us enjoy the magic of twenty-four hours of daylight and the surrealistic beauty of the midnight sun."

Seafarers Expeditions was founded in 1981.

Churchill, Manitoba

Northern Expeditions

P.O. Box 614, Churchill, Manitoba, R0B 0E0 Canada; (204) 675–2793

Whales:	Beluga
Season:	July and August

Boats:	A 17-foot aluminum boat with outboard motor and a 36-foot cabin cruiser; 6 and 15 passengers respectively
Trips:	Two or three trips a day, depending on weather and tides in Hudson Bay. Trips cross the Churchill River for watching whales and visiting historic Fort Prince of Wales.
Fare:	$25 (Canadian) per person for a 2$1/2$-hour tour. Reservations required 45 days before tour date.
Departure:	Boats leave from the lower dock, behind the port of Churchill.
Naturalist:	Naturalist on board

"Northern Expeditions has designed special sightseeing tours," says tour operator Dwight Allen. Transportation by boat, van, all-terrain vehicle, or snowmobile ensures that vacationers see the highlights of each passing season. "Our tours are provided in both English and French. We have something for everyone, provided through an economical, courteous, and efficient tour company."

Riding Mountain Nature Tours
P.O. Box 429, Erickson, Manitoba, R0J 0P0 Canada; (204) 636–2968

Whales:	Beluga
Season:	June 1 to August 30
Boats:	Aluminum boats or rigid-hull inflatable rafts; 10 to 30 passengers each
Trips:	Several multiple-day tours of Manitoba each year include at least one day of whale watching on the Churchill River or in Hudson Bay. Tours also include bird-watching and viewing wildlife on the tundra.

Fare:	A 6-day tour of tundra, including whale watching, costs $1,275 (Canadian). Includes food, lodging, guides, equipment, and transportation from Winnipeg, where tour originates. Reservations required.
Departure:	Participants fly to Churchill from Winnipeg.
Naturalist:	Naturalist accompanies tour.

"We are Manitoba's finest nature tour company—and one of the only," says Daniel Weedon, owner and tour leader. "We have complete package tours—deluxe design."

Sea North Tours Ltd.

P.O. Box 222, Churchill, Manitoba, R0B 0E0 Canada;
(204) 675–2195

Whales:	Beluga
Season:	July 1 to August 14
Boats:	Four boats; capacity range from 10 to 30 passengers
Trips:	Daily trips on Churchill River and Hudson Bay, weather and tides permitting. Trips last 2$^{1}/_{2}$, 4, or 5 hours.
Fare:	Fares start at $25 (Canadian) for adults, $12.50 for children 12 and younger. Reservations advised. Package tours that include lodging are available through North Star Tours, P.O. Box 520, Churchill, Manitoba, Canada R0B 0E0; (204) 675–2629; or through Frontiers North Inc., 774 Bronx Avenue, Winnipeg, Manitoba, Canada R2K 4E9; (204) 663–1411.
Departure:	Trips leave from 39 Franklin Street in center of town of Churchill.

Naturalist: Captain serves as naturalist.

Mike and Doreen Macri say, "Our boats are frequently surrounded by hundreds of belugas during a tour. All boats are hydrophone-equipped to listen to their incredible vocalizations.

"Our captain (Mike) is also a professional wildlife photographer. He recently photographed underwater a mother beluga swimming with her calf on her back." The Macris rent passengers 30mm underwater camera housings for taking pictures.

Museums, Aquariums, and Science Centers

British Columbia

Maritime Museum/Whale Center
411 Campbell Street, P.O. Box 393, Tofino, British Columbia,
V0R 2Z0 Canada; (604) 725–3163

The Maritime Museum displays artifacts from early native cultures, the first European explorers, traders, settlers, fishermen, and shipwrecks. The Whale Center, situated on the main floor, exhibits information, research developments, and artwork about living whales as well as whale bones, artifacts, and historical accounts from the early whaling era. The center offers guided tours, films, and lectures for groups; a marine charter reservation service; and a gift shop.

Hours are 8:30 A.M. to 6 P.M. daily from early March to mid-October. Admission is free.

Wickaninnish Centre
Pacific Rim National Park, P.O. Box 280, Ucluelet, British
Columbia, V0R 3A0 Canada; (604) 726–7721

The center is situated at the surf line on the bay for which it was named. A window on the ocean side allows a view of whales, seals, and sea lions. Within the center are exhibits, displays, and films presented by park interpreters.

From mid-June to mid-September, open 10 A.M. to 6 P.M. daily. From early March to mid-June and from mid-September to mid-October, open noon to 5 P.M. Thursday through Monday. Admission is free.

During March and April the communities along the west coast of Vancouver Island celebrate the spring migration of the gray whale with the Pacific Rim Whale Festival. Among the activities in the park are guided hikes, slide shows, movies, guest lectures, plays, dances, and concerts. For specific dates and more information write Box 948, Ucluelet, British Columbia, V0R 3A0 Canada or phone (604) 726–7336.

Vancouver Aquarium

P.O. Box 3232, Vancouver, British Columbia, V6B 3X8 Canada; (604) 685–3364 or 682–1118 (recording)

Situated downtown in Stanley Park, the aquarium showcases aquatic life from the Arctic Ocean to the north Pacific Ocean. Three orcas inhabit a four-million-liter re-creation of a west coast Gulf Islands habitat. Two belugas live in a similar-sized re-creation of Lancaster Sound, in the Canadian high Arctic. Both exhibits have above- and underwater viewing and interpretive galleries with hands-on exhibits. Whales are fed publicly several times a day.

The aquarium is open 365 days a year, 9:30 A.M. to 8 P.M. in July and August and 10 A.M. to 5:30 P.M. the remainder of the year. Admission is $7 (Canadian) for adults, $6 for seniors and youths 13 to 18, $4.50 for children 5 to 12, $3.75 for disabled people and their attendants, and free to children 4 and younger. Group rates are available.

Manitoba

Manitoba Museum of Man & Nature
190 Rupert Avenue, Winnipeg, Manitoba, R3B 0N2 Canada;
(204) 956–2830 or 943–3139 (recording)

This is an interpretive museum of the natural and human history of the province of Manitoba. Visitors walk through three-dimensional exhibits that depict the various areas of the province from the north to the south. The whale exhibit features the history of the beluga in Hudson Bay.

June 15 through Labor Day, open 10 A.M. to 8 P.M. The remainder of the year, closed Monday; open 10 A.M. to 5 P.M. Tuesday through Friday, noon to 6 P.M. Saturday, Sunday, and holidays. Admission is $3 (Canadian) for adults, $2 for students, $1.75 for seniors and children 12 and under, and free to children under 3. Group rates are available.

Eastern Canada

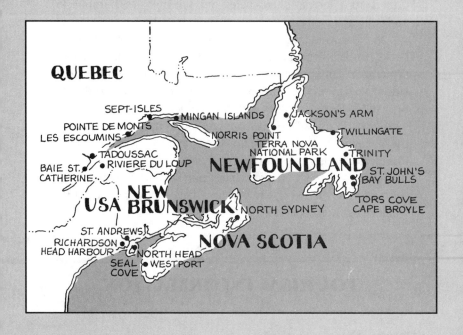

Eastern Canada

Visitors to Western Canada expect to see orcas and gray whales, but whale watchers must travel to the coastal areas of Eastern Canada for a look at blue whales, rare right whales, humpbacks, and belugas.

In Newfoundland, tour operators take people to see humpbacks, finbacks, minkes, and pilot whales from May through September. Those same species, plus right whales and the occasional sperm whale, can be seen off Nova Scotia and New Brunswick from June through September. Blue whales, along with finback, minke, and belugas, are found near the junction of the St. Lawrence Seaway and the Saguenay River, just off Quebec, from June through September.

As in Western Canada, whales may often be sighted from shore or encountered in the wild well beyond the reaches of the whale-watch tour operators.

TOURISM INFORMATION

New Brunswick

Tourism New Brunswick
P.O. Box 12345, Fredericton, New Brunswick, E3B 5C3 Canada
(800) 561–0123

Newfoundland

Tourism Newfoundland
P.O. Box 2016, St. John's, Newfoundland, A1C 5R8 Canada
(800) 563–6353

Nova Scotia

Nova Scotia Tourism
Information Office, 129 Commercial Street, Portland, ME 04101
(800) 341–6096

Quebec

Tourisme Quebec
C.P. 20 000, Quebec City, Quebec, G1K 7X2 Canada
(800) 443–7000

Rivière-du-Loup, Quebec

Linnaean Society

1675 Avenue de Parc, St. Foy, Quebec, G1W 4S3 Canada;
(418) 653–8186

Whales:	Finback, minke, beluga
Season:	Late June to early October
Boats:	One boat, *Samuel de Champlain*; 80 passengers
Trips:	One 5-hour trip on the St. Lawrence River daily at 1:30 P.M.
Fare:	Adults, $35 (Canadian); students 15 to 25, $30; children: 7 to 14, $15; 6 and under, free.
Departure:	Boat leaves from the Yacht Club on rue Mackay in Rivière-du-Loup.
Naturalist:	Naturalist gives commentary in English and French.

Sylvie Brouard of the Linnaean Society says the most important thing to remember is to wear warm clothes. "And I'm talking about winter clothes," she says. "It's really, really cold on the St. Lawrence River."

Tadoussac and Baie St. Catherine, Quebec

Compagnie de la Baie de Tadoussac

145 Bord-de-l'eau, Tadoussac, Quebec, G0T 2A0 Canada;
(418) 235–4548

Whales:	Mostly fin and minke, some blue
Season:	May 1 to October 15 (June is best month)

Boats:	Three rigid-hull inflatable rafts; 10 or 12 passengers each; cruise suits provided.
Trips:	Three trips a day on the St. Lawrence River at 8:30 A.M., 12:30 P.M., and 4:30 P.M. Special trips at 5 A.M.
Fare:	$15 (Canadian) per person for 1¹/₂ hours; $30 for 3 hours. Ten percent discount for groups and students with IDs. No children under 12. Reservations advised.
Departure:	Boats leave from Tadoussac and Baie St. Catherine.
Naturalist:	Naturalist on board

"We use inflatable boats, a smaller boat, closer to the marine environment and with smaller groups aboard. We offer a more intimate experience," says staff member Virginie Chadenet.

Croisières Du Grand Fleuve
1495 Volt, Charlesbourg, Quebec, G2L 1H8 Canada;
(418) 622–2566

Whales:	Fin, beluga, blue, minke, and humpback
Season:	Mid-June to mid-October
Boats:	One boat, *Grand Fleuve*; 250 passengers
Trips:	Three 3-hour trips daily on the St. Lawrence River. Leave from Tadoussac at 8:30 A.M., 12:30 P.M., and 4:30 P.M.; from Baie St. Catherine at 9 A.M., 12:55 P.M., and 4:05 P.M.
Fare:	Adults, $30 (Canadian); children: 6–13, $15; below 6, free. Reservations advised. Charters also available. Hotel package available at La Maison Hovington. Write tour operator for details.
Departure:	Boat leaves from the docks in Tadoussac and Baie St. Catherine.

Where the Whales Are

Naturalist: Scientists from the Research and Educational Group on Marine Environment accompany each trip.

"We have the biggest boat, the most spacious," says office manager Michel Fortin. "We have an orientation in education and interpretation. It's not a tour boat."

Croisières Navimex Inc.
25 Place Marche Champlain, Suite 101, Quebec City, Quebec, G1R 2C8 Canada; (418) 692–4643

Whales:	Beluga, minke, fin, occasionally blue
Season:	June 1 to October 15
Boats:	Two boats; 350 and 300 passengers
Trips:	Three 3-hour trips on the St. Lawrence River daily at 10 A.M., 1:15 P.M., and 4:30 P.M.
Fare:	Adults, $30 (Canadian); children: 5 to 12, $15; under 5, free. Group discounts, charters available. Reservations advised.
Departure:	Trips leave from the village wharves in Tadoussac and Baie St. Catherine.
Naturalist:	Two naturalists on board

"A discovery cruise will allow you to explore a major whale refuge, the mouth of the Saguenay River," says owner Guy Gagnon. "You will be able to observe first-hand several species of whales, such as the beluga, minkes, finbacks, and on occasion five other species.

"Occasionally during August and September, we offer a special six-hour photo-safari cruise allowing you to discover the largest living animal on earth, the spectacular and peaceful blue whale."

Tadoussac, Quebec

Famille DeFour Hotel Tadoussac

165 Bord-de-l'Eau, Tadoussac, Quebec, G0T 2A0 Canada;
(800) 463–5250, (418) 235–4421

Whales:	Beluga, blue
Season:	May 1 to October 31
Boats:	Two boats, one of them the historic 130-foot schooner *Marie-Clarisse*; 145 passengers total
Trips:	Three 3-hour trips on the St. Lawrence River daily at 9 A.M., 1 P.M., and 4 P.M.
Fare:	Adults, $30 (Canadian); children, $15. Group rates available. Reservations required. Packages available at Hotel Tadoussac.
Departure:	Departure from Hotel Tadoussac.
Naturalist:	Naturalist on board

Tadoussac is situated at the confluence of the freshwater Saguenay River and the saltwater St. Lawrence River. For this "whale sightseeing safari," owner Alain DuFour says, "Bring along your cameras and experience the thrill of a fascinating encounter with these giant nomads.

"Every summer, the whales return to the very rich and fertile waters of the St. Lawrence. After having given birth to their young in the waters of warmer climes during the winter, they find here the great quantities of food they must have."

Les Escoumins, Quebec

Base Plein Air Sault-au-Mouton Inc.
81, rue Principale, Sault-au-Mouton, Quebec, G0T 1Z0 Canada;
(418) 231–2214

Whales:	Blue
Season:	April 15 to October 15
Boats:	One motor boat; 10 passengers
Trips:	Two 3-hour trips on the St. Lawrence River scheduled daily according to tides. Passengers are outfitted in full-length isothermic suits.
Fare:	Adults, $25 (Canadian); children 6 to 14, $20. Reservations required. Package including seafood supper, bed, breakfast, and whale watching available at the Base Plein Air Sault-au-Mouton lodge. Week-long packages are available at the hotel.
Departure:	Boat leaves from Petits Escoumins, about 10 miles east of Les Escoumins.
Naturalist:	Yes

Base Plein Air Sault-au-Mouton is a former youth hostel on the St. Lawrence River that has been renovated as a resort for families and groups.

Compagnie de la Baie des Escoumins
100, rue St. Marcellin, Les Escoumins, Quebec, G0T 2A0 Canada;
(418) 233–3151 or 233–2835

Whales:	Mostly fin and minke, some blue
Season:	May 1 to October 15

Boats: Six rigid-hull inflatable rafts; 10 or 12 passengers each; cruise suits provided.

Trips: Three trips on the St. Lawrence River daily at 9 A.M., 1 P.M., and 4 P.M.

Fare: $30 (Canadian) per person for 3 hours. No children under 12. Reservations advised.

Departure: Boats leave from Les Escoumins.

Naturalist: Trips narrated by naturalist, guide, or captain.

The Zodiac boats are equipped with the latest technology and allow for an intimate experience with the whales.

Tan Incorporated

29, rue des Pilotes, Les Escoumins, Quebec, G0T 1K0 Canada; (418) 233–3488

Whales: Blue, beluga, minke

Season: June to October

Boats: An 8-passenger 20-foot Zodiac, a 15-passenger 22-foot hard-bottom inflatable Zeppelin raft, and a 12-passenger 27-foot cruiser

Trips: Nine trips per day, with three options to choose from: a 2½-to-3-hour whale-watch cruise, a 4-hour trip to watch blue whales, and a 1-day whale-watch cruise up the Saguenay Fjord. The 2½-hour trips on Sundays are the most popular.

Fare: Prices vary depending on the boat. For the two shorter trips: adults, $20 to $45 (Canadian); children, $12 to $35. For the day-long trip: adults, $95 (Canadian); children 14 and younger, $85; children 6 or younger, $15. Reservations are advised.

Departure: Trips depart from L'Auberge de la Mer, a resort just west of Les Escoumins, 250 kilometers downriver from Quebec City.

Naturalist: A guide provides commentary on all trips.

"The natural beauty and abundance of the marine life in the St. Lawrence River makes the harbor of Les Escoumins one of the most sought-after sites in North America," a representative from Tan Inc. says. "And we love whales!"

Pointe des Monts, Quebec

Le Gite du Phare de Pointe des Monts

1684 Joliet Boulevard, Baie Comeau, Quebec, G5C 1P8 Canada; (418) 589–8408

Whales: Blue, humpback

Season: June 1 to September 30

Boats: Three boats; 3 to 12 passengers respectively

Trips: Two trips on the St. Lawrence River on weekdays, three trips each Saturday and Sunday; times depend on tides.

Fare: $24 (Canadian) for 4-hour trip, $12 for 2-hour trip. Half price for children. Reservations required. Lodge and chalets available at the same address.

Departure: Boats leave from Pointe des Monts on Trinity Bay.

Naturalist: Guide serves as naturalist.

Owner Jean Louis Frenette says, "For English unilingual customers, Pointe des Monts might be a difficult place to visit. Everything is in French, and the guides on the sea are less bilingual than I am myself.

"In the future, I will try to make a better place for the English tourists because Pointe des Monts is a very splendid place. The sea is rich, pure, and wild. It is very deep next to the shoreline, so you see and hear the whales from your bedroom."

Frenette's lodge is a restored 1830 lighthouse that he rents from the government.

Sept-Iles, Quebec

Canadian Nature Tours

Federation of Ontario Naturalists, 355 Lesmill Road, Don Mills, Ontario, M3B 2W8 Canada; (416) 444-8419

Whales:	Blue, humpback, minke, fin
Season:	Summer
Boats:	Rigid-hull inflatable rafts and sailboats
Trips:	One 9-day trip exploring the Gulf of St. Lawrence with a group of about 10 people. Trip concludes at Sept-Iles.
Fare:	$1,725 (Canadian) per person. Price includes transportation on land and water, meals, and shared-bath rustic accommodation. Reservations required.
Departure:	Trip starts at Sept-Iles, Quebec.
Naturalist:	Biologists from the Mingan Island Cetacean Study

"The deep water of the Gulf of St. Lawrence is one of the few habitats left for the giant blue whale, the friendly humpback whale, as well as minkes and finbacks," notes a spokesman. "This is a chance to join field biologists from the Mingan Island Cetacean Study hoping for close encounters with whales. On bad-weather days we'll explore the rocky coast by van and on foot to investigate waterfalls and interesting plants, beachcomb in the sheltered coves, and watch for puffins, murres, eider ducks, and other seabirds."

Canadian Nature Tours offers trips to many other parts of Canada and the world; several include whale watching among other outdoor activities.

Seafarers Expeditions
P.O. Box 691, Bangor, ME 04401; (207) 942–7942

Whales:	Blue, fin, humpback, minke
Season:	August
Boats:	Twenty-foot rigid-hull inflatable rafts
Trips:	One 8-day trip. Participants live on shore at night.
Fare:	$1,195 (U.S.) per person. Price includes double occupancy, lodging, meals, ground transportation, and guides. Reservations required.
Departure:	Tour begins and ends in Sept-Iles, Quebec.
Naturalist:	Yes

"On this extraordinary expedition, you will have the rare opportunity to observe the grandeur of the largest animals on earth—blue whales—from 20-foot inflatable boats!" says Scott Marion, founder and head naturalist of Seafarers Expeditions.

"Participants have the added bonus of working with the Mingan Island Cetacean Study, helping to support their efforts in understanding the St. Lawrence estuary and its marine inhabitants."

Mingan Islands, Quebec

Mingan Island Cetacean Study

Summer: P.O. Box 159, Sept-Iles, Quebec, G4R 4K3 Canada;
(418) 949–2845
Winter: 285 rue Green, St. Lambert, Quebec, J4P 1T3 Canada;
(514) 465–9176

Whales:	Blue, humpback, fin, minke
Season:	June to October
Boats:	Several 16- to 20-foot rigid-hull inflatable rafts and 40- to 60-foot sailboats
Trips:	Several 7- to 10-day sessions with the Mingan Island Cetacean Study, a nonprofit research group in the Gulf of St. Lawrence. Participants live among and observe the work of research scientists in a coastal village or camp or on a sailboat. Day trips on the St. Lawrence River for 35 to 40 passengers from late June to late October.
Fare:	$120 (U.S.) per person per day for multiday trips. Day trip: adults, $60; students, $45; groups of four or more, $50 a person. Reservations required.
Departure:	Trips depart from Long Point, the gateway to the Mingan Islands, east of Sept-Iles. Representatives of MICS will meet participants who arrive by air at Sept-Iles.
Naturalist:	Naturalists are scientists with the research group.

MICS is said to be the first organization in the world to have carried out long-term studies of the blue whale. Through photo-identification techniques developed by MICS, a catalog of over 200 blue whales now exists for the northwest Atlantic.

Director Richard Sears says, "Our research sessions offer the public the opportunity to get away to the solitude of the sea and immerse themselves in an educational adventure."

The group is expanding its research station to include an interpretive center with illustrations, skeletons, and interactive displays.

Norris Point, Newfoundland

Bontours
Norris Point, Newfoundland, A0K 3V0 Canada; (709) 458–2256

Whales:	Humpback
Season:	June 1 to September 30
Boats:	One motor cruiser; 46 passengers
Trips:	One 2-hour trip daily at 1 P.M.
Fare:	Adults, $20 (Canadian); children 12 or younger, $5. Group rates available. Reservations advised.
Departure:	Boat leaves from the government wharf at Norris Point on Newfoundland's west coast, on the Gulf of St. Lawrence.
Naturalist:	No naturalist on board

Owner Reg Williams says, "Cruise the spectacularly beautiful Bonne Bay. This two-hour cruise along the eastern and western arms of Bonne Bay affords vistas of Gros Morne, Killdevil, the Tablelands, and the Long Range Mountains. We pass over the deepest water in the area—756 feet deep—which gives opportunity for cod jigging and mackerel fishing. Photographic opportunities abound."

Jackson's Arm, Newfoundland

Pelley Inn

P.O. Box 428, Springdale, Newfoundland, A0J 1T0 Canada;
(709) 673-3931

Whales:	Humpback, pilot
Season:	May 1 to September 30
Boats:	One; 6 to 10 passengers
Trips:	Whale watching included in week-long visit that starts at Pelley Inn in Springdale and moves to Little Harbour Deep Wilderness Lodge on White Bay. On shorter visits, whales may be seen during the 2-hour cruise to the lodge.
Fare:	$250 (Canadian) a day for single accommodations, $450 a day for double. $1,575 for single for 7 days, 6 nights; $2,975 for double. Reservations required.
Departure:	Boat leaves from Jackson's Arm, a 1-hour drive from Springdale.
Naturalist:	Naturalist available upon request

Cyril R. Pelley says, "We own and operate the Pelley Inn, a twenty-two-room inn at Springdale, on the northeast coast of our island province. Our customers usually drive or fly via Deer Lake or Gander airport, where they are picked up by our limousine service and returned to the inn. However, our emphasis is on our new wilderness lodge in the great White Bay, just north of Springdale.
"A one-hour drive and a two-hour cruise get visitors to the lodge, where they may hike, fish, relax, or go on whale-watching or bird-watching excursions," Pelley says.

Twillingate, Newfoundland

Twillingate Island Boat Tours Ltd.

P.O. Box 127, Twillingate, Newfoundland, A0G 4M0 Canada;
(709) 884–2317

Whales:	Humpback, fin, pilot, minke
Season:	Late May to late September
Boats:	One boat; up to 10 passengers
Trips:	Two 1½-hour trips a day at 9:30 A.M. and 2 P.M. into Notre Dame Bay, on the "iceberg alley" route.
Fare:	Adults, $25 (Canadian); children, $15. Reservations advised.
Departure:	Boat leaves from Twillingate dock.
Naturalist:	No naturalist on board

Owner Cecil G. Stockley says, "Whales swim around this island all year round on their migratory routes. Any place on this 15-mile-diameter island, whales can be seen a stone's throw away from the island's shore."

He adds that icebergs in all sizes and shapes—from peaked to pancake flat—usually appear in May, having taken two to three years to travel from Greenland, where the great ice packs break up and unleash their frozen landscape piece by piece into the southbound Labrador Current.

"As they pass by, the icebergs growl, rumble, and crackle like thunder. Sometimes they split in half or roll over. But mostly they just sail off into the sun to meet their fate—a final meltdown in the warmer waters off the Grand Banks."

Terra Nova National Park, Newfoundland

Ocean Watch Tours
Squid Tickle, Burnside, Newfoundland, A0G 1K0 Canada; (709) 677–2327

Whales:	Humpback, minke
Season:	Late June to Labor Day
Boats:	One boat, the *Northern Fulmar*; 25 passengers
Trips:	One 3-hour trip daily at 9 A.M. in Bonavista Bay on the northeast coast. Weekdays are busiest.
Fare:	Adults, $25 (Canadian); children, $12.50. Reservations advised.
Departure:	Boat leaves from Headquarters Wharf in Terra Nova National Park.
Naturalist:	Yes

"Terra Nova National Park is Canada's most easterly national park," notes Fraser Carpenter of Ocean Watch. "The waters are fed by the rich Labrador Current, which brings an annual explosion of life to the fjords and bay of the park.

"Because the coastline is deeply cut by fjords, whale watching is done in comfort in all kinds of weather, often only 100 meters from shore!"

In addition to the morning wildlife expedition, Ocean Watch offers two fjord cruises and a sunset cruise, and whales are occasionally viewed on both.

Trinity, Newfoundland

Ocean Contact Ltd.

P.O. Box 10, Trinity, Newfoundland, A0C 2S0 Canada;
(709) 464–3269

Whales:	Humpback, fin, minke, pilot
Season:	May to October
Boats:	Eight boats; 6 to 30 passengers each; cruise suits provided for passengers in rigid-hull inflatable rafts.
Trips:	Half-day or whole-day excursions and multiday expeditions offered.
Fare:	For excursions, rates start at $35 (Canadian) for adults, $24 for youths 13 to 15, $18 for children 4 to 12. Meal included. Multiday expedition rates start (for 3 days) at $465, $339, and $254, respectively by age. Reservations required. Hotel packages are available at the Village Inn. Write for details.
Departure:	Boats leave from Trinity, on Trinity Bay on the east coast.
Naturalist:	Naturalist on board

Dr. Peter Beamish of Ocean Contact says, "Whale watching is free in Newfoundland! You can sit on a cliff near Trinity all day and watch whales. We, on the other hand, guide people into our spectacular marine environment so that the whales can watch them!"

Beamish, who has decades of experience at this, offers passengers the opportunity to make contact with whales by means of a computer-driven acoustic signal. "The ensuing communications," he says, "may involve full breaches, tail or flipper slaps, exhalations, etc., and these are then easily predictable in time, allowing for spectacular photographs."

St. John's, Tors Cove, and Cape Broyle, Newfoundland

Eastern Edge Outfitters Ltd.

P.O. Box 13981, Station A, St. John's, Newfoundland, A2B 4G8 Canada; (709) 368–9720

Whales:	Humpback, minke, pilot, and the possibility of twenty other species
Season:	June 2 to September 30
Boats:	Eleven sea kayaks
Trips:	One-day trips on weekdays during June and July, 9 A.M. to 5 P.M. Four- and 10-day trips kayaking and camping along the coast of Newfoundland and Labrador.
Fare:	One day, $95 (Canadian), lunch included. Four days, $440; 10 days, $1,400. Reservations required.
Departure:	Departures from St. John's, Tors Cove, or Cape Broyle, depending on trip.
Naturalist:	Guides serve as naturalists.

"We are the only company in Newfoundland offering bird- and whale-watching tours by sea kayak," says co-owner Jim Price. "On all our tours we give initial instruction so guests will be able to paddle their kayaks on their own. We will paddle alongside whales and near towering icebergs and will view thundering waterfalls crashing into the sea. All this while learning the skills of ocean kayak travel and breathing the clear zesty ocean air."

St. John's, Newfoundland

Harbor Charters

P.O. Box 5395, St. John's, Newfoundland, A1C 5W2 Canada;
(709) 754–1672

Whales:	Humpback, fin
Season:	May 1 to October 1
Boats:	One Grand Bank schooner and one longliner; 75 and 25 passengers respectively
Trips:	Four 2-hour trips daily at 10 A.M., noon, 2 P.M., and 7 P.M. The busiest day is Saturday.
Fare:	Adults, $25 (Canadian); seniors and children under 12, $15. Reservations advised. Several local hotels offer packages; write for information.
Departure:	Departure from Pier No. 7 in St. John's downtown harbor.
Naturalist:	No

Owner Charles Anonsen says that in addition to whale watching, his tours offer "listening to Newfoundland traditional music; meeting Bosun, our Newfoundland dog; sailing around North America's most easterly point; and enjoying the hospitality of the people from one of the oldest cities in North America, St. John's."

Wildland Tours

P.O. Box 383, Station C, St. John's, Newfoundland, A1C 5J9 Canada; (709) 722–3335

Whales:	Humpback, minke, fin
Season:	Early May to mid-August

Boats:	Four boats; about 25 passengers each
Trips:	Tours of 3, 5, and 7 days to watch whales and view other wildlife in Newfoundland. August is busiest month.
Fare:	Prices depend on package but start at $100 (Canadian). Reservations required. Hotel packages offered with Battery Motel in St. John's. Write for details.
Departure:	All tours start in St. John's.
Naturalist:	Biologist accompanies each trip.

David Snow, president, says, "Whales are a very special part of our product, but we do not ignore North America's largest puffin colony, the world's largest murre colonies, the world's largest storm petrel colonies, and huge collections of seabirds—numbering in the millions—visiting from the Arctic and Antarctic."

His company offers "probably the best marine wildlife–watching opportunities in the world, combined with small group travel. We are Canada's best-kept secret," Snow says.

Cape Broyle, Newfoundland

Great Island Tours
P.O. Box 21, Cape Broyle, Newfoundland, A0A 1P0 Canada; (800) 563–2355, (709) 432–2355

Whales:	Humpback, minke, fin, sperm
Season:	May 15 to October 31
Boats:	One boat, the *Historic Venture*; 18 passengers
Trips:	Three 3-hour trips daily at 10 A.M., 2 P.M., and 6 P.M. Weekends are busiest.

Fare:	Adults, $20 (Canadian); children: ages 6 to 14, $10; 5 and under, $5. Reservations advised.
Departure:	Boat leaves from Cape Broyle Harbor. From St. John's, take scenic Route 10.
Naturalist:	Yes

"We offer unique outdoor, scenic, life-style, and cultural experiences of historic Newfoundland," says owner Sylvester Hawkins.

The tour to Great Island, which has the largest Atlantic puffin colony in North American, is a must for birdwatchers as well as whale watchers, he says. The tour of Cape Broyle harbor offers passengers beautiful scenery as well as the opportunity to try their luck at jigging a cod, sculpin, squid, or flounder.

Bay Bulls, Newfoundland

Bird Island Charters
Bay Bulls, Newfoundland, A0A 1C0 Canada; (709) 753–4850

Whales:	Humpback, minke, fin
Season:	May through September
Boats:	Three boats; 8, 12, and 50 passengers respectively
Trips:	Three or four 2¹/₂-hour trips daily at 10 A.M., 2 P.M., 5 P.M., 7:30 P.M.
Fare:	Adults, $22 (Canadian); children: 15 or younger, $11; under 5, free. Reservations advised. If booked with Bird Island Charters, guests receive 10 percent discount at the Radisson Plaza Hotel in St. John's. Write or call the tour operator for more information.

Departure: Boats leave from Bay Bulls, south of St. John's. There are lots of signs on the lower road.

Naturalist: Naturalist on board

"We are working on photographing whales that come to our area," says Captain Loyola O'Brien, president. Researchers identify the flukes of individual whales "so that we can put names on [those] that travel along the coast."

On board, the captain will sing for you and dance with you as part of the entire cultural experience.

Gatherall's Sanctuary Boat Charters
Bay Bulls, Newfoundland, A0A 1C0 Canada; (709) 334–2887

Whales: Humpback, minke

Season: June and July

Boats: One boat; 50 passengers

Trips: At least three 2-hour trips in Witless Bay daily at 10 A.M., 2:30 P.M., and 5 P.M. Additional trips scheduled according to demand.

Fare: Adults, $20 (Canadian); children: 14 and under, $15; children 5 and younger, $5. Reservations advised.

Departure: Departure from North Side Road in Bay Bulls, south of St. John's.

Naturalist: Guide serves as naturalist.

"This is a guided boat tour—the guide is a well-qualified 'amateur' naturalist," says owner Rosemary Gatherall.

"Gatherall's has been singled out for its whale watching and sensitivity to the marine environment and its wildlife," she notes.

The Canadian government has named the Gatherall family "Canadian Tourism Ambassadors" for "outstanding hospitality to international visitors."

St. Andrews, Richardson, and Head Harbour, New Brunswick

Cline Marine

Leonardville, Deer Island, New Brunswick, E0G 2G0 Canada;
(506) 529–4188

Whales:	Fin, minke, humpback, right
Season:	June to Labor Day
Boats:	One boat; 60 passengers
Trips:	Open water and sheltered water tours in the Bay of Fundy twice daily. Departure times vary according to point of departure. Trips last 3 to 11 hours. Sunday is the busiest day.
Fare:	Fares range from $18 (Canadian) for adults, $15 for senior citizens, $12 for children ages 12 to 17, and $9 for children under 12 for a 3-hour trip to $66, $55, $44, and $33, respectively, for 11 hours. Reservations advised.
Departure:	Boat picks up at the St. Andrews town wharf, the Deer Island Wharf at Richardson, and Campobello Wharf at Head Harbour.
Naturalist:	No naturalist on board

Says Captain R. Conrad Cline, "We are quite easygoing, and I don't think we offer much of a 'slick' approach. We try to be happy, sincere, and responsible so you can really feel that you have had a whale of a time."

A 1^1/$_2$- to 2-hour sunset cruise is available for "young romantics and the young in heart." Captain Cline advises, "Please allow little children to stay with a baby-sitter at home!"

North Head, New Brunswick

Ocean Search Ltd.

P.O. Box 129, North Head, Grand Manan Island,
New Brunswick, E0G 2M0 Canada; (506) 662–8144

Whales:	North Atlantic right, fin, humpback
Season:	Mid-July to mid-September
Boats:	One schooner, *D'Sonoqua*; 20 passengers
Trips:	One 6^1/$_2$-hour trip daily at 9:30 A.M.
Fare:	Adults, $69; children under 12 accompanied by a parent, $25. Lunch, evening lecture included. Group rates offered. Reservations required. Guests at the Marathon Inn in Grand Manan receive a discount.
Departure:	Boat leaves from North Head Wharf on Grand Manan Island, close to the ferry terminal.
Naturalist:	Naturalist on board is marine biologist.

"Ocean Search tours offer more than a search," owner James Leslie says. "They offer an exciting sailing adventure aboard a traditionally rigged oceangoing schooner, expertly manned and equipped for your safety and comfort.

"Grand Manan is a special place—an island set aside in time and beauty. The magic of an island, the romance of sailing, and the thrill of marine life are all part of your holiday."

Seal Cove, New Brunswick

Sea Watch Tours

Seal Cove, Grand Manan Island, New Brunswick, E0G 3B0
Canada; (506) 662–8296

Whales:	Minke, fin, humpback, right
Season:	August 1 to September 30
Boats:	One boat, *Sea Watcher*; 30 passengers
Trips:	At least one 6- to 7-hour trip leaves by 9 A.M. daily, Monday through Saturday. Bring your own lunch. Shorter evening trip added if demand justifies.
Fare:	$40 (Canadian) per person. Reservations required.
Departure:	Boat leaves from Fishermens Wharf in Seal Cove on Grand Manan Island. Upon arriving in Seal Cove, turn down the road across from the two churches. Follow this road as it takes a sharp right, over to the last pier.
Naturalist:	Naturalist on board

Peter Wilcox, son of owner Preston Wilcox, says, "There are very few North Atlantic right whales left, perhaps as few as 250. The Grand Manan Basin has become one of the most concentrated areas of right whales during the months of August and September, perhaps with 50 or 60 different animals.

"Their location is so predictable that it is almost certain that we will see them. In seven years of whale watching, we have had only one day that we have not seen a whale."

Sea Watch Tours offers a seven-day package tour the third week of September, with three days on land and four on a boat. Write for more information.

North Sydney, Nova Scotia

Seafarers Expeditions
P.O. Box 691, Bangor, ME 04401; (207) 942–7942

Whales:	Humpback, fin, minke, pilot
Season:	July
Boats:	Different boats at different locations
Trips:	One 12-day trip to various parts of Newfoundland in July, with land and sea expeditions. Participants stay overnight in lodges. Trip concludes in North Sydney, Nova Scotia.
Fare:	$1,575 (U.S.) per person. Price includes double occupancy lodging, meals, ground transportation, and guides. Does not include airfare.
Departure:	Trip leaves from North Sydney, Nova Scotia.
Naturalist:	Yes

"A unique mix of abundant marine life, spectacular land forms, and local culture make Newfoundland a place of limitless wonder," says Seafarers Expeditions founder Scott Marion. "The Avalon Peninsula will astound even the most experienced birders. Here you can observe thousands of northern gannets, murres, and kittiwakes as well as the largest puffin colony on the east coast of North America.

"Gros Morne National Park, described as the `Banff of the East,' is a region of unsurpassed beauty. One of the most memorable aspects of our tour will be the warm welcome of the local people of Newfoundland."

Seafarers Expeditions was founded in 1981.

Westport, Nova Scotia

Brier Island Whale and Seabird Cruises, Ltd.

Westport, Brier Island, Nova Scotia, B0V 1H0 Canada;
(902) 839–2995

Whales:	Humpback, fin, minke, pilot, North Atlantic right
Season:	June to October
Boats:	One 45-foot boat, *Cetacean Venture;* up to 50 passengers
Trips:	Two 4-hour trips a day at 8:30 A.M. and 1:30 P.M. Sunset trips sometimes available. Weekends are busiest.
Fare:	$30 (Canadian) per person. Charter, group, and family rates available. Reservations required.
Departure:	Departure from Westport, on Brier Island, at the southwestern end of Nova Scotia.
Naturalist:	Field researcher or scientist from the Brier Island Ocean Study accompanies each trip.

Carl Haycock and Harold Graham, co-owners/operators, say their whale-watching trips are unusual in that the whales are normally close to the island and the four-hour trips are especially convenient.

"Brier Island is located at the southwestern tip of Nova Scotia. Highly saline marine water flows into the Bay of Fundy along the Nova Scotia coast, bringing large numbers of zooplankton. Plankton and fish productivity is enhanced by the nutrients brought to the surface by the strong tidal currents, which average 25 feet or more. Local tide rips and eddies concentrate plankton; these, in turn, attract large schools of herring and mackerel which the whales, dolphins, and seabirds feed on."

Museums, Aquariums, and Science Centers

Quebec

The Interpretative Center of Mileau Marin
102 rue de la Cale-seche, Tadoussac, Quebec, G0T 2A0 Canada;
(418) 235–4646

Using exhibits, an aquarium, marine mammal skeletons, posters, videos, and slide shows, the center teaches about whales and their marine environment. A movie features the endangered beluga whales of the St. Lawrence River. The center is associated with the Group of Research and Education on the Marine Environment, a nonprofit organization dedicated to preserving the marine environment and educating the public.

The center is situated near the marina in Tadoussac. Hours are 10 A.M. to 6 P.M. from late June through mid-October. Admission is $2 (Canadian) for adults, 50 cents per child, and $1 per group member.

Nova Scotia

Nova Scotia Museum
1747 Summer Street, Halifax, Nova Scotia, B3H 3A6 Canada;
(902) 429–4610 or 424–6099 (recording)

An Aquatic Environments gallery features freshwater and salt-water exhibits with specimens or models of Nova Scotia seaweeds, invertebrates, amphibians, reptiles, fish, and mammals. Among these are the skeleton of a pilot whale and life-sized models of sharks and a 48-foot sei whale.

May 15 to October 31, the museum is open 9:30 A.M. to 5:30 P.M. daily except Wednesday, when it is open 9:30 A.M. to 8 P.M., and Sunday, when the hours are 1 P.M. to 5:30 P.M. November 1 to May 14, the museum is closed on Monday and closes at 5 P.M. Sunday, Tuesday, Thursday, Friday, and Saturday. Admission is free.

Newfoundland

Ocean Sciences Centre
Memorial University of Newfoundland, St. John's, Newfoundland, A1C 5S7 Canada; (709) 726–4888

Situated in a building designed to resemble the internal anatomy of a sea anemone, the center is a research unit of the Science Faculty of Memorial University. The focus of study is cold oceans. Guides offer hour-long tours of the research facility. Among the sights are working laboratories, special exhibits, videos, a seal tank, aquariums, and a display of diving gear. The Discovery Room has a "touch tank" filled with sea creatures.

Tours are available every half hour from 10 A.M. to 5 P.M., seven days a week from early June to early September. Admission is $2 (Canadian) for adults, $1 for children, and free to seniors, school groups, and children under 6.

Mexico

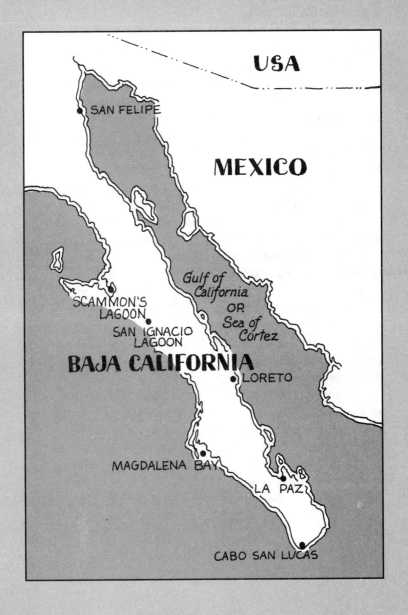

USA

SAN FELIPE

MEXICO

SCAMMON'S
LAGOON

Gulf of
California
OR
Sea of
Cortez

SAN IGNACIO
LAGOON

BAJA CALIFORNIA

LORETO

MAGDALENA BAY

LA PAZ

CABO SAN LUCAS

Mexico

Those photographs that you've seen of exhilarated whale watchers leaning out of tiny boats to pet gray whales were taken in the lagoons off Baja California, in Mexico. Every year the grays migrate south from the Bering and Chukchi seas, supporting a flourishing whale-watch industry along the entire Pacific Coast of the United States. Once in the calm, warm waters of Mexico, the whales mate and give birth, and people watch.

Aluminum skiffs, Zodiac rafts, and sea kayaks now dot Scammon's Lagoon, San Ignacio Lagoon, and Magdalena Bay in February, March, and part of April. On the other side of the peninsula, in the Sea of Cortez, boats go forth in March and April to see blue, humpback, fin, and pilot whales.

As it's unlikely that anyone would go to Baja California by chance—it's difficult to reach, though well worth the trouble. Most whale-watch trips to the area are a week long. Among the groups sponsoring the trips are commercial tour operators; research organizations and scientific institutions, most of which travel by boat; and adventure outfitters, who offer kayaking and camping.

The sponsoring organizations are primarily based in the United States and Canada. Therefore, **the listings in this chapter are organized by destination rather than by departure point.** Separate index listings are given for destinations and departure points.

Should you find yourself in Baja under other circumstances, you will be able to find a fisherman who will happily take you out in a boat for the afternoon to see the whales. Agree on a price in advance, but by all means go.

Scammon's Lagoon, Mexico

Pacific Sea Fari Tours
2803 Emerson Street, San Diego, CA 92106; (619) 226–8224

Whales:	Gray
Season:	Late December to mid-January
Boats:	Two boats. The 88-foot *Spirit of Adventure* holds 30 passengers in 14 cabins; the 80-foot *Deluxe* carries 20 passengers in 8 cabins. Participants live aboard the boats. Whale watching from skiffs.
Trips:	One 7-day and one 8-day trip; stops at San Benito Islands, Cedros Island, Todos Santos Island, and Ensenada. Trip concludes in San Diego.
Fare:	$995 to $1,175 per person. Price includes meals and snacks, accommodations, related equipment, and services of a naturalist staff. Tips aboard, airfare, and transfers not included.
Departure:	Trips leave from San Diego, California.
Naturalist:	All trips accompanied by naturalists

These trips focus on Scammon's Lagoon, but no two trips are alike. Pacific Sea Fari Tours' natural history program has been developed under the leadership of Dr. Theodore J. Walker, a noted author, lecturer, and researcher. Considered one of the world's foremost experts on gray whales, Dr. Walker wrote *Whale Primer*, the first authoritative work of its kind, and founded the whale observatory at the Cabrillo National Monument. Dr. Walker accompanies about one-third of the trips himself.

San Ignacio Lagoon, Mexico

American Cetacean Society Expeditions
P.O. Box 2639, San Pedro, CA 90731; (213) 548–6279

Whales:	Gray
Season:	February
Boats:	The 95-foot sportfishing vessel *Searcher*; 16 cabins accommodate up to 31 passengers. Participants live aboard. Whale watching from small skiffs.
Trips:	Two trips, one 8-day trip in mid-February and a 9-day trip in late February. Both trips focus on San Ignacio Lagoon with stops at Scammon's Lagoon, San Martin Island, San Benito Islands, Cedros Island, and Todos Santos Island. Trips conclude in San Diego.
Fare:	For ACS members: the 8-day trip, $1,150; the 9-day trip, $1,275; add 10 percent for nonmembers. Fares do not include tips, personal items, or alcohol.
Departure:	Trips leave from San Diego, California.
Naturalist:	Naturalists from American Cetacean Society accompany all trips.

The American Cetacean Society has conducted specialized trips for small groups to see whales since 1973. "Our trips take place in some of the great wilderness areas and are led by experienced naturalists. All our trips are really spectacular!" says a spokeswoman.

"San Ignacio Lagoon is the home of the friendly gray whales; you will enjoy close-encounter whale watching from small skiffs."

Baja Discovery

P.O. Box 152527, San Diego, CA 92115; (800) 829–BAJA,
(619) 262–0700

Whales:	Gray
Season:	Late January through mid-March
Boats:	Fiberglass 22-foot Mexican fishing boats for viewing whales; participants camp in tents, except for two nights in a hotel.
Trips:	Custom 4-day trips with a drive-yourself option or 6- and 7-day trips that include airfare to San Ignacio Lagoon. Trips restricted to 7 to 14 participants.
Fare:	$535 per person for custom 4-day land package; $1,285 for 6-day trip; $1,385 for 7-day trip (based on double occupancy). Call for detailed fees on custom trips. Rates for the 6- and 7-day discovery trips include round-trip airfare via private charter flight between San Diego and San Ignacio, all ground transportation and boat excursions, camp and hotel accommodations, and all meals at camp.
Departure:	All trips leave from Brown Field Municipal Airport in San Diego. Transportation to the airport is provided.
Naturalist:	Knowledgeable hosts and guides for all programs

"The Baja Discovery adventure focuses on one of the most spectacular wildlife phenomena in the world . . . the annual gathering of thousands of gray whales in the shallow, warm waters of the Baja lagoons," says owner Karen Ivey. "Our land-based shore camp, on an inner lagoon island about 600 miles from San Diego, lies adjacent to the largest concentration of whales in Laguna San Ignacio."

Manager and professional photographer Gene Warneke stays in camp with participants to assist or instruct in photography.

Biological Journeys
1696 Ocean Drive, McKinleyville, CA 95521; (800) 548–7555, (707) 839–0178

Whales:	Gray
Season:	Late January through mid-March
Boats:	The 105-foot sportfishing vessel *Searcher*; up to 30 passengers in 15 cabins. Participants live aboard throughout the trip. Whale watching from aluminum skiffs.
Trips:	Four 9-day trips to San Ignacio Lagoon, with stops at Todos Santos Island, San Benito Islands, Cedros Island, and San Martin Island. Trips conclude in San Diego.
Fare:	$1,549 per person. Price includes instructions, accommodations, meals and transportation while aboard the vessels, and a Mexican fishing license. Rate does not include transportation to San Diego, airport departure taxes, meals or lodging en route, or alcoholic beverages or tips. Travel arrangements can be made through the trip operator's agent, Eureka Travel Agency.
Departure:	Trips leave from San Diego, California.
Naturalist:	Naturalist accompanies all trips.

Biological Journeys has visited San Ignacio Lagoon and its gray whales every winter since 1970. Ronn Storro-Patterson, a leading authority on whales, and Ron LeValley, an ornithological expert, head up Biological Journeys, which sponsors these natural history trips to Baja California. "Commitment, commitment, commitment to quality and service" is the hallmark of the organization, says Storro-Patterson.

Oceanic Society Expeditions

Fort Mason Center, Building E, San Francisco, CA 94123;
(415) 441–1106

Whales:	Gray
Season:	Mid-February to late March
Boats:	One of three boats: The 86-foot *Spirit of Adventure* has 14 cabins and accommodates 32 passengers and staff; the 80-foot *Deluxe* has 9 cabins and carries 22 passengers and staff; the 105-foot *Qualifier* has 15 cabins and carries 36 passengers and staff. Participants live aboard. Whale watching from small skiffs.
Trips:	Four 8-day trips to San Ignacio Lagoon, with stops at San Benito Islands, Cedros Island, and Todos Santos Island. Trips conclude in San Diego.
Fare:	$1,250 per person. Price does not include airfare or airport transfers.
Departure:	Trips leave from San Diego, California.
Naturalist:	Two naturalists from the Oceanic Society accompany each trip.

The Oceanic Society is a national nonprofit environmental organization and has conducted nature study trips since 1973. "On this expedition, we will see some of the hundreds of whales that frequent this lagoon," a spokesman said. Trips include slide shows and informal lectures each evening and a choice of optional activities each day.

Pacific Queen/Biological Adventures

Fisherman's Landing, 2838 Garrison, San Diego, CA 92106;
(619) 222–0391

Whales:	Gray, blue, fin, minke, orca, humpback
Season:	December through May

Where the Whales Are

Boats: The 88-foot sportfishing vessel *Pacific Queen*; double, quadruple, and eight-person compartments; participation limited to 30. Participants live aboard.

Trips: Six 9-day trips to San Ignacio Lagoon. Itineraries vary slightly, but most trips include stops at West San Benito Islands, Cedros Island, San Martin Island, and Todos Santos Island. Some trips include Scammon's Lagoon. Trips conclude in San Diego.

Fare: $1,090 per person. Price includes food and lodging and full participation in natural history programs on board each evening.

Departure: Trips leave from San Diego, California.

Naturalist: A staff of biologists accompanies each trip.

Captain Ed McEwen, owner of the *Pacific Queen*, leads each cruise, accompanied by a crew of six and a staff of biologists who are experts in the biology and oceanography of Baja California. Expedition biologist and director Margie Stinson has made more than one hundred such trips, leading expeditions since the late 1960s. "Our philosophy is that each guest is treated as you would wish your parents to be treated by strangers," Margie Stinson notes. "Consequently, friendships are lifelong."

Pacific Sea Fari Tours
2803 Emerson Street, San Diego, CA 92106; (619) 226–8224

Whales: Gray

Season: Late January to late March

Boats: Two boats. The 88-foot *Spirit of Adventure* holds 30 passengers in 14 cabins; the 80-foot *Deluxe* carries 20 passengers in 8 cabins. Participants live aboard the boats. Whale watching from skiffs.

Trips:	Seven, 8- and 9-day trips to San Ignacio Lagoon, with stops at San Martin Island, San Benito Islands, Cedros Island, Todos Santos Island, and Ensenada. Trip concludes in San Diego.
Fare:	$1,175 to $1,335 per person. Price includes meals and snacks, accommodations, related equipment, and services of a naturalist staff. Tips aboard, airfare, and transfers not included.
Departure:	Trips leave from San Diego, California.
Naturalist:	All trips accompanied by naturalists

Pacific Sea Fari Tours' natural history program has been developed under the leadership of Dr. Theodore J. Walker, a noted author, lecturer, and researcher. Considered one of the world's foremost experts on gray whales, Dr. Walker wrote *Whale Primer*, the first authoritative work of its kind, and founded the whale observatory at the Cabrillo National Monument. Dr. Walker accompanies about one-third of the trips himself.

The San Ignacio trips are the most popular and sell out quickly. No two trips are exactly alike.

Smithsonian Associates Travel Program
Smithsonian Institution, Department 0049, Washington, D.C. 20073; (202) 357–4700

Whales:	Gray, several species of dolphin
Season:	Late February
Boats:	The 118-foot sportfishing vessel *Royal Polaris*; double and triple cabins, with room for a total of 35 passengers. Participants live aboard. Whale watching from small skiffs.

Where the Whales Are

Trips: One 8-day trip in late February, with three days at San Ignacio Lagoon and stops at Todos Santos Island, the San Benito Islands, Cedros Island, and San Martin Island. Trips conclude in San Diego.

Fare: $1,650 per person; does not include airfare to San Diego or tips.

Departure: Trips leave from San Diego, California.

Naturalist: Experienced naturalists affiliated with the Smithsonian Associates Travel Program accompany the trip.

The Smithsonian Institution sponsors numerous study tours. The Baja Whale Watch promises "spectacular sunsets, brilliant constellations, and the sights and sounds of porpoises, dolphins, and whales."

Thompson Voyages
P.O. Box 217, Laguna Beach, CA 92652; (714) 497–1055

Whales: Gray

Season: February and March

Boats: The 92-foot *Royal Star;* 12 staterooms accommodate 22 guests. Participants live on the boat. Whale watching from small skiffs.

Trips: Two 9-day trips to San Ignacio Lagoon, with stops at San Benito Islands, Cedros Island, and at least one more. Three days spent exploring San Ignacio Lagoon. Trips conclude in San Diego.

Fare: $1,595 per person. Price includes lodging, meals, equipment, and instruction. Airfare to and from San Diego not included.

Departure: Trips leave from Fisherman's Landing in San Diego, California.

Naturalist: Naturalists accompany both trips.

"Join us for an unforgettable adventure in Baja," says owner and marine wildlife expert Doug Thompson. "You'll bring back tales of whales and dolphins, sunsets and gentle sea breezes, in a land untouched by time." Thompson has been conducting trips to Baja since the 1960s. Informal talks and video shows are held on board each evening.

(Note: Thompson plans to offer Sea of Cortez trips in 1991. Write for information.)

Magdalena Bay, Mexico

Baja Expeditions
2625 Garnet Avenue, San Diego, CA 92109; (619) 581–3311

Whales:	Gray
Season:	January and February
Boats:	One of two boats: The 80-foot *Don Jose* accommodates 20 passengers in 5 staterooms; the 120-foot *Baja Explorador* has 11 staterooms for 20 passengers. Participants live aboard on all trips, except for the last night, which is spent in a hotel. Whale watching from small skiffs.
Trips:	Four 8-day trips to Magdalena Bay, offered from the end of January to the end of February. Restricted to 20 passengers. Trips conclude in La Paz.
Fare:	$1,245 per person. Price includes land arrangements, accommodations, meals, beverages, hotels scheduled in itinerary, fishing permits, and most related trip equipment. Airfare, gratuities, and airport taxes are not included. Air reservations can be made through trip operator.

Where the Whales Are

Departure:	Trips leave from La Paz, with bus transportation to the boat.
Naturalist:	Naturalist accompanies all trips.

"Magdalena Bay is formed by a long, low barrier island barely half a mile wide but 40 miles long," notes a spokesman for Baja Expeditions. "The Pacific shore is wild and windswept, the remains of boats and whales, large and small, can be found buried in the beach or half covered by a dune. On the eastern shore, mangrove-lined estuaries are the winter home of thousands of migratory birds."

Baja Expeditions made its first trip in 1974, in a rented fishing boat with a well-thumbed copy of John Steinbeck's *Log from the Sea of Cortez* aboard. Tim Means, founder, notes that today the company is the largest and oldest outfitter of natural history and adventure travel in Mexico. Kent Madin is Means's partner and general manager.

(Note: For information on Baja Expeditions' kayaking trips, see next listing.)

Baja Expeditions
2625 Garnet Avenue, San Diego, CA 92109; (619) 581–3311

Whales:	Gray
Season:	January through March
Boats:	Sea kayaks. Participants camp, except for the first and last nights, which are spent in a hotel. Skiffs carry the camping supplies throughout the trip.
Trips:	Weekly departures for 9-day trips to Magdalena Bay. Novice paddlers welcome. Trips conclude in La Paz.
Fare:	$799 per person. Price includes land arrangements, accommodations, meals, beverages, hotels scheduled in itinerary, fishing permits, and all specialized equipment, including tents, kayaking gear, cookware, and utensils. Snorkeling gear, wetsuits, and sleeping bags

may be rented. Airfare, gratuities, and airport taxes are not included. Air reservations can be made through trip operator.

Departure:	Trips leave from La Paz, with bus transportation to Magdalena Bay.
Naturalist:	Naturalist accompanies all trips.

"Kayaks allow us to observe at close quarters the fascinating behaviors of the gray whale as we move from camp to camp," says a spokesman at Baja Expeditions. Skiffs are used to carry camping equipment and, if tide or weather dictates their use, to view whales.

Biological Journeys

1696 Ocean Drive, McKinleyville, CA 95521; (800) 548–7555, (707) 839–0178

Whales:	Gray
Season:	Mid-February
Boats:	The 80-foot *Don Jose*; 5 staterooms, each accommodating 4 passengers. Participants live aboard, except for the last night, which is spent in a hotel. Whale watching from aluminum skiffs.
Trips:	One 8-day trip in Magdalena Bay, restricted to 20 participants. Trips conclude in La Paz.
Fare:	$1,549 per person. Price includes instructions, accommodations, meals and transportation while aboard the vessels, and a Mexican fishing license. Rate does not include transportation to La Paz, airport departure taxes, meals or lodging en route, alcoholic beverages, or tips. Travel arrangements can be made through the trip operator's agent, Eureka Travel Agency.
Departure:	Trip leaves from La Paz. Bus transportation provided to the boat.

Where the Whales Are

Naturalist: Naturalist accompanies all trips.

"This is a cruise to fulfill any whale lover's dreams—all the beauty and bliss of Baja's warm-water lagoons complemented by the wonders of the gray whale. A perfect trip for whale lovers who are not enamored of the rolling ocean!" says Biological Journeys.

Ronn Storro-Patterson, a leading authority on whales, and Ron LeValley, an ornithological expert, head up Biological Journeys, which has sponsored natural history trips to Baja California since 1970. "Commitment, commitment, commitment to quality and service" is the hallmark of the organization, says Storro-Patterson.

Ecosummer Expeditions

1516 Duranleau Street, Vancouver, British Columbia, V6H 3S4 Canada; (604) 669–7741

Whales: Gray, blue

Season: Mid-January through mid-March

Boats: Sea kayaks. Participants camp during trip, except for the last two nights, which are spent in a hotel. Group limited to 10 participants; beginners welcome.

Trips: Four 14-day trips that begin in the Sea of Cortez and conclude with 4 days in the lagoons of Magdalena Bay. Trips include visits to Mulege and to Loreto, where trips conclude.

Fare: $1,175 (Canadian). Price includes guide and assistant guide, all group equipment (kayaks, paddles, tents, etc.), all ground transportation, and all meals from lunch on day 2 to supper on day 14. Fare does not include transportation to Loreto or back to your home, hotel accommodations for first and last nights, airport departure tax, or personal expenses. Hotel bookings can be made by tour operator.

Departure: Trips leave from Loreto, Mexico. An Ecosummer guide will meet you at the airport.

Naturalist: Guides familiar with Baja flora and fauna accompany all trips.

"Our kayak explorations in Baja allow you the opportunity to see two distinct sides of this spectacular peninsula from a natural and geographical viewpoint," notes staff member Ed Pearce. "Although the Baja expeditions have a specific whale-watching component, many of our other trips, especially on the British Columbia coast, frequently encounter whales."

Founded in 1976, Ecosummer Expeditions began as an adventure company that promoted environmental education, working primarily with high school students. Founder Jim Allan was soon deluged with requests from adults who wanted activity-oriented natural history wilderness trips—and so Ecosummer Expeditions evolved.

National Audubon Society Travel
950 Third Avenue, New York, NY 10022; (212) 546–9140

Whales: Gray, finback, orca, humpback

Season: Late January and early February

Boats: The 152-foot *Sea Lion*; 70 passengers in 37 outside cabins. Participants live on the boat except for the last night, which is spent in a hotel. Whale watching from motorized inflatable rafts.

Trips: Two 8-day trips to Magdalena Bay, with stops at Santa Catalina Island, Los Islotes Island, Espiritu Santo Island, Cabo San Lucas, and San Carlos. Trips conclude in Los Angeles.

Fare: For Audubon Society members, $1,890 to $2,625, depending on the location of the stateroom. (Non members may join for $30.) Fare includes all meals and accommodations on board and in the hotel; does not include airfare from Los Angeles to Loreto (estimated at $200), tips, or alcohol.

Departure: Trips leave from Los Angeles, California. Participants take a direct flight to Loreto, Mexico.

Naturalist: Natural history staff from the Audubon Society and guest lecturers accompany trips.

"The M.V. *Sea Lion* is ideal for exploring the region. Built to glide effortlessly, it will get you as close as possible to the whales and other sea life," says Audubon senior vice president Susan P. Martin. "Where the *Sea Lion* can't go, the ship's fleet of rubber landing craft will be launched, ready to land you almost anywhere at will."

Sea of Cortez, Mexico

American Cetacean Society Expeditions
P.O. Box 2639, San Pedro, CA 90731; (213) 548–6279

Whales: Blue, finback, minke, pilot, dolphin

Season: March and April

Boats: The 80-foot *Don Jose*; 5 staterooms accommodate 4 passengers each. Participants live aboard the boat.

Trips: Two trips: an 8-day trip in the southern end of the Gulf of California and a 10-day trip to the Midriff Islands of Rasa, Guardian Angel, and San Pedro Martir.

Fare: The 8-day trip, in mid-March, costs $1,245 and is restricted to 22 people. The 10-day trip, in mid-April, costs $1,600 and is restricted to 20 passengers. Fares are for ACS members (add 10 percent for nonmembers) and do not include airfare to Mexico, tips, personal items, or alcohol.

Departure: The 8-day trip leaves from La Paz. The 10-day trip leaves from San Felipe.

Naturalist: Naturalist from the American Cetacean Society accompanies both trips.

The American Cetacean Society has been conducting specialized trips for small groups to see whales since 1973. "Our trips take place in some of the great wilderness areas and are led by experienced naturalists. All of our trips are really spectacular!" comments a spokeswoman. "In the Sea of Cortez, blue whales, fin whales, and dolphins are your everyday companions."

Baja Expeditions
2625 Garnet Avenue, San Diego, CA 92109; (619) 581–3311

Whales: Blue, finback

Season: Early March to early April

Boats: One of two boats: The 80-foot *Don Jose* has 5 cabins that accommodate 4 people each; the 120-foot *Baja Explorador* accommodates 20 passengers in 11 staterooms. Participants live aboard.

Trips: Five 10-day trips in the Sea of Cortez, with stops at Espiritu Santo Island, San Jose Island, Santa Catalina Island, Ildefonso Island, and Raza Island. Trips disembark in San Felipe and passengers board bus back to San Diego.

Fare: $1,245 per person. Price includes land arrangements, accommodations, meals, beverages, hotels scheduled in itinerary (determined according to boat used on trip), fishing permits, and most related trip equipment. Airfare, gratuities, and airport taxes are not included. Air reservations can be made through trip operator.

Departure: Trips leave from La Paz, with bus transportation to the boat.

Naturalist: Naturalist accompanies all trips.

Baja Expeditions made its first trip in 1974, in a rented fishing boat with a well-thumbed copy of John Steinbeck's *Log from the Sea of Cortez* aboard. The company's offerings to the Sea of Cortez recapture the sights, sounds, and experiences of Steinbeck's trip.

Tim Means, founder, notes that today the company is the largest and oldest outfitter of natural history and adventure travel in Mexico. Kent Madin is Means's partner and general manager.

Biological Journeys
1696 Ocean Drive, McKinleyville, CA 95521; (800) 548–7555, (707) 839–0178

Whales: Blue

Season: Mid-March

Boats: The 80-foot *Don Jose*; 5 staterooms accommodate 4 passengers each. Participants live aboard except for the last night, which is spent in a hotel.

Trips: One 8-day trip to the Sea of Cortez, with stops at Espiritu Santo Island, Santa Catalina Island, Los Islotes, and La Paz.

Fare: $1,549 per person. Price includes instructions, accommodations, meals and transportation while aboard the vessel, and a Mexican fishing license. Rate does not include transportation to San Diego or La Paz, airport departure taxes, meals or lodging en route, alcoholic beverages, or tips. Travel arrangements can be

made through the trip operator's agent, Eureka Travel
Agency.

Departure: Trip leaves from La Paz, with transportation to the
boat.

Naturalist: Naturalist accompanies all trips.

"We proudly feature a cruise that combines the color and charm of
Baja with all the might and majesty of the world's largest animals. You
will be awed by their size and astonished by their gentle behavior."

Ronn Storro-Patterson, an authority on whales, and Ron LeValley,
an ornithologist, head up Biological Journeys, which has sponsored
natural history trips to Baja California since 1970. "Commitment,
commitment, commitment to quality and service" is their watch-
word, says Storro-Patterson.

(Note: For other Biological Journeys trips to the Sea of Cortez,
see next two entries.)

Biological Journeys

1696 Ocean Drive, McKinleyville, CA 95521; (800) 548–7555,
(707) 839–0178

Whales: Gray, humpback, blue

Season: Early April to late April

Boats: The 105-foot *Searcher*; 30 passengers in 15 cabins.
Participants live aboard. Whale watching from aluminum skiffs.

Trips: Two 12-day trips to the Sea of Cortez, with stops at
Todos Santos Island, Scammon's Lagoon, San Ignacio
Lagoon, Magdalena Bay, Cabo San Lucas, Gorda Bank,
Bahia Los Frailes, Cerralvo Island, Espiritu Santo
Island, San Francisco Island, and La Paz.

Where the Whales Are

Fare: $2,195 per person. Price includes instructions, accommodations, meals and transportation while aboard the vessel, and a Mexican fishing license. Rate does not include transportation to San Diego, airport departure taxes, meals or lodging en route, alcoholic beverages, or tips. Travel arrangements can be made through the trip operator's agent, Eureka Travel Agency.

Departure: Trip leaves from San Diego, California.

Naturalist: Naturalist accompanies all trips.

"You will cruise from San Diego to La Paz, basking in the great variety of natural history experiences offered by this wilderness area. You may see as many as ten species of whales!" says Biological Journeys.

Ronn Storro-Patterson and Ron LeValley head up Biological Journeys, which has sponsored Baja California trips since 1970.

Biological Journeys
1696 Ocean Drive, McKinleyville, CA 95521; (800) 548–7555, (707) 839–0178

Whales: Humpback

Season: Mid-March

Boats: The 120-foot *Baja Explorador*; 11 cabins for 20 passengers. Participants live aboard except for the last night, which is spent in a hotel.

Trips: One 8-day trip to Cabo San Lucas, with stops at La Paz Bay, Los Islotes Island, Gorda Bank, Bahia de Los Frailes, Cerralvo Island, and Espiritu Santo Island. Trip concludes in La Paz.

Fare: $1,549 per person. Price includes instructions, accommodations, meals and transportation while aboard the vessel, and a Mexican fishing license. Rate does not include transportation to La Paz, airport departure taxes, meals or lodging en route, alcoholic beverages, or tips. Travel arrangements can be made through the trip operator's agent, Eureka Travel Agency.

Departure: Trip leaves from La Paz, with transportation to the boat.

Naturalist: Naturalist accompanies all trips.

This cruise immerses you in the world of the humpback whale in the waters of Cabo San Lucas and the Gorda Bank, at the southern-most point of the Baja peninsula.

Ronn Storro-Patterson and Ron LeValley head up Biological Journeys, which has sponsored Baja California trips since 1970.

Mingan Island Cetacean Study

Summer: P.O. Box 159, Sept-Iles, Quebec, G4R 4K3 Canada; (418) 949–2845

Winter: 285, rue Green, St. Lambert, Quebec, J4P 1T3 Canada; (514) 465–9176

Whales: Blue, finback, several species of dolphin

Season: March and April

Boats: Several 22-foot fiberglass boats

Trips: Several 7-day trips in March and April, with a Loreto hotel as the base of operations.

Fare: $129 per day per person. Airfare to Mexico not included.

Departure: All trips start in Loreto, Mexico.

Naturalist: Naturalist accompanies all trips.

The Mingan Island Cetacean Study operates a research station in the Mingan Island region of the Quebec North Shore from May to

Where the Whales Are

November, studying local populations of blue, humpback, finback, and minke whales. Since 1983, founder Richard Sears has also offered educational research programs in the Sea of Cortez.

"Guests are invited to the coastal community of Loreto on the Sea of Cortez, Mexico, to participate in our winter/spring research season," Dr. Sears says. "The striking blue waters of this area offer a rich environment in which to observe a great variety of marine mammals, birds, and fishes."

Nature Expeditions International
474 Willamette, P.O. Box 11496, Eugene, OR 97440; (503) 484–6529

Whales:	Blue, fin
Season:	April
Boats:	The 120-foot *Baja Explorador*; 8 cabins accommodate a total of 18 passengers. (Trip is restricted to 16.) Participants live on board except for the first and last nights, which are spent in a hotel.
Trips:	One 9-day trip with stops at Puerto Refugio and the islands of Raza, San Esteban, San Pedro Martir, San Ildefonso, Santa Catalina, and Los Islotes. Trip concludes in La Paz.
Fare:	$1,390 per person. Price includes ship transportation and land transfers; hotels in La Paz and San Diego; six breakfasts, six lunches, and six dinners; park fees; fishing licenses; instruction; and leadership. Fare does not include airfare, meals in La Paz or San Diego, tips aboard ship, airport taxes, or personal expenses.
Departure:	Trip leaves from San Diego, California.

Naturalist: Biologists who specialize in the natural history of the Sea of Cortez accompany the trip.

David Roderick is president of Nature Expeditions International, which specializes in wildlife and cultural expeditions to unique environments all over the world. Founded in 1974, NIE requires its trip leaders to hold graduate degrees and teaching experience on the college level as well as broad field experience in the countries where they travel.

"Discover the wilderness islands and waters of the Sea of Cortez, with abundant opportunities to get away from it all, explore, study, photograph, hike, snorkel, and relax among the finest wildlife islands in the Gulf of California."

Oceanic Society Expeditions
Fort Mason Center, Building E, San Francisco, CA 94123; (415) 441–1106

Whales: Blue, finback, humpback, sperm, minke, several species of dolphin

Season: Mid-April

Boats: The 86-foot *Spirit of Adventure*; 32 passengers and staff. Participants live aboard.

Trips: One 8-day trip in mid-April to the Sea of Cortez, with a flexible itinerary that may include visits to the islands of Santa Catalina, Los Islotes, San Pedro Martir, Raza, Partida, and San Jose. Trip concludes in La Paz.

Fare: $1,295 per person. Airfare or airport transfers not included.

Departure: Trip leaves from La Paz, Mexico.

Where the Whales Are

Naturalist:	Two naturalists affiliated with the Oceanic Society accompany the trip.

The volcanic islands scattered throughout Mexico's Sea of Cortez form one of the most pristine and biologically significant archipelagos left on earth. The Sea of Cortez is also a feeding ground for large cetaceans, such as the giant endangered blue, fin, sperm, minke, and humpback whales, as well as for several species of dolphins. Slide shows and informal lectures are presented each evening, and passengers may choose from assorted optional activities each day. Oceanic Society Expeditions has been conducting natural history study tours since 1973. (For other Oceanic Society trips, see next entry.)

Oceanic Society Expeditions

Fort Mason Center, Building E, San Francisco, CA 94123;
(415) 441–1106

Whales:	Blue, finback, several species of dolphin
Season:	Mid-November through early January
Boats:	Several 21-foot sailing boats for day trips. Participants camp.
Trips:	Four 8-day trips, limited to 9 participants each. Base camp is established at Carmen Island and sailing expeditions explore the Sea of Cortez. Trip concludes in Loreto.
Fare:	$875 per person. Price includes meals, equipment (except sleeping bags and pads), airport transfers, and instruction in sailing and wilderness camping. Fare does not include airfare to Loreto.
Departure:	Trip leaves from Loreto, Mexico.
Naturalist:	A naturalist affiliated with the Oceanic Society accompanies the trip.

Oceanic Society Expeditions has been conducting natural history study tours since 1973. No prior sailing experience is necessary to make this trip. Sailing masters run the boats and give informal sailing lessons. Everyone helps establish camp and prepare meals. Informal lectures are presented each evening, and passengers may choose from assorted optional activities each day, including nature walks, bird-watching, and snorkeling.

Pacific Queen/Biological Adventures

Fisherman's Landing, 2838 Garrison, San Diego, CA 92106; (619) 222–0391

Whales:	Gray, blue, fin, minke, orca, humpback
Season:	April
Boats:	The 88-foot sportfishing vessel *Pacific Queen*; double, quadruple, and eight-person compartments; participation limited to 30. Participants live aboard.
Trips:	One 11-day trip to the Gulf of California. Stops include San Ignacio Lagoon and Magdalena Bay, but most of the trip is spent in the Gulf of California, in the Sea of Cortez. Stops there may include these islands: Cerralvo, Espiritu Santo, Partida, San Jose, San Francisco, Santa Cruz, Santa Catalina, Monserrate, Danzante, and Carmen. Trip concludes at La Paz.
Fare:	$1,650 per person. Price includes food, lodging, and full participation in natural history programs presented on board each evening. Fare does not include hotel in La Paz or transportation back to the United States.
Departure:	Trips leave from San Diego, California.
Naturalist:	A staff of biologists accompanies each trip.

Captain Ed McEwen, owner of the *Pacific Queen*, leads each cruise, accompanied by a crew of six and a staff of biologists who are experts in the biology and oceanography of Baja California. Expedition biologist and director Margie Stinson has made more than one hundred such trips, leading expeditions since the late 1960s.

Where the Whales Are

"Our philosophy is that each guest is treated as you would wish your parents to be treated by strangers," Margie Stinson notes. "Consequently, friendships are lifelong."

Pacific Sea Fari Tours
2803 Emerson Street, San Diego, CA 92106; (619) 226–8224

Whales:	Gray
Season:	Late February to mid-April
Boats:	One of two boats: The 88-foot *Spirit of Adventure* holds 30 passengers in 14 cabins; the 80-foot *Deluxe* carries 20 passengers in 8 cabins. Participants live aboard the boats. Whale watching from skiffs.
Trips:	Five-, 8-, and 11-day trips to the Sea of Cortez, with stops at San Benito Islands, San Ignacio Lagoon, Magdalena Bay, Cabo San Lucas, Espiritu Santo Island, San Jose Island, Santa Catalina Island, Ildefonso Island, and La Paz. Trip concludes in La Paz.
Fare:	$1,400 to $1,800 per person includes meals and snacks, accommodations, related equipment, and services of a naturalist staff. Tips aboard, airfare, and transfers not included.
Departure:	Trips leave from San Diego, California.
Naturalist:	All trips accompanied by naturalists

Pacific Sea Fari Tours' natural history program has been developed under the leadership of Dr. Theodore J. Walker, a noted author, lecturer, and researcher. Considered one of the world's foremost experts on gray whales, Dr. Walker wrote *Whale Primer*, the first authoritative work of its kind, and founded the whale observatory at the Cabrillo National Monument. Dr. Walker accompanies about one-third of the trips himself, and no two trips are alike.

San Juan Kayak Expeditions Inc.
3090 Roche Harbor Road, Friday Harbor, WA 98250;
(206) 378–4436

Whales:	Finback, blue
Season:	March
Boats:	Sea kayaks. Participants camp at night.
Trips:	Two 6-day trips to Punta San Marcial and two 6-day trips to Danzante Island. Trips restricted to 10 participants.
Fare:	$550 per person, plus airfare to Loreto, Mexico, for the Punta San Marcial trips; $475 plus airfare to Loreto Mexico, for the Danzante Island trips. Rate includes kayaks, all boating gear, shade and rain tarps, and all cooking gear.
Departure:	Trips leave from Loreto, Mexico.
Naturalist:	Naturalist accompanies trips.

"One of the world's most spectacular and pristine shorelines is found along the Baja Peninsula's eastern seaboard," notes Tim Thomsen. He also says beginners are welcome. The Danzante Island trip is the easier of the two for novice kayakers.

Sea Quest Expeditions
Zoetic Research, P.O. Box 2424, Friday Harbor, WA 98250;
(206) 378–5767

Whales:	Bottlenose dolphin, common dolphin
Season:	November and December
Boats:	Sea kayak
Trips:	Three trips with varied 5- or 7-day itineraries. Participants camp overnight.

Fare:	$499 to $599 per person. Price includes everything but airfare to Mexico. Reservations required.
Departure:	Trips usually leave from Loreto, Mexico.
Naturalist:	Naturalist accompanies trips.

Executive director Mark Lewis schedules Sea Quest Expeditions trips to the Sea of Cortez in late November and December, when the air and sea are still warm and inviting. "That means you'll more fully enjoy what Baja has to offer—swimming among colorful tropical fish and herds of curious sea lions and kayaking with colorful dolphin escorts under warm, sunny skies," Lewis says.

"Also, when oceanic conditions are good and plankton blooms develop near shore, we have been able to closely observe fin whales on these trips. Other species, such as humpbacks, orcas, and others, are seen with less frequency."

Sea Quest Expeditions also offers research trips that qualify for college credit, and they will design custom trips.

Baja Peninsula, East and West Coasts, Mexico

Baja Expeditions
2625 Garnet Avenue, San Diego, CA 92109; (619) 581–3311

Whales:	Gray, blue, humpback, finback
Season:	Mid-January through mid-March
Boats:	One of two boats: The 80-foot *Don Jose* carries 20 passengers in 5 staterooms; the 120-foot *Baja Explorador* has 11 staterooms for 20 passengers. Participants live aboard except for the last night, which is spent in a hotel. Whale watching from skiffs and boats.
Trips:	Eight 8-day trips that combine a visit to Magdalena

Bay with a trip around Cabo San Lucas to the Sea of Cortez, with a stop at Cabo Pulmo and Espiritu Santo Island. Trips restricted to 20 passengers. Trips conclude in either La Paz or Magdalena Bay.

Fare: $1,245 per person. Price includes land arrangements, accommodations, meals, beverages, hotels scheduled in itinerary (determined according to boat used for trip), fishing permits, and most related trip equipment. Airfare, tips, and airport taxes are not included. Air reservations can be made through trip operator.

Departure: Trips leave from La Paz and Magdalena Bay, with bus transportation to the boat.

Naturalist: Naturalist accompanies all trips.

This itinerary combines two days in Magdalena Bay with a trip around the tip of Baja to view humpback whales and others migrating south or to the Sea of Cortez.

Baja Expeditions made its first trip in 1974, inspired by John Steinbeck's *Log from the Sea of Cortez*. Founder Tim Means notes that today the company is the largest and oldest outfitter of natural history and adventure travel in Mexico. Kent Madin is Means's partner and general manager.

Biological Journeys
1696 Ocean Drive, McKinleyville, CA 95521; (800) 548–7555, (707) 839–0178

Whales: Gray, humpback, blue, fin, minke

Season: Mid-February to early March

Boats: Either the 120-foot *Baja Explorador*, which serves 20 passengers with 11 staterooms, or the 80-foot *Don Jose*, with 5 staterooms holding 4 people each. Participants live aboard, except for the last night, which is

291

spent in a hotel. Whale watching from aluminum skiffs and from the boats.

Trips: Two 8-day trips, with stops in Magdalena Bay, Cabo San Lucas, Gorda Bank, Bahia Los Frailes Cerralvo or Los Islotes Islands, and Espiritu Santo Island. Trips conclude in La Paz.

Fare: $1,549 per person. Price includes instructions, accommodations, meals and transportation while aboard the vessel, and a Mexican fishing license. Rate does not include transportation to La Paz, airport departure taxes, meals or lodging en route, alcoholic beverages, or tips. Travel arrangements can be made through the trip operator's agent, Eureka Travel Agency.

Departure: Trip leaves from La Paz, with transportation to the boat.

Naturalist: Naturalist accompanies all trips.

"This cruise offers the potential of encountering more whale species than any comparable trip in the world," says Biological Journeys. "You'll witness sights and sounds that create one of the most exciting spectacles on the face of the earth!"

Ronn Storro-Patterson and Ron LeValley head up Biological Journeys, which has sponsored Baja California trips since 1970.

Oceanic Society Expeditions
Fort Mason Center, Building E, San Francisco, CA 94123; (415) 441–1106

Whales: Blue, fin, humpback, sperm, minke, orca, several species of dolphin

Season: Mid-February through early April

Boats: Either the 86-foot *Spirit of Adventure*, with 14 cabins for 32 passengers and staff; or the 105-foot *Qualifier*, with 15 cabins for 36 passengers and staff. Participants live on board. Whale watching from small skiffs.

Trips: Four 10-day trips with stops at San Benito Islands, San Ignacio Lagoon, Magdalena Bay, Cabo San Lucas, Los Islotes Island, Santa Catalina Island, and San Jose Island. Trip concludes in La Paz.

Fare: $1,795 per person. Price does not include airfare or transfers.

Departure: Trips leave from San Diego.

Naturalist: Experienced naturalists affiliated with the Oceanic Society accompany all trips.

"Our movement from temperate to tropical waters makes this one of the richest and most varied expeditions possible," notes Oceanic Society Expeditions. Slide shows and informal lectures are held each evening on board, and assorted optional activities are available each day. Oceanic Society Expeditions has conducted nature study tours since 1973.

Where Whales
Are When

This chapter is a calendar that tells where whales are when. The time span shown encompasses the early weeks, when a few whales are present; the height of the season; and the end of season, when just a few laggers may still be around. Dolphins' migratory patterns are not as well known as those of the great whales, so the listings here emphasize the whereabouts of the larger animals. This calendar has not been reviewed or approved by whales and may not correspond exactly with their comings and goings. Also, keep in mind that whales do not observe our territorial boundaries and may spill over into neighboring states and even countries other than those listed here.

January

Gray whales: Off the coasts of California and Oregon
Humpback whales: In Hawaiian waters

February

Gray whales: Off the coasts of California and Oregon and in the lagoons off the west coast of Baja California, Mexico
Humpback whales: In Hawaiian waters

March

Blue whales, fin whales, and pilot whales: In the Sea of Cortez, off the east coast of Baja California, Mexico

Gray whales: Off the coasts of California, Oregon, and Washington; in Alaskan waters; in the lagoons off the west coast of Baja California, Mexico; and off British Columbia

Humpback whales: In Hawaiian waters and in the Sea of Cortez, off the east coast of Baja California, Mexico

April

Blue whales: In the Sea of Cortez, off the east coast of Baja California, Mexico

Fin whales: Off the northeast U.S. coast

Gray whales: Off the coasts of northern California, Oregon and Washington; in the lagoons off the west coast of Baja California, Mexico; and off British Columbia

Humpback whales: In Hawaiian waters; in the Sea of Cortez, off the east coast of Baja Californian, Mexico; and off the northeast U.S. coast

Minke whales: Off the northeast U.S. coast

Right whales: Off the northeast U.S. coast

May

Beluga whales: Off the Northwest Territories in Canada

Bowhead whales: Off the Northwest Territories in Canada

Fin whales: Off the northeast U.S. coast

Gray whales: Off the coasts of Oregon and Washington

Humpback whales: In Alaskan waters and off the northeast U.S. coast

Minke whales: In Alaskan waters and off the northeast U.S. coast

Narwhals: Off the Northwest Territories in Canada

Orcas: In Alaskan waters

Right whales: Off the northeast U.S. coast

June

Beluga whales: Off the Northwest Territories and in the St. Lawrence River in Quebec, Canada

Blue whales: In the St. Lawrence River in Quebec, Canada

Bowhead whales: Off the Northwest Territories in Canada

Fin whales: Off the northeast U.S. coast, in Alaskan waters, off Nova Scotia and Newfoundland, and in the St. Lawrence River in Quebec, Canada

Humpback whales: In Alaskan waters, off the northeast U.S. coast, off Newfoundland and Nova Scotia in Canada, and off the Oregon coast

Minke whales: In Alaskan waters, off the northeast U.S. coast, off Nova Scotia and Newfoundland, and in the St. Lawrence River in Quebec, Canada

Narwhals: Off the Northwest Territories in Canada

Orcas: In Alaskan waters, off British Columbia, in the San Juan Islands, and off the Oregon coast

Right whales: Off the northeast U.S. coast and Nova Scotia, Canada

July

Beluga whales: Off the Northwest Territories, in the St. Lawrence River in Quebec, and in Manitoba, Canada

Blue whales: In the St. Lawrence River in Quebec, Canada, and off the coast of California

Fin whales: Off the northeast U.S. coast; off Nova Scotia, Newfoundland, and New Brunswick; and in the St. Lawrence River in Quebec, Canada

Humpback whales: In Alaskan waters; off the northeast U.S. coast; off Newfoundland, New Brunswick, and Nova Scotia in Canada; and off the California and Oregon coasts

Minke whales: In Alaskan waters, off the northeast U.S. coast, off Nova Scotia and Newfoundland, and in the St. Lawrence River in Quebec, Canada

Orcas: In Alaskan waters, off British Columbia, in the San Juan Islands, and off the Oregon coast.

Right whales: Off the northeast U.S. coast and Nova Scotia, Canada

Sperm whales: Off the coast of California

August

Beluga whales: Off the Northwest Territories, in the St. Lawrence River in Quebec, and in Manitoba, Canada

Blue whales: In the St. Lawrence River in Quebec, Canada, and off the coast of California

Fin whales: Off the northeast U.S. coast; off Nova Scotia, Newfoundland, and New Brunswick; and in the St. Lawrence River in Quebec, Canada

Humpback whales: In Alaskan waters; off the northeast U.S. coast; off Newfoundland, New Brunswick, and Nova Scotia in Canada; and off the California and Oregon coasts

Minke whales: In Alaskan waters, off the northeast U.S. coast, off Nova Scotia and Newfoundland, and in the St. Lawrence River in Quebec, Canada

Orcas: In Alaskan waters, off British Columbia, in the San Juan Islands, and off the Oregon coast

Right whales: Off the northeast U.S. coast and Nova Scotia, Canada

Sperm whales: Off the coast of California

September

Beluga whales: In the St. Lawrence River in Quebec, Canada

Blue whales: In the St. Lawrence River in Quebec, Canada, and off the coast of California

Fin whales: Off the northeast U.S. coast, off Nova Scotia and Newfoundland, and in the St. Lawrence River in Quebec, Canada

Humpback whales: In Alaskan waters, off the northeast U.S. coast, off Newfoundland and Nova Scotia in Canada, and off the California and Oregon coasts

Minke whales: In Alaskan waters, off the northeast U.S. coast, off Nova Scotia and Newfoundland, and in the St. Lawrence River in Quebec, Canada

Orcas: In Alaskan waters and off British Columbia

Right whales: Off the northeast U.S. coast and Nova Scotia, Canada

Right whales: Off the Northeast U.S. Coast

October

Beluga whales: In the St. Lawrence River in Quebec, Canada

Blue whales: In the St. Lawrence River in Quebec, Canada

Fin whales: Off the northeast U.S. coast and in the St. Lawrence River in Quebec, Canada

Humpback whales: Off the northeast U.S. coast

Minke whales: Off the northeast U.S. coast and in the St. Lawrence River in Quebec, Canada

Right whales: Off the Northeast U.S. Coast

November

This is a great month to plan whale-watch trips!

December

Gray whales: Off the coast of Oregon

Humpback whales: In Hawaiian waters

Whale-Watch Tours to Additional Destinations

Some tour operators sponsor whale-watch (and other nature study) trips to destinations other than those included in this book. Here is a list of those tour operators and brief information about their varied offerings. Write for more information.

Biological Journeys
1696 Ocean Drive, McKinleyville, CA 95521
(800) 548–7555
(707) 839–0178

In addition to the many destinations listed in this book, Biological Journeys sponsors trips to the Galapagos Islands, the Amazon, the Great Barrier Reef, New Zealand, and Costa Rica.

Bluewater Adventures
#202–1676 Duranleau Street, Vancouver, British Columbia
V6H 3S4 Canada
(604) 684–4575

Bluewater Adventures offers trips to Costa Rica in addition to numerous nature study trips off the western coast of Canada.

Canadian Nature Tours
Federation of Ontario Naturalists
355 Lesmill Road, Don Mills, Ontario, M3B 2W8 Canada
(416) 444–8419

More than fifty trips are available, including canoe and backpacking trips, to such destinations as Cuba, Costa Rica, the Galapagos Islands, and throughout Canada.

Dirigo Cruises
39 Waterside Lane, Clinton, CT 06413
(203) 669–7068

Scheduled and custom-tailored trips are available on twelve sailing ships headed for New England, the Caribbean, and the South Pacific. Teacher-training courses and educational expeditions for teenagers are also available.

Earthwatch
680 Mt. Auburn Street, Box 403N, Watertown, MA 02272
(617) 926–8200

This nonprofit organization sponsors scholarly field research trips that allow volunteers to help scientists. Since its founding in 1971, Earthwatch has overseen hundreds of projects in eighty-seven countries and thirty-six states. Of the 120 projects sponsored in 1990, twenty-one involved marine studies.

Ecosummer Expeditions
1516 Duranleau Street, Vancouver, British Columbia
V6H 3S4 Canada
(604) 669–7741

In addition to trips off the west coast of Canada, Ecosummer Expeditions offers trips to the North Pole; in the Northwest Territories; off the coast of Greenland; and to Iceland, Belize, Patagonia, Africa, and Antarctica.

Nature Expeditions International
474 Willamette, P.O. Box 11496, Eugene, OR 97440
(503) 484–6529

Something on the order of ninety-nine trips are offered each year, to such destinations as Australia, the West Indies, Africa, the Galapagos, Easter Island, Nepal, Peru, Oregon, the Amazon, New Guinea, and Costa Rica.

Northwest Outdoor Center
2100 Westlake Avenue North, Seattle, WA 98109
(206) 281–9694

Founded in October 1980, Northwest Outdoor Center specializes in kayak and canoe classes and nature trips. Day trips and extended vacations are offered throughout the San Juan Islands, in New Zealand, and on area lakes and rivers.

Oceanic Society Expeditions
Fort Mason Center, Building E, San Francisco, CA 94123
(415) 441–1106

Trips are available year round to such destinations as Antarctica, the Virgin Islands, Dominica, the Galapagos Islands, Costa Rica, the Bahamas, Patagonia, and Australia.

Ocean Voyages Inc.
1709 Bridgeway, Sausalito, CA 94965
(415) 332–4681

If you've always wanted to sail around the world, you might contact Ocean Voyages, which offers scheduled and custom-designed trips on more than 150 different sailing vessels of all sorts to destinations all over the world. None of the trips are set up specifically to watch whales, but many of them pass through whale-rich waters.

Seafarers Expeditions
P.O. Box 691, Bangor, ME 04401
(207) 942–7942

In addition to numerous trips off the eastern coast of Canada, Seafarers Expeditions sponsors whale-watch trips to the Azores, Tortola, Dominica, and Venezuela.

Sea Quest Expeditions
Zoetic Research, P.O. Box 2424, Friday Harbor, WA 98250
(206) 378–5767

Sea Quest Expeditions sponsors sailing and kayak trips to the Dry Tortugas, the Florida Keys, and the Everglades in addition to the trips in the San Juan Islands and off the coast of Baja California that are listed in this book.

Sea Safaris
International Oceanographic Foundation, P.O. Box 499900
Miami, FL 33149
(305) 361–4697

The Sea Safaris program offered by the IOF includes European adventures as well as trips in the San Juan Islands, Canada, and Alaska.

Smithsonian Associates Travel Program
Smithsonian Institution/Department 0049,
Washington, D.C. 20073
(202) 357–4700

Domestic and foreign study tours are offered to Alaska, the Grand Canyon, Europe, the West Indies, Africa, Japan, and Jamaica.

Thompson Voyages
P.O. Box 217, Laguna Beach, CA 92652
(714) 497–1055

In addition to trips to San Ignacio Lagoon in Baja California, Thompson Voyages conducts wildlife expeditions to the Galapagos Islands, the Catalina Islands, and the Bahamas.

APPENDIX 2

Whale Conservation and Research Organizations

Like-minded people have come together all over the United States and Canada to work for the conservation of whales and other endangered species. Some of the organizations listed here concentrate on research, some on direct aid to the animals, some on political activism, and some on education; some ably combine all four missions. A few of the organizations sponsor occasional whale-watch trips for members, and some even recruit people to assist in research projects. For details, write to those organizations that interest you.

Alaska Geographic Society
Box 4-EEE, Anchorage, AK 99509

Allied Whale
College of the Atlantic, Bar Harbor, ME 04609

**American Association of Zoological Parks
and Aquariums**
Oglebay Park, Wheeling, WV 26003

American Cetacean Society
P.O. Box 2639, San Pedro, CA 90731

American Oceans Campaign
1427 7th Street, Suite 3, Santa Monica, CA 90401

Animal Protection Institute of America
P.O. Box 22505, Sacramento, CA 95822

Animal Welfare Institute
P.O. Box 3650, Washington, D.C. 20007

Brier Island Ocean Study
Westport, Digby County, Nova Scotia, B0V 1H0 Canada

British Columbia Wildlife Federation
5659 176th Street, Surrey, British Columbia, V3S 4C5 Canada

California Marine Mammal Center
Marin Headlands Ranger Station, Fort Cronkhite, CA 94965

Canadian Nature Federation
453 Sussex Drive, Ottawa, Ontario, K1N 6Z4 Canada

Canadian Wildlife Federation
1673 Carling Avenue, Ottawa, Ontario, K2A 3Z1 Canada

Center for Coastal Studies
59 Commercial Street, Box 1036, Provincetown, MA 02657

Center for Marine Conservation
1725 DeSales Street NW, Washington, D.C. 20036

Center for Whale Research
1359 Smuggler's Cove, Friday Harbor, WA 98250

Cetacean Research Unit
P.O. Box 159, Gloucester, MA 01930

Cetacean Society International
P.O. Box 9145, Wethersfield, CT 06109

Children of the Green Earth
P.O. Box 95219, Seattle, WA 98145

Cousteau Society
930 West 21st Street, Norfolk, VA 23517

Defenders of Wildlife
1244 19th Street NW, Washington, D.C. 20036

Delta Society
P.O. Box 1080, Renton, WA 98057

Earth First!
Box 210, Canyon, CA 94516

Earth Island Institute
300 Broadway, Suite 28, San Francisco, CA 94133

Earthtrust Wildlife Society
2500 Pali Highway, Honolulu, HI 96817

Earthwatch
680 Mt. Auburn Street, Box 403N , Watertown, MA 02272

Elsa Wild Animal Appeal
P.O. Box 4572, North Hollywood, CA 91607

Environmental Defense Fund
257 Park Avenue South, New York, NY 10010

Friends of the Animals
30 Haviland Street, Norwalk, CT 06854

Friends of the Earth
218 D Street SE, Washington, D.C. 20077

Fund for Animals
200 W. 57th Street, New York, NY 10019

Greenpeace USA
1436 U Street NW, Washington, D.C. 20009

Humane Society of the United States
2100 L Street NW, Washington, D.C. 20037

International Fund for Animal Welfare
P.O. Box 193, Yarmouthport, MA 02675

International Oceanographic Foundation
4600 Rickenbacker Causeway, P.O. Box 499900, Miami, FL 33149

International Wildlife Coalition
634 North Falmouth Highway, P.O. Box 388, North Falmouth, MA 02556

Intersea Research
P.O. Box 1667, Friday Harbor, WA 98250

Long Island Sound Taskforce
Stamford Marine Center, Magee Avenue, Stamford, CT 06902

Manitoba Wildlife Federation
1770 Notre Dame Avenue, Winnipeg, Manitoba, R3E 3K2 Canada

Marine Mammal Fund
Fort Mason Center, Building E, San Francisco, CA 94123

Marine Mammal Stranding Center
P.O. Box 773, 3625 Brigantine Boulevard, Brigantine, NJ 08203

Mingan Island Cetacean Study
Summer:
P.O. Box 159, Sept-Iles, Quebec, G4R 4K3 Canada
Winter:
285, rue Green, St. Lambert, Quebec, J4P 1T3 Canada

Monitor
1506 19th Street NW, Washington, D.C. 20036

National Council for Environmental Balance
P.O. Box 7732, 4169 Westport Road, Louisville, KY 40207

National Audubon Society
950 Third Avenue, New York, NY 10022

National Wildlife Federation
1412 16th Street NW, Washington, D.C. 20036

Natural Resources Defense Council
122 East 42nd Street, New York, NY 10168

Nature Center for Environmental Activities
P.O. Box 165, Westport, CT 06881

New Brunswick Wildlife Federation
190 Cameron Street, Moncton, New Brunswick, E1C 5Z2 Canada

Newfoundland Labrador Wildlife Federation
c/o P.O. Box 1041, Corner Brook, Newfoundland, A2H 6C6 Canada

Northwest Territories Wildlife Federation
Box 495, Hay River, Northwest Territories, X0E 0R0 Canada

Nova Scotia Wildlife Federation
P.O. Box 654, Halifax, Nova Scotia, B3J 2T3 Canada

Ocean Alliance
Fort Mason Center, Building E, San Francisco, CA 94123

Ocean Research and Conservation Association
720 Olive Way, Suite 900, Seattle, WA 98101

Ocean Research Information Society
2 Whittington Court, Ajax, Ontario, L1S 4L4 Canada

Okeanos Ocean Research Foundation
Box 776, Hampton Bays, NY 11946

Oregon Natural Resources Council
1050 Yeon Building, 522 Southwest Fifth Avenue, Portland, OR 97204

Pacific Whale Foundation
Kealia Beach Plaza, Suite 21, 101 North Kihei Road, Kihei Maui, HI 96753

Where the Whales Are

Quebec Wildlife Federation
319 Est, rue St. Zotique, Montreal, Quebec , H2S 1L5 Canada

St. Lawrence National Institute of Ecotoxicology
310, avenue des Ursulines, Rimouski, Quebec, G5L 3A1 Canada

Save the Whales
P.O. Box 3650 , Washington, D.C. 20007

Sea Search, Ltd.
P.O. Box 210093, Auke Bay, AK 99821

Sea Shepherd Conservation Society
P.O. Box 7000-S, Redondo Beach, CA 90277

Sierra Club
730 Polk Street, San Francisco, CA 94109

Society for Animal Protective Legislation
P.O. Box 3719 , Georgetown Station, Washington, D.C. 20007

Society for Marine Mammalogy
c/o Robert L. Brownell Jr.
U.S. Fish and Wildlife Service, P.O. Box 70, San Simeon, CA 93452

Whale and Dolphin Conservation Society
191 Weston Road, Lincoln, MA 01773

Whale Center
411 Campbell Street, Tofino, British Columbia, V0R 2Z0 Canada

Whale Fund
The Bronx Zoo, 185th and South Boulevard, Bronx, NY 10460

The Wilderness Society
1400 Eye Street NW, Washington, D.C. 20005

Wildlife Conservation International
New York Zoological Society
185th Street and South Boulevard, Building A, Bronx, NY 10460

Wildlife Preservation Trust
34th Street and Girard, Philadelphia, PA 19104

Wildlife Society
5410 Grosvenor Lane, Betheseda, MD 20814

Worldwatch Institute
1776 Massachusetts Avenue NW, Washington, D.C. 20036

World Wildlife Fund
1250 24th Street NW, Washington, D.C. 20037

Adopt-a-Whale
Programs

If whales have captured your heart or your imagination, you may want to support whale conservation programs by "adopting" a whale for yourself or as a gift for a friend or family member. The sponsoring organizations typically provide adoptive parents with a photo of the adoptee, an official certificate, news about sightings of your whale, a one-year membership in the organization, a newsletter subscription, and other materials related to whale research and conservation.

When you adopt a whale, you aren't signing up to help save a nameless, faceless whale. Research scientists who study annual whale migrations recognize individual animals year after year, based on cross-referenced photo-identification files. Whales can be distinguished from one another by specific markings, coloring, scars from boat propellers, and—for humpbacks—the unique patterns on the underside of the tails. If you go whale watching at the right time in the right place, you may very well meet your adopted whale.

Write or call the organizations listed here for more information.

Beluga Whales

Adopt A Beluga
St. Lawrence National Institute of Ecotoxicology
310, avenue des Ursulines, Rimouski, Quebec, G5L 3A1 Canada;
(418) 724–1746

Nearly 80 individuals of the 400 to 500 belugas in the St. Lawrence River have been identified. The minimum donation to adopt a beluga is $5,000.

Blue Whales

Adopt A Giant
Mingan Island Cetacean Study
Summer:
P.O. Box 159, Sept-Iles, Quebec, G4R 4K3 Canada;
(418) 949–2845
Winter:
285 rue Green, St. Lambert, Quebec, J4P 1T3 Canada;
(514) 465–9176

The Adopt A Giant program offers 210 blue whales that live in the Gulf of St. Lawrence and 160 in the Sea of Cortez. Each whale costs $100 per person, $1,000 for a corporate adoption, and a minimum of $50 for school children. Blue whales are the largest creatures ever to live on earth.

Finback Whales

Adopt-A-Finback-Whale Program
Allied Whale, College of the Atlantic, Bar Harbor, ME 04609;
(207) 288–5644

About thirty-five individual finback whales are available for $30; a mother and calf cost $50. The finback is the second largest animal ever to live on earth.

Gray Whales

Gray Whale Adoption Program
Ocean Alliance, Fort Mason Center, Building E, San Francisco, CA 94123; (800) 388–7327

Some 250 gray whales that migrate past the city by the bay each year are available for adoption for $50 each.

Humpback Whales

Adopt-A-Whale Project
Pacific Whale Foundation, Kealia Beach Plaza, Suite 21, 101 North Kihei Road, Kihei, Maui, HI 96753; (800) 942–5311

Nine humpback whales from Hawaii and three from Australian waters are available. There is a $15 annual support fee plus $15 for a nonexclusive adoption or $75 for an exclusive adoption.

Save the Whales International
Earthtrust, P.O.Box 1358, Lahaina, Maui, HI 96767; (808) 661–8755

Save the Whales International, a project under the auspices of Earthtrust, calls its adoption program a "hanai" program, wherein interested people welcome a Hawaiian humpback whale into their extended family without knowing exactly which whale they have adopted. "We're not a research institution. We shepherd the whole flock," a spokesman said. Participants do receive a photograph. Adoption costs a one-time fee of $35.

Whale Adoption Project
International Wildlife Coalition
634 North Falmouth Highway, P.O. Box 388, North Falmouth, MA 02556; (508) 564–9980

More than sixty-five individual humpback whales that linger in the Gulf of Maine from April to November are available for $15 each.

Orcas

Orca Adoption Program
The Whale Museum, P.O. Box 945, Friday Harbor, WA 98250; (206) 378–4710

More than 80 orcas (killer whales) that spend summers in the San Juan Islands are available for adoption. For $35, you receive a museum membership as well as an adoption; $20 covers just an adoption.

Right Whales

Right Whale Adoption Program
New England Aquarium, Central Wharf, Boston, MA 02110; (617) 973–6582

Ten individuals are available for $45 each, or you can adopt a mother whale and her calves for $100. The northern right whale is the rarest whale on earth, very close to extinction.

Bibliography

Nonfiction

Baker, Mary L. *Whales, Dolphins, and Porpoises of the World.* Doubleday, 1987.

Balcomb, Kenneth C. III. *The Whales of Hawaii.* Marine Mammal Fund, 1987.

Bennett, Ben. *Oceanic Society Field Guide to the Gray Whale.* Legacy, 1983.

Bonner, Nigel. *Whales.* Blanford Press, 1980.

Bonner, Nigel. *Whales of the World.* Facts on File, 1989.

Brower, Kenneth. *Wake of the Whale.* Friends of the Earth/Dutton, 1979.

Burton, Robert. *The Life and Death of Whales.* 2d ed. Universe Books, 1980.

Caldwell, D.K. and M.C. *The World of the Bottlenosed Dolphin.* Lippincott, 1972.

Cousteau, Jacques. *The Whale—Mighty Monarch of the Sea.* Doubleday, 1972.

Cousteau, Jacques, and Yves Paccalet. *Whales.* Harry N. Abrams, 1988.

Daugherty, A.E. *Marine Mammals of California.* Rev. ed. California Department of Fish and Game, 1972.

Day, David. *The Whale War.* Sierra Club Books, 1987.

Dietz, Tim. *Tales of the Sea.* Guy Gannett, 1983.

Dietz, Tim. *Whales and Man.* Yankee Books, 1987.

Doak, Wade. *Encounters with Whales and Dolphins.* Sheridan House, 1989.

D'Vincent, Cynthia. *Voyaging with the Whales.* Oakwell Boulton, 1989.

Ellis, Richard. *The Book of Whales.* Alfred A. Knopf, 1980.

Ellis, Richard. *Dolphins and Porpoises.* Alfred A. Knopf, 1982.

Gatenby, Greg. *Whales: A Celebration.* Little, Brown and Company, 1983.

Gilmore, R.M. *The Story of the Gray Whale.* Gilmore, 1961, rev. 1972.

Gormley, Gerald. *Orcas of the Gulf: A Natural History.* Sierra Club Books, 1990.

Harrison, Richard, and Michael Bryden. *Whales, Dolphins, and Porpoises.* Intercontinental Publishing, 1988.

Hoyt, Erich. *Seasons of the Whale.* Chelsea Green, 1990.

Hoyt, Erich. *Orca: The Whale Called Killer.* Rev. Ed. E. P. Dutton, 1990.

Hoyt, Erich. *The Whale Watcher's Handbook.* Doubleday, 1984.

Jones, Mary Lou, Steven L. Swartz, and Stephen Leatherwood. *The Gray Whale.* Academic Press, 1984.

Katona, Steven K., Valerie Rough, and David T. Richardson. *A Field Guide to the Whales, Porpoises, and Seals of the Gulf of Maine and Eastern Canada.* 3d ed. Scribner's, 1983.

Kelly, John E., Scott Mercer, and Steve Wolf. *The Great Whale Book.* Center for Environmental Education, 1981.

Leatherwood, Stephen, and Randall R. Reeves. *The Bottlenose Dolphin.* Academic Press, 1989.

Leatherwood, Stephen, and Randall R. Reeves. *The Sierra Club Handbook of Whales and Dolphins.* Sierra Club Books, 1983.

Leatherwood, Stephen, Randall R. Reeves, William F. Perrin, and William E. Evans. *Whales, Dolphins, and Porpoises of the Eastern North Pacific and Adjacent Arctic Waters.* 2d ed. Dover, 1988.

Lilly, John. *Man and Dolphin.* Doubleday and Company, 1961.

Matthews, L. H. *The Natural History of the Whale.* Columbia University Press, 1978.

Matthews, L. H. *The Whale.* Simon and Schuster, 1968.

McIntyre, Joan. *Mind in the Waters.* Scribner's/Sierra Club, 1974.

McIntyre, Joan. *The Delicate Art of Whale Watching.* Sierra Club Books, 1982.

McNally, Robert. *So Remorseless a Havoc.* Little, Brown and Company, 1981.

Miller, Tom. *The World of the California Gray Whale.* Baja Trail Publications, 1975.

Minasian, Stanley M., Kenneth C. Balcomb III, and Larry Foster. *The World's Whales.* Smithsonian, 1984.

Mowat, Farley. *A Whale for the Killing.* Bantam Books, 1972.

Nakamura, Tsuneo. *Gentle Giant: At Sea with the Humpback Whale.* Chronicle Books. 1984.

Nickerson, Roy. *Brother Whale.* Chronicle Books, 1977.

Nickerson, Roy. *The Friendly Whales: A Whale Watcher's Guide to the Gray Whales of Baja California.* Chronicle Books, 1987.

Norris, K. *Whales, Dolphins and Porpoises.* University of California Press, 1966.

Reeves, Randall R., and Stephen Leatherwood. *The Sea World Book of Dolphins.* Harcourt, Brace, Jovanovich, 1987.

Scammon, Charles M. *The Marine Mammals of the Northwest Coast of North America.* Reprinted by Dover, 1968; originally published in 1874.

Scheffer, Victor. *A Natural History of Marine Mammals*. Scribner's Sons, 1976.

Small, G. L. *The Blue Whale*. Columbia University Press, 1971.

Walker, Theodore J. *Whale Primer*. Cabrillo Historical Association, 1962 (since revised several times).

Watson, Lyall. *A Sea Guide to Whales of the World*. E. P. Dutton, 1982.

Watson, Paul. *Sea Shepherd: My Fight for Whales and Seals*. Norton, 1982.

Weyler, Rex. *Song of the Whale*. Anchor Press, 1986.

Whitehead, Hal. *Voyage to the Whales*. Stoddart Publishing, 1989.

Williams, Heathcote. *Falling for a Dolphin*. Harmony Books, 1989.

Williams, Heathcote. *Whale Nation*. Harmony Books, 1988.

Winn, Lois King, and Howard E. Winn. *Wings in the Sea: The Humpback Whale*. University Press of New England, 1985.

Yates, Steve. *Marine Life of Puget Sound, the San Juans, and the Strait of Georgia*. Globe Pequot Press, 1988.

Fiction

Abbey, Lloyd. *The Last Whales*. Grove Weidenfeld, 1989.

Carrighar, Sally. *The Twilight Seas*. Dutton, 1989.

Lucas, Jeremy. *Whale*. Summit Books, 1981.

Melville, Herman. *Moby-Dick; or The Whale*. Numerous editions and publishers, 1851.

Scheffer, Victor. *The Year of the Whale*. Scribner's, 1969.

Searls, Hank. *Sounding*. Ballantine, 1982.

Siegel, Robert. *Whalesong*. Berkley, 1981.

Spain, Stanley. *Rajac: A Story*. MacMillan, 1982.

Indexes

Northeast U.S. Coast Points of Departure

Northeast U.S. Coast Tour Operators

Where the Whales Are

Pacific Northwest Points of Departure

Pacific Northwest Tour Operators

California Points of Departure

California Tour Operators

Allen Barry Boat Company (Sausalito), 112
American Cetacean Society Expeditions (Balboa), 137
Bagheera Sailing Adventures (San Diego), 140
Belmont Pier Sportfishing (Long Beach), 131
Captain Dave's Waterfront Cruises (Oxnard), 126
Captain Jack (Fort Bragg), 110
Capt. Don's Coastal Cruises (Santa Barbara), 123
Catalina Cruises (Long Beach), 131
Catalina Passenger Service (Balboa), 135
Celtic Charter Service (Eureka), 109
Chris' Fishing Trips (Monterey), 119
Cisco's Sportfishing (Oxnard), 127
Classic Sailing Adventures (San Diego), 141
Dana Wharf Sportfishing (Dana Point), 138
Davey's Locker Sportfishing (Balboa), 136
Dolphin Charters (Berkeley), 113
Footloose Forays (San Francisco), 114
H&M Landing (San Diego), 142
Harbor Sailboats (San Diego), 142
Helgren's Sportfishing (Oceanside), 139
Huck Finn Sportfishing (Half Moon Bay), 116
Invader Cruises Inc. (San Diego), 143
Islandia Sportfishing (San Diego), 144
Island Packers (Ventura), 125
Lady Irma II (Fort Bragg), 110
L.A. Harbor Sportfishing (San Pedro), 128
Long Beach Sportfishing (Long Beach), 132
Misty II Charters (Fort Bragg), 111
Monterey Sport Fishing (Monterey), 120
Newport Landing Sportfishing (Balboa), 134
Oceanic Society Expeditions (Half Moon Bay and San Francisco), 115, 117
Orion Charters Inc. (San Diego), 144
Pacific Yachting (Santa Cruz), 117
Princess Monterey Cruises (Monterey), 120
Randy's Fishing Trips (Monterey), 121
Rain Song Sportfishing (Santa Cruz), 118
Redondo Sport Fishing (Redondo Beach), 127
San Diego Harbor Excursion (San Diego), 145
San Diego Natural History Museum (San Diego), 146
Seaforth Sportfishing (San Diego), 147

Alaska Points of Departure

Note: Tours that depart from points outside of Alaska are found on pages 182 to 184.

Alaska Tour Operators

Western Canada Points of Departure

*Tour destination; see tour listing for departure point.

Western Canada Tour Operators

Eastern Canada Points of Departure

Eastern Canada Tour Operators

Mexico Destinations

Points of Departure for Mexico Tours

Mexico Tour Operators

About the Author

PATRICIA CORRIGAN, secretly a mermaid, lives in landlocked St. Louis, Missouri, with her teenage son and two orange cats that love water. Right now she is fulfilling a childhood dream—working as a news reporter for the *St. Louis Post-Dispatch*. As soon as her son graduates from high school, she intends to avoid empty-nest syndrome and at the same time begin fulfilling a more recent dream by moving to the southern coast of Oregon. There she plans to watch whales from her living room window when she isn't out on a boat in some equally whale-rich area of the world.

About the Illustrator

DAVID PETERS is a commercial artist and author and illustrator of *Giants of Land, Sea and Air—Past and Present* (Sierra Club/Alfred A. Knopf, 1986); *A Gallery of Dinosaurs and Other Prehistoric Reptiles* (Albert A. Knopf, 1988); *From the Beginning: The Story of Evolution* (Morrow Junior Books, 1990); and *The Strangest Animals of All Times* (Morrow Junior Books, Christmas 1991). He lives in St. Louis, Missouri, with his wife and two daughters.

. . .

Note: Ten percent of the author's income from this book will go to whale conservation and research organizations working to ensure that the world's whales do not become extinct.

. . .

In an effort to include every whale-watch tour operator serving customers in the geographical areas delineated in this book, the author has checked, rechecked, and cross-checked with known tour operators, local chambers of commerce, state and local tourist bureaus, museums, aquariums, and conservation organizations and foundations. If you were inadvertently left out, or if you know someone who was, please make sure the omission will be remedied in revised editions by writing immediately to Patricia Corrigan in care of The Globe Pequot Press, 138 West Main Street, P.O. Box Q, Chester, Connecticut 06412.